Praise for *The Snowball System*

"Full of steps that you can follow to grow your business without feeling like a sleazy salesperson."

—Adam Grant, *New York Times* bestselling author
of *Give and Take* and *Originals*

"Of all the skills that the thousands of entrepreneurs I have worked with struggle with the most, selling tops the list. *The Snowball System* presents a clear, effective, and ethical way to sell that will turn your fear of selling into joy of serving."

—Pamela Slim, author of *Body of Work*
and *Escape from Cubicle Nation*

"*The Snowball System* is one of the best books on sales I have ever read. If you implement the practical tools from this book, your business generation results will improve dramatically. Successful professionals have a system and *The Snowball System* will help readers be successful. Mo's system has significantly helped me and many of lawyers at our firm."

—Mike Duffy, Director of Client Services, King and Spalding

"Building relationships is the cornerstone of good business but few people understand how to actually build them and keep them strong. *The Snowball System* provides the science and methodology behind making relations real and valuable. Bunnell has written a relationship guide for business people and anyone wanting to have an impact on the world." **—Greg Becker, CEO of Silicon Valley Bank**

"Great professional services firms invest many years developing their people to solve problems and to accumulate domain expertise. But too often, these same firms invest far too little in training those same people the skills required to do sophisticated business development as partners. *The Snowball System* outlines a learnable approach to doing business development the right way, a way that will be embraced as authentic, proactive, and impactful to clients. This is a must-read."

—Mike Deimler, Senior Partner and
Managing Director of Boston Consulting Group

"*The Snowball System* is a practical book you can use right from the first chapter—*and* is a great read—too rare in today's world. This book isn't just for business developers, it's for anyone needing to influence others in an authentic, helpful way. Mo's book applies our Whole Brain® Thinking approach to a business process as well or better than I've ever seen. If you haven't heard of the HBDI® or the Whole Brain® Thinking model, this is a great introduction. If you have, and always wondered how it could be used in business development, this will be a goldmine."

—Ann Hermann, CEO of Herrmann International

"Individuals and organizations can no longer rely on impressions and interruptions to drive sales–they need a strategy and a plan to find their ideal customers. *The Snowball System* will not only teach you how to think differently about growing your business—it provides tools and processes you can use to thrive in our experience-driven economy."

—**Brian Colucci, Chief Business Development &**
Marketing Officer of Kilpatrick Townsend

"As someone with over 20 years of experience in corporate sales training, I was convinced there was nothing new under the sun when it came to business development approaches. Then I met Mo Bunnell. His techniques have the unique combination of being easy to understand and implement while at the same time wildly and immediately impactful. *The Snowball System* has been a game changer in helping our sales teams strengthen client relationships and close business."

—**Joby Gendron, Sales Development Director, Aetna**

"*The Snowball System* is an exceptionally engaging and practical resource containing a wealth of actionable tips for how to effectively develop new business. I highly recommend Mo's book for anyone looking to strengthen and grow client relationships." —**Jeff Berardi, CMO of K&L Gates**

"I've always thought there was a great opportunity to create a business development system that aligns with what I truly believe are the core principles for success in creating great relationships: transparency, respect, commitment, honesty, trust, and integrity. I'm very excited to have found this in *The Snowball System*. This incredibly compelling and immensely valuable book provides a proactive framework and process to create wins for others, significantly grow your influence, and feel great about the profound impact you've had on others."

—**Kevin C. Conroy, Founder of Conroy Media**

"If you struggle to find time to grow your business while maintaining your current client portfolio, then *The Snowball System* is for you. Bunnell helps you reflect on your current behaviors and rethink how you can be more effective. He provides unique solutions to some of your greatest challenges in the balancing act of serving existing clients while hunting for new ones."

—**Sandy Lutton, Chief Revenue Officer**
of Washington Speakers Bureau

"*The Snowball System* is essential reading for anyone looking for a comprehensive, step by step guide to business development success. Mo's wit and conversational tone makes for an enjoyable yet highly practical read."

—**Marty Fagan, Senior Vice President,**
Sales & Business Development, TransUnion

"I was lucky. I met Mo through a chance encounter that accelerated my career. Since then I've become one of the top 10 residential real estate agents out of over a million in the US. And now, *The Snowball System* can teach you what Mo taught me. Don't just buy this book, devour every word and put the concepts to work. You won't regret it." —**Bonneau Ashley, CEO of Ansley Atlanta**

The Snowball System

THE
SNOWBALL
SYSTEM

*How to Win More Business
and Turn Clients into Raving Fans*

MO BUNNELL

PUBLICAFFAIRS
New York

PublicAffairs
Hachette Book Group
1290 Avenue of the Americas, New York, NY 10104
www.publicaffairsbooks.com
@Public_Affairs

Printed in the United States of America

First Edition: September 2018

Published by PublicAffairs, an imprint of Perseus Books, LLC, a subsidiary of Hachette Book Group, Inc. The PublicAffairs name and logo is a trademark of the Hachette Book Group.

The publisher is not responsible for websites (or their content) that are not owned by the publisher.

Print book interior design by Jeff Williams

Library of Congress Cataloging-in-Publication Data
Names: Bunnell, Mo, author.
Title: The snowball system : how to win more business and turn clients into raving fans / Mo Bunnell.
Description: First edition. | New York, NY : PublicAffairs, an imprint of Perseus Books, LLC, [2018] | Includes bibliographical references and index.
Identifiers: LCCN 2018017032| ISBN 9781610399609 (hardcover) | ISBN 9781610399593 (ebook) | ISBN 9781549142116 (downloadable audio)
Subjects: LCSH: Relationship marketing. | Customer relations—Management.| Technological innovations—Management.
Classification: LCC HF5415.55 .B86 2018 | DDC 658.8/12--dc23
LC record available at https://lccn.loc.gov/2018017032
ISBNs: 978-1-61039-960-9 (HC), 978-1-61039-959-3 (ebook), 978-1-54914-211-6 (downloadable audio)

LSC-C

10 9 8 7 6 5 4 3

To Becky, for putting up with my boundless curiosity while guiding me to be my best self.

Contents

More Business, Less Busy-ness

• • •

Believe it or not, *you* are a salesperson. Don't think so? Nowadays there are more of us than you might think, though we go by different names—lawyers, consultants, marketers, and accountants as well as wedding photographers, Brazilian jiujitsu instructors, graphic designers, and chiropractors. Even account managers that manage big, ongoing relationships are in sales, managing existing work and on the hook for expanding it. If you're good at doing something and need paying clients to do it for, call it sales, call it business development—whatever you like—welcome to the club. This book is for you. Every day I teach people like you how to sell their services—without selling their souls.

You're reading this book because you want your business to grow. You want to win more clients and do more business with the clients you already have. You want more of the *right* work for the *right* money with the *right* clients. I'm going to show you a proven system for making all this happen and then making it a habit for life.

•

Picture twelve senior partners at a prestigious professional services firm sitting around a round table. Like you, they're just getting started learning this really awesome system. One of my company's facilitators asks the first question:

"How many hours have you spent building your expertise?"

After a short pause one of the partners raises his hand.

"Fifty thousand." Our facilitator raises an eyebrow. The man squints a little doing the math in his head: "I work three thousand hours a year, and I've been doing this fifteen years. Throw in my degrees, and you're easily at fifty K."

"Great," the facilitator replies. "Now, how many hours have you invested in learning *business development*? You know—generating leads, turning prospects into clients, developing strong client relationships that lead to more and more work."

No pause at all this time: "Seven. Including the five so far today."

Everyone at the table laughs uncomfortably. The truth hurts.

That said, maybe you're not starting from scratch. Maybe you've read some books and established effective business development techniques that have helped you get where you are today. That's great. But however much you already understand about the principles of effective business development, the only gap that truly matters is the one between knowledge and *action*. Be honest: In a typical workday how many hours do you actually spend growing your business?

Add it up. I'll wait.

If you're anything like the thousands of skilled client-facing professionals I've trained over the last decade, the answer is: less than an hour.

It's okay. Don't be too hard on yourself. This is a universal problem. We are not very good at balancing the time we spend doing the work against the time we spend drumming up more.

In an earlier era a lackadaisical approach to growing your business worked fine. If you did good work, the phone would ring. There were fewer local experts in most fields, and clients were loyal. You'd take a few people to lunch each week, send out those holiday cards every year, and, boom, a steady roster of happy clients would be yours to serve.

Today, clients are savvier. They put more work out to bid or do in-depth comparative research online. The marketplace is flooded with expertise.

The result? Your hard-won knowledge is only table stakes. Today, we are "seller-expert" hybrids responsible for (1) meeting the needs of current clients, (2) developing those relationships to deliver more work, and (3) attracting and retaining new clients. Organizations expect their experts to fill their own pipelines with a steady flow of new work. Client relationship skills matter more than ever.

We need to manage doing the work while also convincing people to let us do the work for them. That doesn't even include the time it takes to reply to hundreds of emails a day, attend interminable meetings, and file detailed expense reports. If you're anything like most of the people I train, right now you're probably thinking, *I didn't become a* _____ *to sell myself!* True. But like it or not, once your expertise and professionalism elevate you to a certain level, your ability to grow client relationships largely determines your success. Your capacity for business development will only increase in importance as your career progresses. To rise, experts need to sell.

From the other side, professional salespeople are finding it more and more necessary to develop a foundation of strategic thinking and insights around the products and services they sell. Gone are the days when you could smile-and-dial in the morning and golf in the afternoon.

Experts need to understand how to sell their own services, and salespeople need to understand the services they're trying to sell. Ultimately, service and selling are becoming one craft, one universal set of skills and practices around finding people who need your help and then helping them as effectively as possible. The question is: Are you going to grow your business at the same high level of skill and professionalism you display in your own area of expertise?

Here's the good news: I can show you how. I've been a highly successful seller-expert myself and have since taught thousands of other professionals how to achieve growth with world-class proficiency. That's because I've been right where you are.

This may be hard to believe right now, but when I transitioned from expert to seller-expert, I found that I came to love growing my business. This surprised me. Sure, business development was overwhelming at first because I didn't know where to begin—after all, this book didn't exist yet. What changed everything for me was discovering that real, sustainable business development isn't about selling as it's traditionally understood at all. It's about being *strategically helpful.*

As experts, we like helping people. Selling—being helpful—should be second nature. So why do we find it so difficult to sell ourselves? Showing someone what we can do for them doesn't have to be a bad thing at all. Yet you can't be blamed for feeling otherwise, especially if you've ever read a typical book or attended a seminar on sales. Traditional sales training has always been about "closing the deal," as though anything that happens afterward is beside the point. Use these techniques in this order, you're told, and the rube will sign on the dotted line. Once the sale is made, mark it up on the board and get that set of steak knives.

This attitude has its roots in a different era, when salespeople faced intense pressure to meet monthly quotas no matter how they did it and reaped lavish rewards for doing so. It placed short-term performance ahead of long-term relationships.

Today, the quotas and bonuses are still around, but this attitude has become antiquated. Consumer protections have increased, and review sites and social media mean that our relationships with *all* our clients, past and present, are never really over, even if we've completed the work and parted ways. Clients are free to share about their experience working with us the next day, week, month, or year. If a former client comes to regret their decision to buy long after that high-pressure sales lunch, it takes only a few minutes to inform any prospective client curious enough to Google your company. Today, news travels fast, and bad news travels even faster.

This shift goes both ways, thankfully. Where old-school selling is eternally vulnerable to online retaliation, being strategically helpful by using the Snowball System will reap benefits long after the work is over. The approach you will learn in this book is broad, generous, efficient, and long lasting. It's about building a relationship based on trust and mutual reciprocity that will last for years. People *love* doing business with someone who really understands them and helps them solve their problems—including the ones they didn't even know they had. And they will tell the world.

•

Clearly, no one can afford to let business development activities slide. Yet, because we cringe at the idea of selling, we let our day-to-day work get in the way. When we're really buried, the very idea of *more*—more clients, more work, more emails—can trigger migraines. Why pour gasoline on a fire? Instead, we put our heads down and focus on what's in front of us. Let tomorrow worry about tomorrow.

Sooner or later, of course, we clear our plates. In the meantime the new-business flywheel has run down. We realize it's been weeks or longer since our last new lead. Our inbox is empty—of promising client opportunities, anyway. We panic. Suddenly, and with no particular plan, we start making calls and setting up lunches at a breakneck pace until the flywheel spins up again.

Problem solved, right? Except it hasn't been. We've just kicked the can down the road. We'll end up back in the same position in a few weeks or months. Meanwhile our output looks unreliable and inconsistent no matter how productive we are at points. The only steady metric is our anxiety level.

As we've seen, the capacity to attract and retain clients, win their trust and appreciation, and keep their business determines the arc of a career. Yet we spend almost no time learning how to do it—at least relative to how important it is. I call this the *business development paradox*.

On the bright side, the paradox promises rapid gains for students of the Snowball System. When you're just starting out, investing even a modest amount of time and energy promises a substantial return. Because every chapter of this book walks you through implementing a set of key tools, you will start to see results long before you reach the final page.

At this point you might be thinking: *Not me, pal. I picked this book up out of desperation, but the one thing you're not going to do is teach me how to "like" selling, let alone see growing my business as some kind of fun game. Some people are natural salespeople, and others aren't.*

Sure, some people have stronger innate selling skills than others. But show me any rainmaker, and I guarantee you'll find that they worked very hard to get that way. Rainmakers approach selling as a craft, mastering it as methodically as they did their core expertise. No matter the starting point, it's always possible to improve.

Anders Ericsson at Florida State University is a world-famous researcher who studies expertise. He's the expert on how people become experts. Ericsson's research shows that people develop expertise through what he calls "deliberate practice." Put simply, they break down the individual aspects of their craft so they can improve each area and then put it all back together. It isn't enough to just perform a task over and over again; you need to *deliberately* attack the difficult components one by one and improve them. Doing so drives progress. It develops expertise. The only difference between you and the "born" rainmaker is that one of you used deliberate practice to get better at selling.

While we muster the effort to push ourselves now and then, without steady reinforcement, these heroic efforts dwindle until the next motivational speech—or the next scary gap between paid work. To thrive, you need to build the capacity to sell consistently and in all weathers. To sell consistently we need that change of perspective I mentioned: we need to understand selling as one of the most valuable and generous things you can do with your time.

Some potential clients know they need someone with your expertise but don't know exactly how you can address their specific situation. Others may not even realize what they need yet or how much better things could be with your help. Then there are your current clients, anchored on the services you've performed in the past and not even thinking about what you could do for them next. The point is, *people don't know what they don't know.* Bringing your services to the appropriate person's attention and helping them figure out how to get the most value out of it is at the heart of business development.

True rainmakers always have the client's best interests in mind. I believe that. It's what I practice and what I teach.

Before we dive into the specifics of the Snowball System, let's start with the simple idea that ties it together: the buyer should feel like it's their birthday.

I don't know about you, but I love my birthday. It's the one day of the year that's all about *me.* Weeks before, my wife and daughters ask me how

I'd like to spend my special day. That morning they give me handwritten cards telling me how awesome I am. During the day I get thoughtful gifts, cards, and Facebook messages from friends and family around the world. When I return home from some self-indulgent adventure or another, my daughters look me in the eye and ask me how it went.

Did I mention they look me in the eye? That means they actually put down their phones for a minute.

I'd tell you to put yourself in a client's or prospect's shoes, but you already know what it's like. Like you, they're getting beat up all day— meetings, emails, performance reviews. The pressure never stops. If they're at a big organization, there's a re-org every few months. These are the people you're selling to, people just like you, people who work very hard for very long hours, constantly worrying about meeting expectations and hitting numbers.

Buying is the one time at work when you're put on a pedestal. Someone else is finally paying attention to what you want, asking questions about your opinion—even taking notes! It doesn't sound like a lot, but if you've ever been in a position to buy and haven't been treated this way, you know how disappointing it can feel.

This is the essence of the Snowball System: making the client feel special. How? *By listening to what they want and then giving it to them.* What could be better than that?

Once you learn how to make people feel important, the rest of the selling process will become so much easier that you'll wonder why you ever dreaded doing it in the first place.

•

At this point you might be wondering how I learned to be effective at business development in the face of all these obstacles. The time has come for an admission.

My name is Mo Bunnell, and I used to be a practicing actuary.

As professions go, well, actuaries make accountants look like rock stars, and for good reason. Becoming an actuary requires learning and retaining vast amounts of information. I even had to miss our family Halloween parties because of the tests that always happened the following week. (I still hear stories about those parties. Apparently they were great. Probably because there weren't any actuaries around to spoil the fun.)

If the idea of memorizing inch-thick tomes on calculating disability reserves, analyzing risk-adjusted decrements, and using the Poisson Distribution for queue analysis doesn't thrill you, be glad you're not an actuary. Personally, I can't get enough of scientific research and *Moneyball*-like analyses. That's my happy place. (We'll talk more about the different thinking preferences and how they affect business development in another chapter. It's a game changer.)

I entered my profession only to slam headfirst into the business development paradox. When I finished my exams, I moved into the broader role of managing consultant. Promoted from a deeply technical role to one where I had to interface with C-suite HR professionals at Fortune 500 companies, I learned immediately that I was out of my depth. My firm suddenly expected me to develop and manage big client relationships instead of, you know, doing actuarial stuff all day. Huh? Suddenly I went from expert to seller-expert and was on the hook for a whole new set of outcomes.

Talk about intimidating. Before the promotion I only had to know about the offerings of my own department. After, I had to know about hundreds of offerings across dozens of departments. I'd typically worked with a client's head of benefits, but now I'd be connecting directly with a C-suite executive, usually someone with at least two decades' experience over me. Overnight I went from working on employee benefits to handling all of a client's top talent initiatives.

When I moved to my new role, I naively assumed that someone would just hand me a manual. *Here's how you do business development,* they'd say. *Just memorize this.* After all, I'd just spent nearly a decade learning my primary craft by stuffing massive amounts of information into my brain. Why should this be any different?

To my surprise, I discovered that there was no manual. Just a desk with a computer and a phone. Now I was really scared. My entire future suddenly depended on my ability to sell, and I had no idea how to go about learning to do it. Thank goodness I had some great mentors to help me through the transition, but I wanted even more. I wanted a process, and I wanted it based on science.

I'm a systems guy, so I decided to begin by drafting a simple selling process document, something to make business development a little more automatic. I knew that, without putting my business development efforts "on rails," I'd never be able to maintain momentum in the face of my day-to-day demands.

Sure, I wanted to succeed. But I was even more motivated to *not fail*. So I did what any good actuary would do: I studied like crazy. Passing the actuarial exams when I took them required me to memorize as many as twelve hundred pages of technical information every six months and then take exams that had a pass rate of about 35 percent. To make it, I needed to learn how to learn quickly and effectively. So I learned.

I began with psychology: motivation. Why people buy. Why "seller-experts" procrastinate and give up too early. More than anything else, I wanted to solve the business development paradox for myself. So I threw myself into the books and then into the peer-reviewed research papers cited by those books. I did everything I could to break the relationship-building process down into small steps that I could perform over and over. I hadn't discovered Ericsson's deliberate practice research yet, but I was instinctively following his advice. Turns out, fear is a powerful motivator.

Early on in creating my business development process, I faced one particularly important meeting. I was at Hewitt Associates (now part of Aon) and had recently been promoted to my first broader client management role. Because my annual revenue goals were so aggressive, only one client I managed had the room for growth needed to allow me to reach my goals. The good news was that we did little for this Fortune 500 client, so I had the upside I needed. Unfortunately, that was the bad news too. The work we did have was buried down in the organization, and the people we knew couldn't buy enough for me to significantly grow the relationship. Through some hard work and a stroke of luck, I landed a meeting with their chief human resource officer, who only one person in our organization knew. I *had* to connect with her. I had one shot, one meeting. If it didn't work, no annual bonus. Pressure!

Desperate for an edge, I interviewed successful peers. What helped win the day for an important initial meeting you had? I went to lunch with a great mentor. What do you see people do in their first meetings they shouldn't? I even asked my other clients for their advice. How could I have improved on the experience you had with me in our first meeting? I distilled everything I learned into a set of concrete steps, and then I methodically followed those steps one by one, like a pilot preparing for takeoff.

On the day of the meeting I arrived even earlier than I would normally. When her assistant called me into the office, I walked on air, full of optimism, entering the hallowed ground of the executive suite on the 52nd floor, so special that it had its own guard station. I even had an upbeat theme song playing in my mind, knowing I had prepared for this meeting more than any other in my life. I sat down with my well-prepared list, written a second time so it looked neater, and opened my new, supple, leather portfolio, looking up to say my well-rehearsed opening to the meeting. That's when my mind's theme song screeched to a halt, with the imaginary needle ripping across the entire record.

My prospective client looked me sternly in the eye, announcing that she had all the resources she needed in the HR space and that she didn't need to know me.

She told me that she had an executive compensation consultant, a healthcare advisor, a retirement plan actuary, and that they weren't planning on moving any of their benefits administration work anytime soon. She went on about the various talent experts she loved at other firms, which she listed in detail to make the point. The first ten minutes of our meeting were spent with her telling me she didn't need this meeting or my services. Beneath her words I could tell she was clearly wondering how I had gotten this meeting, and she would make sure this kind of time waster wouldn't happen in the future.

Though my heart was racing, I didn't let it shake me. I couldn't. The stakes were too high. I stuck to my process faithfully and tried to reframe the meeting. I told her I wasn't there to sell anything but instead that our team had already put together some ideas about what could be done to improve her business and that hearing them would only take a few minutes of her time. I assured her again: every idea would be on our dime. She relaxed a little, and as I began filling her in, I could tell she was curious. She liked my first idea, and my second. I kept going. In the end I left with a dozen action items to follow up on.

I still remember the ride back to the office. I euphorically sang "Shake Your Rump" by the Beastie Boys (more volume makes a good song great). My system had worked, and it had worked despite some serious opposition—which was good, because I wasn't going to make it as a rapper.

I'd hit upon the answer to my problems—a repeatable selling process that I could practice and hone. After all, I didn't want to make *a* sale, no matter how important; I wanted to change my entire approach to selling. I wanted to crush my numbers. I wanted to enjoy my new job. I wanted my clients to tell their friends and colleagues about how much they enjoyed working with me.

Now I was off to the races, taking in the latest research on the psychology of relationships, trust, and communication and using it to develop a systematic approach to every aspect of the business development process. I continued breaking things down, building methods and tools for each important rainmaking skill.

The rapid improvement I experienced led my company to select me to take charge of two of its four largest worldwide accounts. Around that same time I was asked to lead an office of seven hundred associates, including hundreds of senior seller-experts in various practices. Using this prototype system, the teams I was fortunate to lead—teams of really, really talented experts—delivered hundreds of millions of dollars of large, complex outsourcing projects and highly customized consulting. That's when I realized I was on to something *big*.

I decided to take a leap. I left my career behind and started Bunnell Idea Group (BIG). I spent the next ten years building out and teaching a complete methodology that *anyone* could use to land new clients and grow the relationships they already had. In that time the Snowball System has proven its worth for people in nearly every profession and at every level.

It all started with a friend hiring me to teach him "how I did it." Now I'm grateful to say that BIG has become very successful. Over the past decade we have trained over ten thousand people at over three hundred organizations. We work with many of the most prestigious professional service firms and with Fortune 500 companies around the world, entrusted with their most valuable account executives and leaders. It's been a wild ride.

But there was one question that still nagged me. I knew that the seller-expert problem I'd solved had spread much more widely than the rarified circuit of international consultancies, high-powered law firms, and global brands we now serve at BIG. I started to wonder whether the system that worked so well for pros at the highest levels of the largest businesses would work for *any* client-facing professional.

What about small businesses that can't afford to send their key employees out for corporate training? What about the growing ranks of freelancers? Could this system help anyone from a piano teacher to a hypnotherapist, from a web copywriter to a small-business marketing consultant? We're living in the dawn of the gig economy. More than ever, people are forging out on their own and working for themselves. Could I help them too?

One of the key themes of the Snowball System is the regular pursuit of goals. I practice goal setting myself, as I practice every other tool I teach. A year ago I wrote down a new professional goal for myself: "Write a book that documents our system, bringing it to everyone who needs it." As you read this, I can mark that goal accomplished.

Many professionals think sales skills can't be taught. They think you've either "got it" or you don't. I thrive on proving them wrong. The truth is, *you* can do this. All you need to do is learn and integrate a set of new behaviors. Think of selling as a craft, one that is worthy of study and deliberate practice. If you learned your core discipline, you can learn this too.

At BIG we've helped experts across industries master the client pipeline—from gregarious people to introverts and from small consulting practices to immensely complex offerings from multinational companies. Providing the aha moment to sales-shy professionals has become my passion. Whether you're an account executive at a large corporation or a full-time freelancer or you're a professional salesperson or working a side hustle with an eye toward leaving the corporate world, the skills in this book will spell the difference between scraping by and scaling up.

The approach in this book is both effective and practical, easily integrated into your day-to-day work. Once you make these tools and practices a part of your routine, they will feel like second nature.

The real beauty of the Snowball System is that your clients end up so happy with your work that they can't stop talking about it to anyone who will listen. They do your marketing for you, way better than you ever could. Instead of feeling like you're struggling to push your business uphill, it'll start to feel like your business is rolling along with a momentum all its own, growing bigger and bigger like, well, a snowball. Over the years, this system has helped thousands of experts and hundreds of organizations build and maintain their businesses. So how big do you want your snowball to be?

CHAPTER 1

Think Big, Start Small, Scale Up

. . .

Experts are always made, not born.

—ANDERS ERICSSON, *The Making of an Expert*

THE SNOWBALL SYSTEM contains strategies, tools, and tactics that work together as a self-reinforcing, integrated system. It isn't just a collection of tips for dealing with clients—it's a *machine for growing your business*. Once the parts are in place, the system will drive progress with only regular maintenance from you.

Effective business development, or BD, requires a small but regular investment of time. To get the most out of that time, we want to put in additional effort now to get things up and running so that you encounter zero friction when it's time to put in the work. Many things demand our attention and pull us away from growth-oriented activities. A successful BD system requires a foundation of habits. Because habits are automatic and don't drain our willpower and attention the way completing normal tasks do, they won't slide off the agenda when things get busy.

Researching what they call "psychological momentum," Seppo Iso-Ahola and Charles Dotson found that when establishing new habits, successfully doing something small each day—instead of a big effort every week, for example—is much more likely to build a behavior that sticks. They say these small wins generate a feeling of psychological momentum, similar to what a sports team may feel when they go on a run: everything feels like it's going their way, and that feeling is powerful. Build your own momentum with small actions completed consistently over time, and you'll get that feeling too. Each time you successfully perform a habit, you will feel more energized to perform that habit the next time. You can expand on the behavior once it's firmly established.

Now it's time to get you started on the Snowball System in a small but powerful way. As a professional who attended my training put it: "Think big, start small, scale up."

Why

Take out a blank sheet of paper and, in a few words, write down *why* you want to get better at business development.

Some of those who train with us initially write that they want to "make more money." But that's not specific enough—I always ask them to take it a step or two further. What's the money for? Sending your kids to college? Retiring early? Buying that awesome vacation home? Be clear. Be specific. Be *honest.*

For some, getting better at business development is about rising in the ranks. Once a professional begins to lead client relationships, BD skills become as important as one's primary expertise. Sometimes these skills become *the* most important factor in a career's progression.

Whatever your true goal is, acknowledge it now. Then, in a sentence, explain why the effort to learn business development will be worth it. The more personal your reason, the more likely you will stick with the system. Getting great at selling your expertise is a craft—and a challenging one. It won't usually provide fun behavioral reinforcements for doing the right things. Understanding why you're deliberately developing this skill can power you through the tough times.

So what's your *why*?

Who

Now take another blank piece of paper and write down along the left side the seven most important people in your sphere as they relate to your BD efforts. This can be a mix of current clients, key people you'd like to meet, and sources of referrals. It's easy to fixate on those you spend time with now. Don't. Instead, write down the people with whom you *should* be investing your primary outreach time.

Who are the seven people with the greatest potential to benefit your business?

What

Let's get ready to act. For each relationship write down the next step—the very next action you can take to serve that person. Frame it in terms of the benefit to *them*. This could be an introduction to someone they'd find useful to meet or an asset like a relevant industry article that might be of interest to them. Perhaps it could be an invitation to lunch to talk about how you can help them solve a problem they're facing. Use your imagination. What kind of offer would delight them?

Make each outreach action specific, something you can accomplish in a short time and is 100 percent under your control. If it feels more like a long-term project than a task, break it down to the next specific action.

Instead of "Foster relationship with Jennifer" (too big) or even "Have lunch with Jennifer" (too vague), write, "Email Jennifer with potential times to talk about her goals and ways I can help her." No matter how overwhelmed you might be on any given day, you can knock out a task like that in a couple of minutes.

Now circle the three most important, potentially valuable actions on your list. Just three. These will be your Most Important Things (MITs) for this week.

When

We've found that the busy professionals who train with us are more likely to do something when they've blocked out a set time on their calendar for it. But most people don't do any planning around business development, instead taking action only when inspiration strikes. You wouldn't manage your most important project this way, would you? Yet over the long term, business development *is* your most important project.

Want to be more effective at execution? Then put your MITs on your calendar right now. Set aside an adequate amount of time to accomplish each one, or batch them into one BD-focused session. Whatever works best for you.

Next, schedule a session at the end of the week both to review how these three actions went and to decide on three new MITs for the following week. During each weekly review keep a running tally of your success rate. How many did you accomplish this week? If you got all three—great! Missed one, two, or all three? Refocus. The good news is, you can do better next week. If you take nothing else away, this habit of selecting and then completing your three most important business development actions each week will keep your BD machine running.

For your weekly review I find that thirty minutes is sufficient once you get the hang of it. You may want to do this review at home—on Sunday evening, for example—so you can complete it free of distraction and begin the following week with a solid plan in place. But Friday afternoon may work for you too. It all depends on your schedule and the nature of your workplace.

Once you instill in yourself the habit of weekly BD planning and review, you'll never understand how you were able to get anything important done without it.

Where and How

Hopefully the steps I've asked you to take so far sound doable—you may even be excited to try them. But perhaps your cynical side is already wondering whether you're going to be able to keep it all up past the first week. That psychological momentum is the key to your success, and that's where the *how* comes in.

One proven technique for habit building is doing the same thing in the same place at the same time, every time. Where are you going to do your weekly review? If you work in an office, this may be an easy one, but you may decide to do it from your home office or to conduct it on the commuter train into the city. This may be a good idea, particularly if your workplace is highly prone to interruptions, noisy, or otherwise distracting.

The important thing is to be consistent and to make sure in advance that you have all the necessary materials at hand. If you work with pen and paper, you'll need your planner and other physical materials within reach. If you're on a laptop, you'll want to make sure your contacts, calendar, and other info can sync properly—this may rule out Amtrak and its spotty Wi-Fi.

People keep track of their to-dos in all kinds of ways, from sophisticated productivity software to a fringe of curling Post-it Notes around a computer monitor. However you manage your current workload, *this system works best when it is tracked separately from your everyday tasks, in its own self-contained system.* This might mean a different app, a separate project within a sophisticated task management app, a different notebook, or Post-it Notes of a different color.

To see my current app recommendations, go to **mobunnell.com /apps**. The important thing is to not get bogged down. Some of the most astonishingly productive rainmakers use nothing but pen and paper.

Note: Whenever I refer to the name of a specific worksheet in **bold**, you will find it available for free download at **mobunnell.com/work sheets**. *You do not want to skip the worksheets.* They are designed to help you implement the system. And although I've made it easy to re-create the worksheets on blank pieces of paper, there's a lot of nuance you'll miss if you do it without seeing the worksheets themselves. Even if you choose to handwrite them or re-create them in your favorite app, you'll want to see the perfect format first.

Okay, now that I've made my pitch for the worksheets, I realize they aren't for everyone. Or you might not have internet access at the moment. No problem—keep reading. We've made it easy for you to read the book and make progress with the simplest of tools, paper and a pen. You can circle back to the downloads later.

Whether worksheets, technology, or starting with blank paper, having everything in one place will help you implement the Snowball System. I want you up and running quickly so you can start seeing benefits right away. I want to get you *hooked*. This is how I do my live training. The people in the room are high earners, and their time is too valuable to waste. (Isn't yours?) We work with real objectives and real metrics so that everyone can return to their desks at the end of the workshop well on their way to implementation and results.

But before we get started with your personal strategic planning, we need to cover something else first: the somewhat secret science behind how people think. We're all different in how we think, with only about 3 percent of people thinking in a balanced way. That's critical for our personal strategic plan because, without it, 97 percent of us will likely leave something important out.

We need to think with our whole brain. Learning how to do this changed my approach to business development and, more broadly, to just about everything I do.

Whole Brain® Thinking*

The heart of the Snowball System is people. To understand people, you need to understand how they think or, more accurately, how they *prefer* to think. The most important person you need to figure out? You! That's why this section is so early in the book. We'll use it immediately to improve your personal strategic plan, making sure it's balanced in its approach. We'll use it throughout the book to improve just about everything else. This is foundational.

Ned Herrmann was at General Electric in the early 1980s when he developed the HBDI® (Herrmann Brain Dominance Instrument®*), an assessment based on research on thinking and the brain. I rely on it in every client interaction and in most of my methods. It's rocket fuel for relationships, and when I stumbled on it, it changed *everything*.

Have you ever tried to win the interest of a new prospect but ran into a brick wall? Think of the last time you sent the email or delivered the pitch that usually sparks interest in even the most skeptical recipient and yet, for some inexplicable reason, your words seemed to fall on deaf ears. So frustrating.

When things don't click, we tend to focus on the substance of the message. But problems connecting with others are typically about the

---

* Whole Brain® Thinking, HBDI®, and Herrmann Brain Dominance Instrument® are registered trademarks of Herrmann Global, LLC.

way you delivered your message, not the message itself. Often what you say just isn't tuned to the way your audience prefers to receive and process it. I had many such disconnects in my own work as a seller-expert. Like you, I chalked these incidents up to some nebulous personality mismatch or perhaps bad conference room cold cuts. Then I discovered the uniqueness of this model, which measures how an individual prefers to communicate, learn, and solve problems. Crucially, it doesn't measure ability—just preferences.

One thing I love about this model is that it was born of solid research. It was developed using extensive research from Nobel Prize–winning neuroscientists as well as Ned Herrmann's own work at Berkeley. Since its inception it has been rigorously validated and updated.

The power of this approach is not limited to the assessment itself; it is also a metaphor for how the brain works. The emphasis is on the *whole* brain, not the oversimplified "left brain/right brain" dichotomy you often see.

Here's the model:

THE WHOLE BRAIN® MODEL

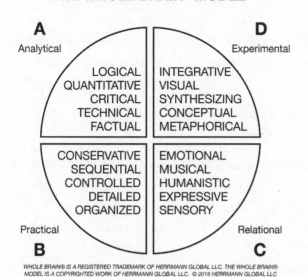

Each quadrant represents a preference for using one mode of thought over the others.

People with Strong A-Quadrant Thinking Preferences
Are More Analytical Thinkers

They tend to be logical and fact based in their decision making. They weigh risks and benefits. Think of an actuary calculating the probability of an event or a litigator structuring a precise legal argument. These folks address the "what" of a question. They are more likely to judge a meeting successful if budgets are agreed upon and clear performance goals are established. Oh, and if the food was purchased at a discount.

People with Strong B-Quadrant Preferences
Are More Practical Thinkers

They tend to be process oriented and tactical. If those with an analytic preference have a calculator running in their mind, practical thinkers have a Gantt chart. You know the type: you say, "Oh, looks like we'll need to reschedule the meeting," and they say, "Right. But we can't do it next week because Bob will be in Los Angeles and Betsy will be on vacation. The following week is okay, but remember, the conference room won't be available that Monday." Folks with a practical preference address "How?" and "When?" For them a successful meeting is one where timelines, steps to complete the goal, resources, policies, and quality guidelines were covered. Making a checklist and checking things off. Let's get some things *done!*

Those with Strong C-Quadrant Preferences
Are More Relational Thinkers

They are intuiting and incorporating others' perspectives and points of view into their decisions. They know just how to phrase a message so the audience will understand. They *get* people. They're asking "Who?" Typically, relational thinkers consider a meeting successful if all the participants have communicated their perspectives and if they enjoyed the experience: "Jim, I noticed you're out of tea. Would you like someone to run out and get more? Organic green dragon, right? You haven't spoken up in a while. What do you think of Jane's suggestion?"

Those with Strong D-Quadrant Preferences Are More Experimental Thinkers

They skew toward creative and strategic solutions. They're the people who ask "Why?" They are typically comfortable synthesizing concepts, identifying important themes, and generating new ideas. For them a successful meeting usually involves people creating or aligning with the big picture, the vision, the solution. "Let's start by reviewing our ten-year plan and then brainstorm using the new floor-to-ceiling whiteboards! We can write in the windows too!"

•

Take a moment and think about yourself. Offhand, based on the way you communicate and solve problems, your approach to making decisions and your overall priorities, how would you assess your own degree of thinking preference for each quadrant? Remember, these are preferences, not abilities. In which of these quadrants are you most *comfortable*? And which quadrants, if any, make you *cringe*?

This model is one of the first things we cover in our training. This is because most people project how *they* think onto the buyer and communicate *their* value in ways that would convince themselves. The better way? Communicate your value in the way the buyer prefers to receive it.

Ann Herrmann-Nehdi is Ned Herrmann's daughter, the CEO of Herrmann International, and the world's foremost expert on using their models. I asked her about the importance of this methodology for seller-experts. She put it very simply: "Your client's buying decision is directly related to the thinking that is going on in their head. It is equally important for you to know how *you* think so that you can properly adapt to your customers, accelerating the process for both of you."

I love Ann's perspective here. It's gold.

If you learn to identify these different thinking processes in yourself as well as in others, you will develop a sixth sense for communicating and working collaboratively. That's the magic of Whole Brain® Thinking for business development. You will see its influence in almost every chapter of this book.

One last fact: over 3 million people have taken the assessment, and of those, about 95 percent reveal *more than one* dominant thinking preference: two, three, or, in some cases, even four. Almost everyone! Thinking is nuanced, and we need to avoid the incorrect simplicity of statements like "Jim's an experimental thinker." Jim might bias toward that way of thinking, but the statistics show he likely has one or more other strong preferences too, and even if he doesn't, he'll probably greatly benefit from hearing from the other perspectives *precisely because he'd likely leave them out himself.*

I'll show you later in the book how to implement all four ways of thinking in your client interactions. Doing this will be your insurance policy, a hedge against multiple thinking preferences among one or more people in the room. Communicating in all four modes of thinking increases your probability of success.

If you're interested in getting an HBDI® Profile* yourself, visit **mobunnell.com/HBDI** for more information. Although taking the assessment would be ideal, you don't need your HBDI® Profile to use this book. Understanding in broad strokes, however, how your clients and prospects prefer to think, communicate, and *be communicated with* will rapidly accelerate your success at building rapport. This model is going to enhance everything we do.

For now our task is to get you thinking about your growth plan, and using the principles we've just learned is going to make it even better. The best plans incorporate all four ways of thinking—that way you won't overemphasize or underemphasize different aspects of the plan. This is planning like you've never seen it before.

Personal Strategic Planning

Earlier you wrote down the why that drives you to get better at business development. Your *why* is your ultimate purpose in learning to be

---

* Whole Brain® Thinking, HBDI®, and Herrmann Brain Dominance Instrument® are registered trademarks of Herrmann Global, LLC.

a rainmaker, your endgame, the objective that transcends your current project, your current role, even your current career. Deciding on your why can be incredibly motivating and inspiring, but you don't want to stop there. To succeed, you need to step back and figure out how you're actually going to pursue your objective—day by day, month by month, year by year. All the tactics in this book won't do you any good unless they're aligned with a clear and purposeful *strategy*. So how do you build one?

Although there are many different definitions of the term "strategy," with regard to business development, I like to keep it simple. A strategy is a top-down plan for getting from where you are to where you want to be. It's what you'll emphasize over all else.

First, we need to figure out where we are. Get the **Beginning State Scorecard** worksheet—remember: bold means a worksheet is available at **mobunnell.com/worksheets**—to complete the following 100-point self-evaluation, or just tally your score on a notepad. If you're not able to download it at the moment, below is a quick and dirty version to keep you moving forward in the meantime.

As you fill out this first scorecard, don't worry about perfection in your scoring. Don't sweat too much over if something's a 3 or a 4. You don't need to do this (or any part of the Snowball System) perfectly—that will slow you down too much. You just want to create a rough snapshot of the state of your BD efforts today. Think of Olympic judges assigning numerical scores to artistic events like diving or gymnastics. It's an analytical approach to evaluating a subjective performance. Is it perfect? No. But quantitative evaluation can help track and improve nearly any kind of performance. That's our goal here: to create a quick analysis of your current BD state so we can improve it.

Relationships

Our success at business development rests on a foundation of relationships, so let's start there. Score yourself from 1 to 5 on each of these, for a maximum possible score of 20.

+ Have I identified—and written down—the key characteristics of my ideal clients? (Score 1 to 5)
+ Have I used these key characteristics of my ideal clients to identify and write down the organizations I'd like to get introduced to? (Score 1 to 5)
+ Do I have a method for investing in and being helpful to the most important people who will help me grow (clients, strategic partners, influencers)? (Score 1 to 5)
+ Do I have an appropriate number of touch points to stay top of mind with these most important people, and do I track my touch points? (Score 1 to 5)

Vision

How clear is your vision to grow your business? Score yourself from 1 to 5 on each of these, for a maximum possible score of 20.

+ Have I defined the areas where my ideal clients will be spending money in the future? (Score 1 to 5)
+ Do I have a clear brand I promote in the marketplace that is aligned with these areas? (Score 1 to 5)
+ Do I have a clear BD strategy for each step in the process, from generating leads to closing deals, and do I follow it consistently? (Score 1 to 5)
+ Do I have a vision for integrating current clients, strategic partners, and colleagues with my overall business strategy? (Score 1 to 5)

Measurement

Next let's figure out what we can measure so we know whether we're on track. We need to collect a few numbers:

+ How much money would you have liked to have brought in over the last year?
+ How much money did you actually bring in?

If you don't know these numbers and can't find them easily, make a quick estimate. Now let's compare them. If you brought in as much money or more than you would have liked to over the last year, give yourself a 5. Earning 90 to 99 percent of your goal is a 4, 80 to 89 percent is a 3, 70 to 79 percent is a 2, and less than 70 percent is a 1.

Now we'll use a similar process to look at how much time you invested in BD activities and how effective that time was:

+ How many hours per year do you think you should be investing in growing your business? What investment of time would be best? (Keep reading through the next paragraph if you're not sure).
+ How many hours did you actually invest in growing your business?

Working forty hours a week for fifty weeks a year adds up to two thousand work hours annually. Use that as a rough benchmark to determine these numbers. An expert changing firms and under a nonsolicitation agreement might invest two thousand hours in business development during their first year because they are starting from scratch. A forty-year veteran consultant who gets pulled into larger projects by others might invest very little—but they also might not be doing the work they'd like and might not be moving up in the organization.

I think a good annual minimum for most seller-experts is two hundred to four hundred hours, and that's after you have a stable, thriving book of business. For many, it's more. Below that and, even if you're busy, you're likely not attracting the high-value, high-margin work you'd like. Or, if you're an account manager or account executive, you're likely not growing your accounts as quickly as your leadership would like.

Whatever you do, pay attention to the time you're spending on business development, including setting goals. Time is the most precious resource you have, and the professionals I work with find this evaluation powerful when we analyze it in our classes. Don't skip this step. If you do, you'll let the world determine your time and fate—instead, design the life you want.

Now let's compare how many hours you invested versus how many you would have liked to have invested. If you invested as much time or more than you would have liked over the last year, give yourself a 5. Investing 90 to 99 percent of your goal is a 4, 80 to 89 percent is a 3, 70 to 79 percent is a 2, and less than 70 percent is a 1.

Here are two final questions to round out the measurement section:

+ Do I have an ongoing process for measuring and reinforcing my personal success? (Score 1 to 5)
+ Do I have an ongoing process for measuring and reinforcing my team's success or, if solo, my success with my outside collaborators and strategic partners? (Score 1 to 5)

Action

Let's close by looking at how you've been doing on implementation: getting the plan right and then executing.

Important: These questions are each worth 10 points, not 5. That's because consistency is vital when filling your pipeline and winning more work. As a result, we weigh process heavily.

+ Do I have an ongoing series of meetings to measure and track my success? These "meetings" can be just with yourself, with an accountability partner, or with your team. The key is that you allot time to managing your pipeline just as you do for managing any important project. (Score 1 to 10)
+ Do I have an easy-to-use system to measure and track my success? (Score 1 to 10)
+ Do I hold myself accountable for my commitments? (Score 1 to 10)
+ Do I celebrate my *incremental* successes (not just the end goal of closing business deals but also the progress toward that end) personally and with my colleagues? (Score 1 to 10)

Add up your quadrants. Remember that the Action section can add up to as many as 40 points and the other quadrants can add up to 20.

How close to 100 did you get?

It can be painful to see your weak spots exposed like this, but don't let it overwhelm you. This scorecard is comprehensive. No one hits all these marks perfectly, no matter their level of experience. In our classes most professionals score between 40 and 60. They don't stay there, of course. (Hold on to your score because you're going to want to check at intervals to see how much you've improved and what still needs work. I update and review my scorecard annually, but you might want to do it as frequently as quarterly as you get the Snowball System up and running.)

Now it's time to set some goals to get better. This is an opportunity to use the insights you've gained from assessing your current situation to outline a plan for the coming year. Get the **Future State Scorecard** worksheet, or take out a blank sheet of paper and draw a big plus sign in the middle, then add a title for Relationships (lower right), Vision (upper right), Measurement (upper left), and Action (lower left). Feel free to duplicate this in an electronic document if you like.

Relationships

+ Describe your ideal prospects, including the best role to approach when first entering a new company.
+ Describe your ideal strategic partners, the people positioned to refer prospects to you or who have influence in the decision to choose you.
+ Describe the ways you'll consistently invest in being helpful and staying top of mind to these prospects and partners.

Vision

+ Describe what your ideal prospects will be spending money on in the coming years. What are the strongest trends in your industry?
+ Describe the brand you will be known for and how it will align with these spending patterns.

Measurement

✦ Quantify how much revenue you will generate next year.

✦ Pick the one or two BD metrics that are under your direct control. The two I usually recommend starting with are the time you spend on business development (BD hours) and the selection and number of MITs you complete (MITs completed). These two work well together, giving both a quantity and quality perspective. Get creative and choose a different set of measures if that works better for you.

Action

✦ Describe the BD rituals you'll implement.

✦ Describe how you'll hold yourself accountable for completing your BD work.

Let's work through this entire process using an example. Say you're a consultant who facilitates the development of strategic plans. You've just gone out on your own, having worked in strategic planning roles *inside* four large organizations over the past decade. You have fifty-six contacts in high-level leadership roles with significant budgetary authority. These leaders are now scattered across seventeen different organizations.

The good news: you know lots of well-positioned people who hold you in high esteem.

The bad news: your pipeline is at zero, no one is paying you a salary, and you'd like to afford your kids' college education and the occasional visit to a decent coffee shop.

Here's what your planning might look like:

Relationships

✦ Ideal prospect: My perfect prospect is someone in a leadership role, preferably with one-hundred-plus people reporting up to them. That's where I think budgetary levels will fit with my pricing.

+ Ideal strategic partners: I will be working this first quarter on defining my perfect strategic partner, as I'm not sure who that is yet. I think it will be other experts who call on senior leaders, possibly in areas of expertise like communication skills or executive search (headhunters).
+ Network investment: I'll be constantly investing in my network by sharing advice and articles on strategic planning and team management that I've collected over the years. I hope to ping each of my fifty-six contacts once a month with something valuable that's not a pitch to hire me but instead emphasizes my expertise.

Focus

+ Future spend at ideal prospects: Senior leaders are being pushed to be more strategic, and of all their responsibilities, this is one area that's easy to justify spending money on.
+ My brand: My expertise is the facilitation of strategic planning. Because I don't have an army of analysts to help me, I'll focus on strategic meeting facilitation this year, letting the client dig into the data and allowing me focus on conducting interactive planning sessions using the process I've developed. It features early interactive sessions that create team alignment and relationship building along with an iterative approach to finalize the plan. To state my brand concisely, *I am the person who can efficiently lead a team to craft a strategic plan, taking them from dysfunctional or less than ideal to high performing.*

Measurement

+ Revenue: I'd like to bring in $1,000,000 this first year. Because I'll charge about $100,000 for a strategy facilitation project, I need to sell and deliver eight or nine of those, making up the remainder with smaller, onetime meeting facilitations and presentations. If I get a 50 percent acceptance rate, I'll need to propose $2,000,000 of new business. Lots to do!
+ Trackable metrics: I'll offer a free one-hour strategic analysis using the method I've created to each of the fifty-six qualified contacts I've

identified. My contacts can use them or offer them to someone else they know who might need it. I'll only count offers I make in person or on the phone, as I want to get into a deeper conversation with each person. Quality over quantity, so no offers over email. I'll reach out to thirty in the first month, fifteen in month two, and the final eleven in month three. I'll likely revisit what I should track at the end of the first three months. I'm a little scared of my commitment here, but I'm going for it. I need the momentum, or else I'll fail. I do *not* want to fail. My family and friends are watching.

Action

+ My BD rituals: I will conduct a weekly review of progress with my free analysis offers and with advice and articles sent out as part of my broader outreach efforts. Keep the focus on asking for and getting these meetings and making these offers. Reminders to myself: I'm being helpful, not salesy. And I need to keep the consistency on outreach, even if I land a project or two early. Nights and weekends belong to my pipeline these first three months, not me.
+ Accountability: I'll hold myself accountable by sending my accountability partner my weekly data. He's a few years ahead of me in starting his own business and has agreed to review my data weekly. It's due to him at 4 p.m. every Friday. Our call at 4:30 p.m. each week to review my progress—or lack of progress—is really going to keep me going. He has promised to get in my grill if I don't do what I need to do and to celebrate when I do. We're focused on what's *in my control*. If I do what I've set out to do here, the work will come. I can hardly wait to help my clients succeed!

Don't be afraid to set your sights high. Although your goals should feel achievable, the most effective and motivating goals feel *challenging*. Don't set the bar so low that you can step over it.

Now, write your plan.

Done? Congratulations! You've created a vision for the future. Science shows that this act alone has a powerful effect.

Harnessing the *Power of Habits*

With some of your goals in place, it's time to look at the other core behavioral tool that makes this system so effective. Although good goals are critical, establishing the right habits—and eliminating the wrong ones—are fundamental to executing it.

As discussed earlier in the chapter, habits are amazingly powerful. Research shows that we spend more of our time on "autopilot" than we realize. Think about it: What did you do when you first woke up this morning? Have your first cup of coffee? Check your email? Hug the large, black dog sleeping in your bed? (Okay, maybe that's just me.)

Now compare this morning's activities to the ones you performed yesterday. Chances are they look very similar. The brain loves a good routine. When it's following a routine for the hundredth or thousandth time, it knows exactly what to do and how to do it. It feels great to accomplish things well and smoothly—you're in a groove. You learn to crave the sensation of accomplishing tasks easily, without too much cognitive effort. Habits are also rewarding because they usually end with actual rewards: positive sensations like the clean, minty sensation you get from brushing your teeth.

Your brain is constantly looking for ways to save energy by finding rewarding patterns and establishing habits around them. Makes sense, right? But there's another part to this story, as explained by Dan and Chip Heath in their book *Switch*. The Heath brothers use the metaphor of a rider steering an elephant. The rider is the rational part of our minds, the conscious "I" that thinks it's in charge and making all the decisions. The elephant is the subconscious, emotional part of the mind. As you might guess from the metaphor, the subconscious part is more powerful than the rational mind.

To a certain degree the rider can steer behavior. Go ahead: look up from this page and stare at the wall for a count of three. Then continue reading.

Did it work? Your rider made the conscious decision to perform that behavior. All well and good for something as simple as staring at the wall, but when things get difficult or stressful, the elephant is going to go pretty much where it wants. Let yourself get too hungry while on your diet, and the elephant is going to push you straight for the cookie jar. It's in moments like these when you can feel how limited the rider's influence truly is.

In a way the rider aligns with the upper part of the HBDI® Profile, the analytical and experimental quadrants that involve logic and strategy. You know how many calories each cookie contains (analytical), and you have a vision for the beach body you want to attain (experimental and, in this case, the visionary part of experimentation). Yet the elephant, represented by the lower practical and relational quadrants, wants dessert because dinner should end with dessert (practical—in this case, a process) and because, heck, today was a really hard day (relational—in this case, a sense of our own feelings). A moment later the cookie is gone. Yum! Wait, I shouldn't have eaten that cookie! Dang it. Elephant got me again.

So when it comes to building good habits and removing negative ones, routines (practical) and emotions (relational) rule. These are the elephant quadrants. Over the long term, fighting them is a losing battle. Harness them, and you can achieve almost anything. You just need to work with the power of your elephant.

In this system we use the word "rituals" to refer to productive habits that help you accomplish your goals. Specifically, a ritual is a chain of behaviors that, once triggered, are performed habitually and without much additional cognitive effort.

A ritual can be triggered by the calendar. For example, you might start your laundry on Sunday mornings. It can also be driven by an event. Receiving your employer's W-2 might be your cue to start work on your taxes.

What are some of your calendar-triggered habits? What are some of your event-driven habits? Which propel you toward success, and which are holding you back?

Before we start designing BD rituals to achieve your specific goals, there are two important points about habit building. First, the easiest way to start a new habit is to chain it to something that already happens without fail. This effectively skips a step because you already have a cue, or trigger, to build from. Second, always reward yourself immediately after performing a ritual. While the rider in your brain may see the connection between a reward and a ritual performed earlier in the day, the elephant won't. So make it quick and fun: your second coffee of the morning, a walk around the building, five minutes on social media.

Let's look at two examples, one calendar driven and one event driven.

Let's say you want to establish a calendar-driven weekly ritual to proactively send something valuable to one important client each week. You might plan to do this before your Monday morning team stand-up meeting. Focusing on getting it done before the meeting will give you a deadline, with a little rush to get things finished before the meeting starts. You'll feel that clock ticking, which is good. Doing this first thing will start your week off with momentum, accomplishing the hard thing first. That's a reward in itself. The trigger: meeting coming! The reward: satisfaction knowing you knocked out the hard thing.

Now, an event-driven ritual. Let's say you've been told that you over-emphasize analytical thinking, so you want to improve at the relational aspects of client development. From now on, every time you're going to talk to a client, decide in advance on one thing to ask that client—and not the typical "How was your weekend? Great! Down to business!" An authentic question with follow-up questions that show interest. Use what you've learned about the client so far. For example, if you've learned that your client plays a particular sport avidly, you might ask if there was a match this weekend. It's a subtle difference, but it shows forethought and genuine curiosity. Don't know anything about this client? Social media is no help? Start by asking a question about their interests and hobbies.

The trigger to prepare a question will be "every phone call or in-person meeting with a client." Your ritual might be writing a question down on a Post-it and putting it where you can't miss it. The reward? You could have a piece of paper tallying your opportunities and how many times you successfully asked your question, with it only counting for a score if you truly listened and followed up with a question or two to show that you did.

You could even sum up your results at the end of the week, a weekly relationship scoreboard of sorts. The key is immediately tallying the opportunity and, if you deserve it, the success. Solid trigger, immediate reward. (You might find yourself worrying about it sounding inauthentic, but the more you do it, the easier and more authentic it will feel.) At the end of each week you can add up the number of opportunities you've had, increasing or decreasing your success percentages over time. It'll feel great to watch your numbers increase along with the quality of your relationships.

With these examples in mind, it's time to design your rituals. Get the **Rituals** worksheet, or simply write these words at the top of a blank piece of paper:

Ritual	Calendar or Event Trigger	Reward

Now design a few rituals that will build some BD momentum for you. Picking just a couple will be enough to get started; once you start seeing your rituals become truly habitual, you will be motivated to create more.

Done? Perfect. You'll revise and improve these as you go, but it's a great start. Your initial plan is important—it's essential to get started in the right direction, with the right priorities. But designing and actually *performing* your rituals is where you'll succeed or fail.

●

If you're like most of the professionals who train with us, you already feel pushed to the limit with your current workload. However certain you are of the need to grow your business, deep down you may also be wondering: *What if this system actually* works? *Then I'll really be in trouble.*

Boy, it's ironic. You're reading a book on growing your business, desperate to find something that works—and half-afraid that it will. *After all, if this is as effective as Mo says it is, it may bring in more work than I can handle! Then what?*

In my experience, growing your business changes the nature of the work for the better, even if the transition is rocky. More qualified leads and more new clients translate into more of the challenging, highly profitable work you enjoy doing, while you delegate the rest, often by expanding your own team. And if you refer less-than-ideal prospects out to other organizations instead? They have a strong motivator to refer the work you want most back to you. Either way, it's a win.

In addition, the skills you will learn throughout this book will make you more efficient in general. Although at times it may seem like I'm adding a lot of work to your plate, by learning to be more strategic and to only invest your efforts where they will be most effective, you'll find yourself clearing away much of the busywork that had been clogging up your day with little to show for it. Your work life may get downright serene, even as the floodgates widen. I've seen it happen. It's the difference between the doggy paddle and the breaststroke.

The fact is, *you already sell*. In fact, you have a BD strategy—for most people it's just a hodgepodge of tactics and preconceived notions accumulated over the course of your career. The time has come for an upgrade. When you're finished, your only regret will be that you didn't start learning the Snowball System sooner.

CHAPTER 2

The Flywheel

. . .

> If your ladder is not leaning against the right wall, every step you take gets
> you to the wrong place faster.
>
> —STEPHEN COVEY, *The 7 Habits of Highly Effective People*

EVEN THE BEST tool in the world is useless if you don't use it. When I
made the transition from actuary to account manager, I knew I needed a
true business development *system* to take my career to the next level. I also
knew that it would have to be bulletproof, something I could stick to no
matter how hectic things got. Otherwise I'd eventually run out of steam.

When your work involves clients, regardless of your industry or profession, there's a certain amount of flexibility required. People reschedule
lunch at the last minute. People hold meetings without setting agendas.
People dial in to conference calls fifteen minutes late and spend the remaining time discussing everything *but* the deal on the table. Some days
it can feel like your progress has gone missing like a set of car keys.

No matter how organized and disciplined *you* might be, it's the nature
of client work that things will get out of hand now and then. As the actions of others derail your day, week, or even month, it takes more and
more time and energy to get yourself back on track.

In contrast, business development, when done right, works like a flywheel. Once you put the initial effort into cranking it up to speed, your
system only needs a small amount of steady input to keep the business
growing. But if you fail to do so consistently, it will eventually run down.

I got to experience the flywheel firsthand while working at Hewitt when I moved up in its healthcare consulting practice in the 1990s. The work was unpredictable by nature, with some bonus seasonal spikes occurring throughout the year. We would have very little work in the winter and be so busy in the summer that it would be hard to take a single vacation day. And back then the size of our engagements was pretty small, all encompassing, and usually completed within a few weeks, so it was difficult to know what we'd be doing next month, let alone a few months out. Every time we dug ourselves out from a crisis, we'd discover that our pipeline of potential client leads had almost dried up. We'd invest major effort in restarting the flywheel through business development, only to watch it spin back down during the next busy patch as the work forced us all to neglect business development again.

I'd come face-to-face with the dreaded *business development paradox*: hustle to bring in work, get busy, slack off on business development because you're busy, end up right back where you started.

Using Habits and Goals to Drive Continuous Progress

As I started to lead my own client relationships, I was scared. I had to address the paradox, so I decided to focus on behavior. Not client behavior, which is unpredictable and essentially out of my control. Instead, I zeroed in on my own behavior. What could I do differently? At first I tried brute force. I started working seventy- and eighty-hour weeks to ensure that my business development got done no matter how busy things got. I made sure to keep the flywheel going *no matter what.*

But throwing quantity at the problem was not the answer. As burnout set in, I knew there had to be a way to get my BD work done while still seeing my family now and again and perhaps sleeping more than four hours a night.

Eventually I began to look at my habits. They're the gift that keep on giving. Once you've developed a strong habit, it provides all the benefits of the behavior with none of the mental drain. While it took years to evolve them, it started with small changes with a big impact.

So how would I build some positive new BD habits? On the surface the kinds of things I did for business development didn't seem to translate into the habits I was reading about. Creating a new prospect pitch deck isn't the same thing as remembering to floss. Thankfully, as I dug deeper, the research provided me with some clues.

In the last chapter we talked about how a few early successes create a kind of psychological momentum. It turns out that a couple of quick wins not only make you more likely to continue doing a certain behavior, but they even make the activity *feel* easier. In short, *early success breeds long-term resilience.* But the research also found that this gain can be easily squandered—break the momentum before the habit is firmly established, and you're likely to stop doing it completely.

With this concept in mind, I decided to set small goals to start. That way I'd have no excuse not to do them no matter how busy I was. I needed to rack up wins early on to create momentum. This would make the tasks feel easier and more enjoyable, making me more likely to continue and making the habit itself stronger. Consistency would be key; I didn't want to skip a day under any circumstances.

As you'll see in the coming chapters, this is the framework for how we will build all the positive BD behaviors you'll rely on as a rainmaker: start small, target early wins, and place consistency above all. If you've never deliberately grown a habit like this before, you may be surprised how quickly a behavior can go from awkward to automatic.

Of course, the more complex or challenging the behavior, the longer it can take to become hardwired—my clients tell me two or three months practicing a new BD habit usually cements it. They usually continue to improve after that, but the snowball is already rolling downhill with its own momentum. So be patient with yourself, especially at first, because every new behavior will feel uncomfortable and frustrating at first. But your efforts will pay dividends for the rest of your career.

This isn't just something I've experienced—the research bears it out too. My favorite researcher on this topic is Teresa Amabile at Harvard. Her aptly titled book *The Progress Principle* details that workers focused on making small, incremental improvements—and celebrating their progress frequently—are both the most productive *and* happiest workers.

That's why think big, start small, scale up works. You begin with a small improvement, celebrate it, and continue to grow from there. After a while you can't stop.

In the end, habits are powerful but limited. Although they can propel you, they won't help you steer. I next considered how to direct my daily efforts toward the overarching objective: more of the right clients and more of the right work with those clients. Habits promised steady forward momentum, but without a clear direction, I could easily establish counterproductive behaviors that led nowhere. That meant I needed to establish goals.

It's become fashionable among some productivity experts to scoff at goal setting. They're wrong: goals work. I teach BD goal setting in my training and continue to marvel at the results. The science backs this up: research into the effectiveness of goal setting gained momentum in the 1960s. Psychologists wanted to understand why some people perform significantly better, both personally and professionally, than the rest of us. Many studies were performed over the years, but macro answers remained elusive. Many studies found goal setting powerful, but a few said otherwise. Then researcher Edwin Locke reviewed over one hundred studies performed using decades of data and found an *extremely strong* statistical correlation between goal setting and performance. Taken together, the research made clear that writing down the things you want to accomplish increases your odds of success at doing those things. I can't think of a better use for a Post-it Note.

The secret to sustainable, successful business development is twofold: well-designed habits to keep you moving through thick and thin, and clear, ambitious goals to know where you're going. Amabile plus Locke. The combination is unstoppable.

Business Development Is a Skill

"Sure, I earned multiple advanced degrees and became one of the foremost experts in my field, but when it comes to client relationships, you've either got it or you don't, and I don't."

This line of thinking is one of my biggest pet peeves. I can't tell you how many times I've heard the "you've either got it or you don't" argument from someone about to begin training in the Snowball System. It's crap. In fact, it's harmful. Being effective at building relationships is not the result of some gene in your DNA, and believing otherwise is nothing but an excuse to avoid learning how.

Just think of a rainmaker in your own profession. You know at least one. Down the hall or at another company, there's a person who does pretty much the same thing you do but grows their business much more quickly. Worst of all, this person makes all of it—finding new opportunities, meeting strategic partners, attracting quality leads, landing big projects—look easy. Even fun. Rainmaking looks, to the rest of us humble mortals, like magic.

This is where one of my favorite quotes comes in. It's from science fiction writer Arthur C. Clarke: "Any sufficiently advanced technology is indistinguishable from magic."

This is why people can jump to the conclusion that BD skills are hidden in some secret strand of DNA, that some people are "born with it." When they see the rainmaker in action, the skills seem too advanced for them to perform. The thing is, they didn't see the rainmaker working on a growth strategy, tired, on a delayed flight home. They didn't see the rainmaker struggling to adapt to a certain thinking style. They didn't see the rainmaker writing down a list of core relationships to maintain—and then keeping in touch with them, month after month. Yes, rainmaking is learned.

We invent all sorts of reasons to explain why the rainmaker gets the great clients, the lucrative projects, the team to lead: natural charm, good looks, "shameless" salesmanship. All this to avoid the uncomfortable truth that, although you may be a better expert, *that isn't enough*. Once you get to a certain level of competency in your area, the fast way up is through business development.

Business development is a skill like any other. Learning it takes study and practice, but those are two things you already know how to do. After all, you've mastered the fundamentals of your profession. Choosing to deliberately study business development just means accepting that once you have enough expertise to talk to clients and prospects, learning business development is your most promising path to growth.

I understand the frustration you may be feeling at this point, as I have hit the same wall myself: "Are you kidding me? I busted my butt for a decade to learn my job, and now I have to start all over again with something new?"

Shoshin is a concept in Zen Buddhism. It means "beginner's mind." To have shoshin is to approach a practice without any preconceived notions or expectations, even after you've reached an advanced level. It takes humility to tackle a new skill once you've become an expert in your field; it's easier to simply rest on your laurels and work with what you've got.

Learning skills at the beginning of your career is so much easier. As an expert, it takes plenty of shoshin to make progress at something new. Every student of business development begins at the beginning, no matter how accomplished they might be in their primary expertise.

One final, important note on your evolution as a rainmaker: with two disciplines to master, one must take priority. So which should come first—your core expertise or business development?

People naturally assume that their expertise—the thing they're actually paid to do—should always take precedence. But from what I've seen while training thousands of seller-experts, putting business development first leads to more success. This happens for a simple reason: if you focus on your core expertise first, you might never improve at business development. But if you treat business development as your number-one priority, you will naturally improve at your craft along the way. It's a buy-one-get-one deal: buy into business development, and you get your craft upgraded for free. You'll be talking to more prospects than ever, speaking at professional conferences, developing collateral materials, having lunch with strategic partners, and so on. As a result, you'll have your finger on the pulse of the industry and a direct line to the most pressing concerns of clients. Business development should become the target of your professional development efforts moving forward. This commitment will pay dividends.

The Hallmarks of a Rainmaker

So business development isn't magic—just a matter of advanced technique. *Business development is the craft of finding the right prospect and then designing the perfect buying experience for that prospect.*

As professionals we shy away from calling this process "selling." That word conjures an image: the dishonest car salesman who offers what's on the lot instead of what you need, who doesn't know much about cars, who doesn't listen, who is nowhere to be found when your new hybrid sedan breaks down.

This is the opposite of what we want to work toward. As professionals who have invested years in developing an expertise, our greatest aspiration is to become trusted advisors. Our notions about traditional selling run counter to that, so the word gets tarnished. (If you haven't read David Maister's book *The Trusted Advisor*, add it to your list. I read it early in my career, and it's stuck with me.)

What does it mean to be a trusted advisor? Think about the advisors you trust in your own life. Do you put great stock in your accountant's advice? In the suggestions of your attorney? In the prescriptions of your doctor? Each of us places our trust in a select few professionals because (1) they're good at what they do, (2) they clearly demonstrate that they have our best interests in mind, and (3) they tell us like it is instead of telling us what we want to hear. You know you can count on your trusted advisors when the stakes are high. You wouldn't think of going to anyone else.

When someone you know has a problem that's in your advisor's wheelhouse, you're going to pull out your pom-poms and start cheering. You're a raving fan. With clients like you, your trusted advisor doesn't need to waste time cold-calling leads.

To become trusted advisors ourselves, we don't want to sell. We want to help. Rainmakers are helpful. When we reframe negative "selling" to positive "helping," our hackles go down about the whole process. We're not seeking out new prospects so we can sell to them but rather offering them assistance they really need. Have a first meeting on the books? Look for ways to help. Going to lunch with someone you'd like to become a client? Look for ways to help. Can't get someone to call you back? Look for ways to help.

Changing your mindset from selling to helping is the critical first step to growth. Someone who thinks of growth as a negative won't move forward. Someone who's genuinely trying to help more and more people in bigger and deeper ways? They'll naturally find and develop opportunities.

With that in mind, let's dig a little deeper into relationships. Too often we invest in the wrong people for the wrong reasons and then wonder why we don't get the results we want. How can we move to trusted advisor and even beyond with the most important people? It's time for a tool to bring focus to your relationship-building efforts.

Investing in Your Most Important Relationships

Your most important task as a professional is to keep each of your key relationships going strong. This goes not only for your client relationships, of course, but also for everyone else with the potential to make a positive impact on your business.

What you need in order to become a true rainmaker is a systematic method for developing your relationships to the fullest. Part of the challenge is figuring out which of many possible relationships to invest in. Time and energy are the most valuable resource, and yet we scatter them widely, focusing on the people who are easy to approach and already want to spend time with us. Becoming successful at business development means taking a rigorous, deliberate approach to building the most important relationships, regardless of how difficult they might appear.

Better relationships will transform every aspect of your life, both personally and professionally. Certainly, nothing will have a more dramatic impact on your business and career than a thoughtful, systematic approach to creating more, stronger, and more valuable relationships. The goal of this system is simple: to turn the people who matter into raving fans.

Management author Ken Blanchard coined the term *raving fans* in his book of the same name. He argued that the best way to beat the competition is to take such extraordinarily good care of your clients and customers that they will not be able to stop talking about you to everyone they know. When you consistently go above and beyond for your clients, they will start raving about you, your integrity, your service, and your company. Raving fans are by far your best marketing strategy. You'll never get a better lead than a warm referral from a thrilled client.

Most of us give the process of investing in relationships very little thought. Typically we secure a first paid engagement with a client thanks to a combination of luck, work, and planning. Then, rather than double down on our success with our new client and find a way to go deeper, we go back to putting out fires with our other clients and let that fragile new relationship wither.

Psychology shows that it takes time and repetition to build a new behavior. Interacting with us and our product or service should become a habit for our new client. That's why the first weeks and months of the relationship are by far the most important. Excel now, and your client relationship will continue on an excellent footing for years to come. This is a broader application of what researchers call the "primacy effect": we remember beginnings disproportionately because they anchor us. The beginning of a relationship is a delicate time: mess it up, and it's very tough to recover. Get it right, and you build momentum that is hard to stop.

Don't take it from me. Allow me to introduce you to Peter Sellers, my business development crash-test dummy. He's here to make mistakes so you don't have to.

Peter has a meeting on the books with Sally Beier. He learns through a mutual friend that Sally already has a negative impression of Peter's company. They've wasted her time in the past, making promises and then failing to deliver. In fact, she has only agreed to meet with Peter because of this mutual friend.

Determined to overcome Sally's skepticism, Peter prepares diligently for the introductory meeting. He knows that he and his organization have a lot to offer her and that there's no reason a previous bad experience should prevent that from happening.

On the day of the meeting Peter dresses to the nines, arrives ten minutes early, and delivers a polished and engaging presentation with the focus squarely on Sally and the pressing needs of her business. As you'd expect, all that prep pays off. Although Sally is chilly at first, she warms up in response to Peter's professionalism and commitment. They end with a great dialogue on possible next steps, the meeting wraps on time, and Peter agrees to call in a few weeks to follow up.

Those weeks pass. Peter is busy preparing for another prospect meeting, an even bigger opportunity than the one he had with Sally Beier. He also has a memo to draft, his in-laws are coming to town for the upcoming holiday, and the family vacation is only a few days away. How will he find the time to—wait, what was he supposed to do for Sally Beier? Send her an email? What exactly was the next step there? *Ah, well. Time will jog my memory*, he falsely decides. He makes a note to follow up, somehow, with Sally as soon as he gets back from vacation.

Cut to two weeks later. What a great trip! The whole family had a great time enjoying the outdoors. Back at his desk, Peter glumly notices his note to himself and decides to just give Sally a call about that meeting from more than a month ago. He'll figure out what he was supposed to have done as he's doing it.

When he gets Sally on the phone, Peter senses right away that something is wrong. She's gone cold on him, just like she was at the start of their first meeting. Her answers are brief and crisp, even to strategic, open-ended questions. The conversation goes nowhere.

Peter's confused. Sally had been impressed when they met.

Peter follows up once more.

Crickets.

This happens all the time. The prospect has preconceived notions. The professional tries to change them at the introductory meeting, making promises about different outcomes. Then those promises are broken and the existing impression is reinforced. Another opportunity lost.

In this case Sally Beier came into the situation with a preexisting negative impression of professionals from Peter's company. Peter, through his behavior at the first meeting, indicated to Sally that he was different. Then he failed to follow up as promised, reinforcing her preexisting beliefs. Game over.

We like to blame our BD failures on the prospects and their beliefs, attitudes, and opinions. After all, if you tried to woo a skeptical prospect like Sally Beier and it didn't pan out, you'd probably chalk it up to her "attitude." If she already had a bone to pick with your organization or with salespeople in general, how is that your fault?

The fact is, it doesn't matter. Even if Sally had a neutral view of Peter's organization, she'd likely have had a negative view of other seller-experts she'd encountered elsewhere. We've been asked to interview our client's clients before, and most of them tell us that first-time meetings are overwhelmingly a bust. That lack of follow-up Peter displayed is, sadly, the norm. You should enter every new relationship expecting a mountain to climb because there usually is.

What would have happened if Peter had handled this prospect differently? Let's rewind the crash test and run it differently.

The day after the introductory meeting Peter sends Sally a thank-you email summarizing the points they'd agreed on and where he still needs to get internal clarification. He also sends a personalized LinkedIn request, noting a few people they know in common.

Three days later Peter sends another follow-up, providing answers on all but one of the remaining points. (That last one needs input from an expert who is on vacation.)

Four days later he sends the follow-up on the remaining point.

The next week Peter sends Sally a link to a *Harvard Business Review* article pertaining to the issue at hand. "Thought you might find this helpful," he tells her. "Check out the quote on page 2 discussing . . . "

Two days after that, Peter introduces Sally by email to an existing client (and raving fan) who has dealt with the same issue and would be willing to discuss Sally's situation with her (plugging Peter along the way).

Finally, right on schedule as promised, Peter calls Sally back to follow up on their introductory meeting.

How would that follow-up call have gone this way? Would Sally still nurse her grudge against the company? Would she still refuse to respond?

Actions speak louder than words. It makes no sense to invest tremendous effort before the first meeting but not on the follow-up. You build trust through repetition and consistency over time. The more time you invest in your prospects, the better your relationships will be.

This doesn't have to mean only face time, either. It can mean sending a research finding, making a helpful introduction, linking to an article of interest. Even though we're pretty much powerless to control other people's overall perceptions, opinions, beliefs, and values, we can control our own behaviors. The easiest way to shape someone's opinion of you is to say what you're going to do and then do what you said you would, over and over and over again.

When you follow through like this, you build trust. Trust is the single most important quality in a relationship. It is also the most fragile; once lost, it is rarely regained. Trust grows slowly, advancing an inch each time you make a promise and keep that promise. And it shrinks rapidly, retreating a foot or more for each promise you break.

Of course, building relationships beyond the level of acquaintance requires more than just consistency. One of the hardest leaps for most professionals is advancing beyond the level of paying client. Once someone signs off on our work, most of us tend to consider the relationship-building job "done," when, in reality, it's just getting started.

Behavioral scientists use R as a shorthand for something that *reinforces* a behavior. R+ is a positive reinforcer, and R–, a negative. When Peter showed up on time for the introductory meeting and delivered a useful, targeted presentation, he created an R+ experience for Sally. When he failed to follow up on time, unintentionally repeating the same behavior she'd experienced with other professionals from his company, he created an R– experience, reinforcing her existing negative opinion.

Although the one R+ didn't hurt, it is only through repeated, sustained, positive reinforcement that a person will change a negative opinion to a positive one. Research indicates that it takes a small mountain of R+ events just to neutralize one R–! Bad is just more powerful than good. In a paper aptly entitled "Bad Is Stronger Than Good," Roy Baumeister and others at Case Western and the Free University of Amsterdam did a meta-analysis of over one hundred psychological studies. They found that the human mind consistently remembered negative events longer and more powerfully than positive ones. (One exception was things we did ourselves, where we tend to overemphasize our positives and underemphasize our negatives. I must be way out of the norm as I only seem to remember my failings!)

How much more powerful is bad than good? It depends on the context and the study. One they quote finds that in romantic relationships, negatives count five times more. In our training we use a ratio of four-to-one as a general rule of thumb. Think of it this way: you might enjoy a couple of great meals in a row at a new restaurant, but one extremely rude server and some food poisoning—chances are you'll never return.

Your goal in every interaction is to create lots of R+ experiences for the other person. This insulates you against the inevitable negative experience, and, of course, you might already have to overcome R– experiences they've had with others in the past. Every relationship is the sum total of all the R+ and R– interactions you've had with that person and what they've heard about you through other sources. Rack up the R+s, and you'll watch your relationships rise.

The Path to Raving Fan

Every growing BD relationship passes through the following seven stages.

Target. This is someone you want to know but don't. Your next step is to get an introduction or otherwise offer them something so valuable that they feel compelled to connect.

Acquaintance. This is someone you've met, but that's about it. It can be a big deal to get here, but you haven't discussed what you do, so the next step is to create curiosity about your expertise.

Curious skeptic. They're interested in learning more but also skeptical whether you're needed. Maybe they think their needs are covered or that there's an easier or better way still out there. The next step is typically to offer a *give-to-get* (more on this later) so they can get a glimpse of the value you offer.

New client. This is someone who has taken a chance on hiring you for an initial paid project, but the relationship is still untested and fragile. Doing a great job is important but not sufficient. You'll want to learn about the client's future goals so you can help them in bigger ways. The next step is ongoing engagement or other projects.

Solid working relationship. This is someone who trusts you to do certain types of work, but the relationship hasn't transcended the paid work. Your value is still limited to the paid work you perform. We see a lot of professionals plateau at this level because they think they can stop investing in the relationship at this point. But when you only provide value specifically for what you are paid to do and not more broadly, you can box yourself into being a commodity—you can easily be replaced. The next step is to continue to add value in new areas, outside of what you're paid to do, especially those that are aligned with the client's personal and business priorities.

Loyal client. The relationship is no longer limited to the specific work at hand—your client now sees you as what business expert David Maister calls a "trusted advisor": someone who helps a client outside of what he is specifically paid to do. The client calls you for advice on important topics. These "above and beyond" interactions are some of the most valuable ways you can help clients. Counterintuitively, the next stage in advancing the relationship is to ask the client to serve as a reference or referral. As we'll see later, *mutually* helpful relationships are the strongest. Your clients at this stage want to help you succeed. You just have to ask.

Raving fan. These are the people who love your helpfulness and your work so much that they can't help but tell everyone who would benefit from knowing you. This is your goal in every important relationship. Raving fans become your own personal sales force. The next step at this level is to ask the client to introduce you to even more people who would benefit from knowing you. Here you're anything but a commodity; you're a vital part of your client's past and future success.

Every relationship in your pipeline exists somewhere along this spectrum, and, as you can see, each step calls for a different strategy to advance to the next. Typically it can take years to move a relationship along from target to raving fan, but when rainmakers tackle it systematically, the path can be shortened to a matter of months. I see it happen all the time thanks to the *Protemoi List.*

The Protemoi List

Relationships are at the core of your future success. Some people let the universe determine who they know, who they will know, and how quickly the connections will be created. Others work a process, always moving incrementally ahead, one week at a time. Guess who brings in more business?

For a seller-expert a raving fan is the ultimate prize. These are the people who proactively try to help you succeed. If budgets dry up, they call you first when money starts flowing again. In a competitive bid they are your in-house champion. When they're talking to their peers, they're talking about how great you are.

The stages from target to raving fan obviously apply to prospects and clients, but, as we'll see, they're also a useful lens for understanding *all* our important business relationships. Think about the people who have made the greatest impact on your business and career trajectory so far. Not just the great, happy clients—what about the boss who saw herself as your mentor and put you up for promotion before you knew you were ready yourself? The well-placed influencer who routinely steers prospects your way? The former colleague who keeps you current on all the industry changes? Some people out there are looking out for you and, if they're in the right position, can have a truly outsized effect.

What do your raving fans have in common? Why do they like you so much that they're willing to go out of their way to help you succeed? For most people these relationships form mysteriously—things either click with somebody new or they don't. In reality, we have far more agency over our relationships than we think.

In fact, it's possible to turn *all* your most important contacts into raving fans—eventually. But these efforts must be sustained over time, as we saw with Sally Beier. You can't wow someone on day one and then come back a year later expecting the relationship to be where it was. Although raving-fan status is almost always attainable, it's rarely easy. Therefore you can't expect to invest and sustain the necessary time and attention with every single prospect, let alone with every person on your contact list (as you might feel obligated to do).

So where do you focus your efforts? On your best clients? Your un-happiest ones? The people who actually say yes when you invite them to lunch? The people with the fanciest job titles?

The correct answer is: on the people on your Protemoi List.

Protemoi (pro'-tuh-moy) is Greek for "first among equals." Your Pro-temoi List will help you invest in your most important relationships, whether there is an active engagement or not. Ultimately some people are more important to your success than others. Your long-term success de-pends on this group. The Protemoi List captures those names and keeps them front of mind.

Your Protemoi List represents your list of potential raving fans, the people most worthy of the investment required to create this special rela-tionship. "Investing" in a relationship might mean anything from emailing a relevant article, to calling with a cool product idea, to an invitation to brainstorm over dinner.

Some people start with five names, and some with twenty-five, but that's about the upper limit. Research shows that new habits stick when the goals stretch us but remain achievable. Remember: think big, start small, scale up.

One of my favorite experts on relationships is Keith Ferrazzi, author of *Never Eat Alone*. In the book Keith talks about the importance of making a list of key relationships: "The truth is, you don't even really need technol-ogy to start getting a grip. What you need is focus and attention."

I had the opportunity to get Keith's take on relationships in the seller-expert world specifically for this book. "Relationships are important for everyone, but especially important to the seller-expert," Keith told me. "Many business developers promote a product, but in the seller-expert's case, many times they *are* the product. This elevates the importance of relationship management to the highest level. And when relationships are of paramount importance, you simply *have* to write them down. *You have to have a plan.*"

You will naturally form a connection with many of the people you come into contact with on a day-to-day basis, like the other parents on your child's Ultimate Frisbee team or the person who happens to sit next to you at work. But for relationship-driven business development we can't rely on serendipity, and we can't rely on memory. A good plan is a necessity, and every good plan starts with a list.

Developing Your Own Protemoi List

So who goes on your Protemoi List? A healthy mix is usually three-quarters clients and prospects and the rest people who can help with your business development indirectly: referrers, your boss, influencers, strategic partners, or other experts you rely on.

This ratio varies by discipline. Some seller-experts do a large amount of work for a particular client, and then that client doesn't need them again—wedding planners and damage-control PR experts come to mind. In these cases a Protemoi List may consist entirely of strategic partners who can refer the right kinds of clients. Compare this to an account manager with one major account to service and grow. That entire Protemoi List might be made up of leaders at the client company. Whatever your discipline, calibrate your mix to the kinds of relationships that will be most valuable to your business over time.

We're now going to create your Protemoi List. Get the **Protemoi List** worksheet or simply take out the quick list of seven names you made in Chapter 1. Look again at the names along the left-hand side: Are these seven people truly the most important ones in your relationship pipeline? Make any edits you need by either making them on the worksheet or editing your initial list. We're going to upgrade it.

Professionals often make the mistake of focusing on people already in their network. It's human nature to prioritize the people we know over the ones we'd like to know. Rainmakers, however, learn to balance existing relationships against the people it would be most useful to know in the future. It may feel a bit odd to add someone you've never met to a list like this, but give it a try and watch valuable new relationships bloom. You'll get hooked on the process of finding and winning over new Protemoi people.

Once a month quickly revise your initial list with all this in mind. Aim for the number of people you think you can invest in—outside of what you're paid to do. Don't get stuck on the selection process; if you need to think that hard to remember someone, they aren't important enough for your Protemoi List. Add any other people you need to your list now. Move fast. Go.

Next, add two more columns on the page: "Relationship Stage" (remember our list above: target, new client, raving fan, etc.) and "Next Step." The Protemoi List is a pipeline. Its purpose is to help you advance your relationships with each of these people over time. Knowing where you are with each person on your Protemoi List tells you what to do next. Be honest with yourself as you do this: Which stage is each relationship in?

The Next Step column is the most important. Here, write down a concrete action you can take to drive that relationship toward the next stage. In practice these might be things like calling to ask how those college visits went with their daughter, emailing a relevant *Harvard Business Review* article, or suggesting a lunch to discuss goals for the upcoming fiscal year. The next steps should be relationship building, not something the client could perceive as a sales call. So avoid things like "follow up on the proposal we sent last week." (I'll introduce you to a separate tool for managing specific opportunities later.)

You've now completed your first Protemoi List. You'll hone it over time as you work with it and come to rely on its power to focus your efforts where they matter most. For now know that you have a major part of the foundation of this system already in place—and we're only in Chapter 2!

Most high-level professionals will tell you that relationships are the most important contributor to success, yet they don't systematically prioritize and invest in them. All too often they just try to juggle this stuff in their heads. Guilty of this yourself? You're driving to work when you suddenly think, "I need to email Karim!" Then something comes up, and the email never gets sent. Five years go by, and Karim is named CEO. Now it looks pretty cheesy to email him. "Hey, remember me? The person who didn't keep in touch? Uh, I just saw you're now in a buying position at a client of mine. Want to go have lunch so I can tell you about what we do?"

There's a better way.

Creating a Positivity Machine with an Asset List

Our most important relationships are lined up and ready to go. Now what? The Protemoi List isn't intended to replace your task list by reminding you to follow up with clients on the work at hand. Rather, it's a *positivity machine*, a tool to sustainably and systematically create R+ experiences for each of your Protemoi people. Sometimes that R+ experience is the offer of your services. More often, however, it comes down to adding value with your next interaction.

Value can take many forms—a business book suggestion, an introduction to someone in your network, a link to the video of a relevant talk, an invitation to coffee. When you add value to an interaction through a tangible item like this, we call it an *asset*.

Waiting for inspiration to strike before you reach out to the dozen or more people on your Protemoi List doesn't work. You'll spend your time researching and digging for something instead of *doing*. This part of the process needs to be as systematic as the rest of your strategy so you can build and sustain a habit. The most effective way to do this is to maintain an *Asset List*, a list of items you always have at hand to quickly send your Protemoi contacts to create easy R+ experiences.

Assets can be anything helpful or interesting to your Protemoi people. Although many of our clients think of business items first, anything that adds value can work great, like information on hobbies, sports teams, and health advice. Look for those commonalities you've identified using the gravitas model (which you'll learn about in Chapter 7) and the other tools you'll learn in the Snowball System. What are your shared passions? That's always a good place to start when selecting an asset to send. Categories of assets include the following.

Interesting People

Connect your Protemoi people with others who share their interests, hobbies, business experiences, and so on. When you make the introduction, you usually get to participate in the first meeting or call and are likely to get endorsed by both parties.

Ideas

You're an expert—you have ideas. One of the best ways to transcend a working client relationship is to offer help outside the context of what you're being paid to do. You might share a back-of-the-napkin sketch explaining a new concept (some of the models I explain later in the book started like this). You might explain a relevant tip or tool of the trade. You might suggest how a successful new technique from another industry might apply to the client's area. You might even propose a solution you've devised but for which you have yet to find an appropriate client. *Ideas in search of clients* are a great way to get a conversation started as the other person helps you brainstorm a good fit.

Industry News

You probably already invest some time each week keeping track of the latest in the industries you work in. Instead of just scrolling past social media updates, blog posts, and news articles, start clipping valuable ones to your Asset List. Chances are, if you consider something relevant, many of your Protemoi people will as well.

Books and Articles

Books and articles always make good assets, especially if they help advance an idea or concept you've already discussed with that person. Be sure to direct the recipient to the specific passages that apply to them. You wouldn't want to send them *Management Theory 101* and say, "You need this." (That might be taken the wrong way!) Instead, be specific by tailoring the suggestion to the person receiving it. That's where the magic is, where the caring comes through. If you're going to send a book, send the actual, physical book along with a handwritten note mentioning the sections they should be sure to read and why. For an article, don't just send a link. For one thing, links sometimes change, or there's a paywall or another technological annoyance that will replace your carefully crafted

R+ with an R–. Print to a PDF file and attach that to your email in addition to the link to make things easy.

Other Media

Nowadays you might also share useful websites, videos, podcasts, webinars, or any number of other digital assets. Again, make this as easy as possible for people. Make sure you have viewed or listened to the entire contents of whatever item you're sending, and direct the recipient to the relevant parts. Instead of simply sending the link to an hour-long webinar they'll never watch, tell them to advance straight to 14:05 to see the speaker spend two minutes and thirty seconds explaining a marketing concept they'll find interesting.

Hobbies

If you've discovered you share an interest or pursuit with the recipient, don't hesitate to bond over that shared passion. Always keep your ears open during conversations for clues. If the client offhandedly mentions having seen an artsy independent movie, you might tell them about an upcoming film festival. If they're a fitness buff, you might tell them about the charity 5K you're going to run—maybe they'll join you!

When you diligently maintain your Asset List you will have so many possibilities to choose from that providing them to your Protemoi people at regular intervals will take only a moment's browsing. Add a bunch right away to get things started, but after that, simply leave your list open during the day and get in the habit of adding to it as items arise while you're browsing the web or after a fruitful brainstorming meeting.

Your Asset List will contain PDFs, links, videos, and other types of files. A document or spreadsheet probably won't suffice. Personally, I use the cross-platform application Pocket to store my Asset List. This allows me to easily capture digital assets of any kind from the web as well as quickly find and send relevant ones, even when I'm on the road. I can even "store" people in Pocket by saving their LinkedIn URL.

I like Pocket, but many software tools have similar features, from Google Keep to Microsoft OneNote, with more options appearing every day. Choose one that suits you, your platform, and your working style. The key is to keep capturing. My trainees tell me that their ability to add value to their clients' lives drastically improved when they started diligently capturing assets. If it's cool, capture it!

Staying in Touch

Congratulations! You've created your Protemoi List and your Asset List. You know how you're going to use the latter to drive the former. Now let's establish your R+ assembly line, your process for sustainably and systemically creating positive experiences for the most important people in your network.

Every month, schedule one hour to work specifically on your Protemoi List. During this session, review the entire list, and make note of each person you haven't yet interacted with in an "I'm thinking about you" way this month.

Next, curate an asset that would add value to several of those people— the more the better. Customize the asset for each person, and send separately. Customization is the key to this step. Everyone's scanning their email to distinguish what was really written for them from all the generic messages they receive. So use specific language. Note why the person will enjoy this. Tell them specifically what to pay attention to. Personalize as much as possible. Then find another asset that would fit several others and so on, until you're caught up with everyone on your list for that month. Done!

For example, let's say you recently added an interesting article that relates to an industry you follow to your Asset List. During your Protemoi session write an email to an appropriate person on your list summarizing the article, accompanied by a link to the original and a PDF version. Wrap up with a quick explanation of why you thought to send it to them specifically. Send it, and then tailor a copy of the same message for every other person on your list who might also find it interesting. Some months, that might be everyone on your list. Remember these three Cs: capture, curate, customize.

Implementing this simple process is like setting up automatic investments into a retirement account. It takes a little effort to get started, but then you stop giving it much thought. A year or two pass, and "suddenly" you realize that your account is chock-full of cash. Where did it all come from? I'm rich! Similarly, after implementing your Protemoi List and Asset List process for a while, you will "suddenly" have thriving relationships with people you barely knew not that long ago, people who are becoming increasingly important to your business.

Of course, just because you have a monthly process doesn't mean you can't send a relevant asset to a Protemoi person at any other time. For example, if you get off the phone with someone and your conversation triggers an idea for an asset, go ahead and send it right away.

•

We've seen how a focus on the right relationships can drive success. Instead of letting the world determine who we'll spend time with, we're in control, investing in the future network we want to have. And we have a plan for being proactive.

Now it's time to look outward. How does the rest of the world see you? How are you currently *positioned* in the marketplace? Are you the clear, number-one choice for prospective clients?

In the next chapter you will learn how to establish a strong and memorable brand, strategically positioning yourself to attract a steady flow of ideal clients. Positioning is the heart of business development. Done right, you'll never need to hustle for prospects again.

CHAPTER 3

Targeting Your Ideal Clients and Positioning Yourself to Win

• • •

BRINGING IN MORE of the kind of business you want begins with your value proposition. If you don't understand your clients' problems or how you're going to position yourself as the best solution to those problems, you're toast.

What are you the very best at doing? How does your offering stand apart from the alternatives? Who are you for, and why should they choose *you*?

A hungry bear plants itself in one spot on the riverbed. If it's in the right place, lunch will deliver itself. That's the beauty of effective positioning. If you place yourself properly, business drops in your lap like a wriggling salmon. If you don't, you end up cold and wet, with nothing to show for it. Without sticking to a bold, strategically crafted position that effectively differentiates you from the competition, growth grinds to a halt. There's an unbridgeable chasm between what you're selling and what prospects are looking to buy.

Mike Deimler knows strategy and focus. For two terms he led Boston Consulting Group's (BCG) global strategy practice, one of the top strategy firms in the world. BCG had to break its own rules to let someone lead a practice for two terms. So although it takes someone pretty special to lead strategy for one of the best worldwide strategy firms, it takes someone *extra* special to do it twice. When I asked Mike about the importance of being unique, of having a differentiated offering in the world of seller-experts, he told me this, and it wasn't at all what I expected. (Emphasis directly from Mike.)

> For twenty years as a partner at BCG, I have always walked around with a thin folder in my briefcase. Open it, and you'll find a *single* sheet of paper for each of my clients, and on each page I scrawl an ever-evolving list of the *top-ten most strategic issues* the CEO at each client *should* be addressing. They are not necessarily all things that BCG should support, but they are all bold, aspirational statements of what I truly believe my clients should be addressing. By thinking *deeply* about the client's agenda and putting their interests first, I can engage with them with a sense of obligation to discuss that list. I don't really sell; I just have the courage to engage my clients with a provocative, deeply informed view of what is in the best interest of their companies. The business takes care of itself.

Mike found his place on the river. He wants to be positioned as the top strategic resource to big-time CEOs. To do so, *he lives the part.* I guarantee this position is unique with nearly all his clients, especially in the way Mike can deliver on it. It shows three things: he *knows their business as well as or better than they do*, he's *proactive*, and he's a *resource for anything important*, not just BCG services. The uniqueness is in Mike's list of ideas. As those ideas are adopted and become successful, the CEO connects them to Mike. And as he or she attaches success to Mike, they'll want his input more often. This puts him in the position as an extremely valuable and unique external resource for all major priorities, not just what BCG does. Remember reading about becoming a trusted advisor? This is how you do it. Mike doesn't have a logo. He doesn't have marketing materials about himself. He's simply figured out what he wants to be known for, and he lives that promise, strengthening it with every interaction.

Let's turn the lens on you. What do *you* want to be known for? In this chapter you will learn how to create your positioning using a battle-tested, five-dimension positioning process I've taught to thousands of seller-experts across the country. All you need to do is follow where it leads. It will show you how to communicate your value. In the eyes of your ideal prospects you will become the obvious choice, the only option. You will use a variation of this process whether positioning your organization, yourself, a specific offering, or an individual deal.

To position yourself properly you will need a clear vision of the kind of clients you want to attract. I'll show you how to target them. But first let's take a closer look at what positioning is, how it works, and why it's so important to an expert like you.

The Power of Positioning

As a service provider your fundamental problem is that you're not the only option in town. If you were, this BD stuff would be *easy*.

"Hey, Bill. I need help with a tax problem. Can you recommend a good accountant?"

"Sure. My friend Jim happens to be the last accountant on Earth."

"On the whole planet? Wow, that was easy. What's his number?"

Jim the accountant is ideally positioned in this scenario. As king of the hill, he has his pick of clients. Everybody—literally everybody—wants to work with him. Jim can charge premium rates, up to and including anything his clients can afford. Unlimited demand and a supply of one—Jim can grow his business as much as he wants. Plus, with accountants such a novelty, he'll be a hit at dinner parties with witty one-liners like, "It's accrual world."

Jim's comfortable state of affairs is unlikely to continue in a free marketplace. What happens when Jen gets her CPA too? Now there are two accountants to choose from. Jim is still busy, but Jen starts luring some of his favorite clients away. What can Jim do to ensure that his ideal clients choose him over his new competitor? (He's gotten feedback that his sparkling sense of humor isn't going to cut it.) This is where positioning comes in: showing potential clients why you are the best (or only!) choice to meet their specific needs.

This isn't just about competitors, either. There is always one more option to position your business against: nobody. Prospects can usually choose to defer a project or do the work internally. People in pain can skip the chiropractic adjustment and pop more Advil. In Jim's case taxpayers can use tax prep software. This isn't about positioning yourself as the least bad option but rather as the one of greatest value. When you do that, prospects will be eager to work with you as soon as possible.

You can position your organization (or yourself, as a solo service provider) as "Jim's Accounting—3.2 Percent More Accurate Than Jen's Accounting." You can position a service, product, or practice as "Jim's Early-Bird Tax Blaster Service Gets You the Fastest Refund." Or you can position a specific deal for a specific client by saying, "Jim is the best choice to streamline QuailCo's corporate tax structure because of his special strategy tailored to the unique needs of the quail egg industry."

Positioning is all about changing buyer perception. This might lead you to suspect that positioning is just a euphemism for advertising. In fact, it's more like the opposite.

The Psychology of Positioning

By the 1970s companies were bombarding Americans with a nearly continuous stream of advertising—on television, in print, and plastered on pretty much every available surface. Consumers were told again and again about the deep cleaning power of Tide, the alluring mystique of Chanel No. 5, the thirst-quenching refreshment inside a can of Coca-Cola.

Marketing strategists Al Ries and Jack Trout started to suspect that features and promises alone couldn't explain why a select few ads effectively swayed consumers while the rest didn't, despite *endless* repetition. There was simply too much advertising going on for any normal person to consciously process all that product information. Ries and Trout decided to investigate how people made sense of this unceasing flow of pitches and taglines.

Their research revealed that the less a product promised to do, the more likely consumers were to believe the ad. The tighter the focus of the message, the more loudly it resonated.

"Positioning," they wrote, "is how you differentiate yourself in the mind of the prospect." It isn't enough to talk about all the ways your product is better—the more you talk, the less customers hear. The art of positioning is saying only the things that will most clearly differentiate and elevate your offering as well as having the discipline to leave the rest out. In other words, focus wins the battle.

More than three decades later Ries and Trout's advice still holds true. It applies to positioning both for clients and for consumers. You'd think everyone would get it by now, but focus is scary because it means leaving things out, even things that sound really convincing. That's one of the reasons crafting a *positioning statement* is one of the most important parts of the BD process. Your positioning statement delivers a simple message— the reason the clients you want should choose you.

Of course, "simple" is easy to see and difficult to do. It means being specific. Focusing on the people you want to reach most means saying no to other, still attractive opportunities. The thing is, brands that are "for everyone" just aren't as successful as brands that are for a very specific customer or client.

Ries and Trout point to Kraft. Kraft is a great company with many great products. But what does the name Kraft actually *mean* to consumers? What are they good at? Could it be caramel? Mac and cheese? Mayonnaise? Shredded cheese? Salad dressing?

The place in the supermarket where I pause, where I actually stand and analyze, is by the barbecue sauce. I look at the new brands and check out my old favorites. I dig in and read the ingredients. One brand I would never, ever buy on that shelf is Kraft. How in the world, in my buyer's mind, could Kraft be as sweet as Sweet Baby Ray's Gourmet Honey Hot Sauce? Or as unique as Stubb's Original Legendary Bar-B-Q Sauce, Stubb being so legendary that they put his picture on the label? Or maybe I should get the "We're Talkin' Serious" Bone Suckin' Sauce.

Kraft's sauce might be just as good as these specialty brands, but it's hard to believe it. It seems average, normal, and unexciting simply because they make so many other things. It feels like it's part of a big corporate machine, not handcrafted by someone who only cares deeply about the happiness of my taste buds. That's the cognitive shortcut we all take: we tend to assume that specialists will be better than generalists. When it really matters—whether hiring an expert for a critical project or having buddies over for a barbecue—we want the specialist because we expect we'll get the best results from them.

So being everything for everyone seems safe but is actually dangerous. Specialization creates demand. To specialize properly, you need to know where you want to create that demand. Who are you for?

Targeting the Right Prospects

Powerful positioning speaks to your prospects' perceptions and needs. But which prospects? Being "for everyone" is akin to being for no one. The step before the first step in the positioning process is to identify and target the kinds of clients you most want to serve. Only once you have a crystal-clear vision of your ideal prospects can you effectively position yourself to attract them.

Targeting is the process of identifying the business value of prospects in order to prioritize your efforts. In one sense it means saying no to potential clients who may be willing to pay you money. Saying no to money is universally difficult. If business is slow, turning down paying work of any kind can feel like an existential threat. Even when revenue is healthy, our survival instinct kicks in whenever we consider steering a prospect to another service provider or ending an existing client relationship that is past its expiration date.

It helps to frame this in terms of *opportunity cost*: putting effort in one area means you can't invest that effort anywhere else. Regardless of what they're paying you, there's always a loss to be counted in terms of potential gain from possible alternatives. As a service provider, you can only work with so many clients. Often we underestimate the bandwidth requirement of any single client or engagement. We may tally up the hours of direct work, but inevitably we ignore the email communication, phone calls, and general mental drain of investing in a relationship. Even if business is slow, an hour per week salvaged from a less-than-ideal client can be invested in lead-generation efforts that might translate into one or more ideal clients.

Here's an example, one I lived through and learned from early in my career. I was a young actuary at the time, leading a large healthcare selection and pricing project with a Fortune 20 company. It was a big deal. Eager to please, I would do about anything for my clients. And with over

250,000 employees relying on their company's healthcare plans, my work would have a big impact.

One night our client contact called with an urgent request. She wanted some comprehensive projections reworked for an eight o'clock meeting the next morning. And she didn't just want them tweaked—she had some new ideas that created a massive amount of work. It would normally take days, and it was already four in the afternoon.

This client had a history of vague directions, last-second requests, and a few emotional outbursts, but this was the worst yet. We were all already scared of her. I asked as many questions as I could, tried to understand her underlying goal, and called my wife, Becky, to let her know I would miss our family dinner. I built the sophisticated underlying models and called the client a few times with questions, trying to clarify what she wanted. I talked to her last around nine at night, when she told me to make assumptions if needed. "Figure it out," she said with an underlying tone of "you're bothering me."

There was much more to do. I kept going. I finished the modeling, made the results as pretty as I could, and checked everything. By four in the morning I had it figured out and fought the fax machine to get the numbers to her. I feared the paper would run out on their side with no one there to refill the paper tray. Success! It worked. I went home, slept a bit, showered, and got back to work for our eight o'clock call with her and her senior team.

Except there was no eight o'clock call. She didn't show. I waited for their call, then started leaving messages with everyone I knew there. Finally I got to her assistant closer to normal work hours around 8:30, and she told me my client wasn't in yet. Her team was waiting in a conference room with my models still sitting on my client's fax machine. Apparently she strolled in later in the morning, admitting to sleeping through the meeting. Some other emergency popped up on her side that morning, and we covered the analysis a few days later.

Being so young, I didn't know how to handle this, but my practice leader did. Because this kind of thing had happened multiple times, he called the client and fired us from the work. My emergency nonemergency work was the last straw. We completed what we were on the hook to do, but nothing more—it wasn't worth it. Our entire team was stressed to the hilt, always trying to please this person, and we had realized there was no pleasing her.

Here's the good news: firing ourselves from the client rippled through the organization. It got people talking. Apparently our client contact had been doing this kind of thing to her internal team too, but they had been afraid to speak up. After we communicated why we were ending our contract, others came out of the woodwork, and our client contact was fired within the week. A few weeks later we were asked to come back for more work with the rest of the team there, who we loved working with. Things grew from there, and within a decade that client became the largest client in our firm.

If a client isn't a good fit and the situation can't be fixed, it's time to start planning toward an eventual severing of that relationship. Saying no to the wrong client makes it possible to say yes to the right one—or even several right ones. Whether we like to admit it or not, difficult clients take up more than their rightful share of time and energy.

This isn't just about saying no to less valuable relationships to make room for new ones; it's also about prioritizing *all* your relationships properly. It goes back to the thinking behind the Protemoi List: we want to systematically develop stronger relationships with the people who will have the greatest impact on our business.

This is another area where rainmakers behave differently from the others. Most people prefer to spend their time reconnecting with the clients and strategic partners they already know. After all, it's always harder to reach out to more important but less solid connections. But get comfortable with this discomfort. With practice it does get easier.

In order to say no to the wrong clients and yes to the right ones you need a clear idea of who the right ones are. This needs to be written down. You may have a gut feel for your ideal prospects, but you need to be able to communicate this targeting to others—colleagues, strategic partners, and so on—so they can send you more of the business you want and less of the business you don't.

It's difficult to position yourself until you know who you're trying to communicate your position to because we need to think from their perspective, prioritizing the value *they* perceive. That's why targeting and positioning are so interrelated. Positioning communicates what *problems you uniquely solve*, while targeting communicates the *types of people who spend money solving that unique problem*. First, we'll nail down your targeting. Then, with that perspective in mind, we'll circle back and fine-tune your positioning.

Defining Ideal New Business

There are two ways to bring in new business:

+ Engage with a new client.
+ Open up a new area or a new relationship within an existing client organization.

The easy path is to spend our time working on existing areas and existing relationships with existing clients. But to bring in new business you need to venture away from the easy path.

Professionals tasked with getting into new organizations understand this right away, but it applies to account managers too. If your work centers around a single large client, your primary growth opportunity may be to expand into other business units or functional areas within that company. From this perspective the "new clients" are new buying centers in the same organization.

For example, let's say your company prints signage and training materials for a large corporation's HR department. If that account is your sole responsibility, your best opportunity might be to expand into creating brochures and pamphlets for their marketing department. Or it might be to invest in new relationships within that HR department. That way, if your primary contact leaves the company, you can seamlessly transition to the replacement. If you focus all your attention on one person, you risk losing the account—and possibly your job—when a new decision maker comes in.

No matter what type of client you manage or what the road to growth looks like for you, the process remains the same: you need to prioritize the most important relationships instead of just talking to the people you already know.

The best rainmakers set clear criteria to rate their opportunities. They might evaluate prospects based on budget, the types of projects typically bought, the industry, or the size of the company, either in revenue or in number of employees. Many people don't use criteria at all or they use them only informally and haphazardly, ignoring them to the extent that they're anxious about meeting revenue and other targets.

Your own selection criteria, if you've set any, will be influenced by your thinking preferences. For example, if you're a heavily analytical thinker, you might tend to prioritize prospects and clients based on their budgets and other easily quantifiable data points. This method risks missing other key elements that don't fit as easily into your calculations—cultural fit, for example, or whether the prospect is too risk averse.

In the end most of us stick too heavily to only one metric: How easy will it be to get to that person? Inevitably, it's human nature to prefer investing in those prospects who are easy to reach over the ones who might be most valuable in the long run. Easy trumps valuable but hard nearly every time. We must fight against this.

No matter the nature of your BD responsibility, you need to establish balanced criteria for evaluating prospects and prioritizing your time. The purpose of this exercise is to identify the most valuable prospects so you can invest your time where it will pay the greatest dividends.

Which criteria would most accurately select an ideal new client for you? Don't focus on your existing client relationships; this will bias you toward people you know now instead of those you should know. We'll incorporate your current network into the targeting process later. Also note that these examples have been organized into our quadrants so you won't under- or over-bias based on your own thinking preferences.

On a piece of paper divided into four quadrants or on the **Brainstorm your business development criteria** worksheet, list at least four criteria *per quadrant* that are specific to your business. See the examples in the adjacent chart.

Here's a simple example. Let's say you're a wedding planner. In the analytical quadrant you'll want a client with the budget to hire you and to

Target Client Criteria Examples

A. Analytical	D. Experimental
• Total revenue of the organization • Amount of money spent in your industry • Amount of money spent with organizations just like yours • Number of employees • Industry • Company type (ex: private vs public)	• Strategic fit between their needs and your solutions • Willingness to take strategic risk • Prestige of their organization's brand • Discipline of organization (ex: innovation, low cost, operational excellence, etc)
B. Practical	**C. Relational**
• Proven expertise we have in this industry • Safety conscious nature of an organization • Documented (or undocumented) procedures for their operations • Ease of their purchasing process	• Cultural alignment between us and the prospect • Health of the organization • Reputation of the CEO or leadership team in our industry • Connections the Board of Directors have with our other business targets • Relationship our strategic partners have to the company • Philanthropical nature of the company

BASED ON THE WHOLE BRAIN® MODEL OF HERRMANN GLOBAL LLC. © 2018 HERRMANN GLOBAL LLC

pay for a wedding of the appropriate scope. Do you have a sense of how much that is? Start thinking through your own analytical criteria. It might be much more than money.

In the practical quadrant you'll want a client who can give you enough advance notice to plan properly. You've learned the hard way that last-minute weddings are a bigger headache than they're worth. Many industries can only succeed when there is adequate time to do their work well, while others are hired at least partly because there *isn't* much time! (Think of the emergency PR expert we talked about.) Start thinking through all the possible practical targeting criteria that are best for you.

Some less direct criteria may not be obvious, especially if you're more of an analytical thinker. Let's think through the experimental quadrant, which we might think of as strategic for the sake of this exercise. You might consider how visible the wedding will be in the local community. A highly publicized wedding will generate more new business for you down the road. Do you take that into consideration in your targeting by actively marketing to country clubs and other hubs of influential local families? If visibility is a factor in your targeting, how heavily do you weigh it against the others? I think this is an interesting perspective: two projects with the same work and profitability don't necessarily deliver the same value. What alignment should you be looking for?

In the relational quadrant you might add criteria about the bride and groom and their in-laws. Oh, the in-laws! Going back to opportunity cost above, difficult and demanding clients can sop up a tremendous amount of bandwidth. Do you really want to receive all-caps text messages at three in the morning because a mother-in-law and daughter can't agree on the groomsmen's socks? Again, how heavily do you weigh the perceived difficulty of a client (relational) against factors like budget and timing (analytical and practical)? Many of my clients rank cultural fit between them and their clients quite high. That fits perfectly in the relational quadrant. Start thinking about your criteria that would fit well here.

The point of working through this now is to get clear in your own mind about what you want in a client. That way you can position yourself to bring in more of the clients you want and less of the rest. You may not always work with clients who meet all your criteria to a T, but specifying what those criteria are and how you plan to weigh them can't help but steer you in a better direction.

Once you've completed the brainstorming process, select the top five criteria from your lists. Most of the professionals in our classes include at least one from each quadrant, but you don't have to. Also, it's okay to choose fewer than five criteria if that works best.

Now write your targeting criteria down, and give each one a percentage indicating its relative importance. They should add up to 100 percent. For example:

✦ Sufficient budget to work with us 45%
✦ Culture fit 35%
✦ Speed of buying cycle 10%
✦ Proximity to our location 10%

Think hard about your current and past clients in light of this rough set of criteria. Where clients haven't matched up, what has been your experience? Think, for example, of the last time you worked with a client who could easily afford you (analytical) but with whom there was a terrible culture fit (relational). In the end were you happy you worked with them, or did you regret having taken it on? Did that painful engagement lead to useful referrals and strategic relationships? Or was it a time- and energy-draining dead end?

I can't promise that this process will prevent you from ever having a frustrating client engagement again. I can guarantee, however, that you'll have fewer opportunities to put your palm to your forehead and wonder, *What was I* thinking?

Proper targeting is a moving, well, target. Your aim will improve over time.

Target List

Let's take your new BD criteria and put them into action. True rainmakers maintain *Target Lists* of prospective clients and organizations to keep the focus of their BD efforts front and center.

Who are the clients it would be most valuable to work with? Who are your dream clients? What are your dream companies? If you could sweep away all your existing clients and replace them with nothing but ideal ones, what would that roster look like? Write these names down on the **Target List** worksheet or on a sheet of paper.

Once you've written your Target List down in black and white, you will finally see whether you are spending your time and energy on bringing in work of the highest value or if you've been taking the easy path and spending time with the people with whom you feel most comfortable.

An insurance brokerage client of mine has experts specializing in various niches. One specializes in restaurant franchises. His clients have unique insurance needs ranging from standard slip-and-fall issues to the risks of preparing and serving food. This expert knows the language, the patter, of the food service industry. He understands the risks. Most important, he knows the insurance clauses by heart: which boilerplate provisions must be revised and which can remain as is. If the risk manager at a franchise talks to experts at two insurance brokerages, one a generalist and the other my client, it becomes an easy choice: this expert knows who he is for, and the right prospects see that right away.

For now think about what this process has shown you. What insights did prioritizing your targets give you? In light of the rankings, would you say you've been spending your efforts where they have been most likely to bring in ideal clients?

Here's what our students say in nearly every class: they've been spending most of their time chasing the wrong organizations and the wrong people. The subconscious pull of "spending time with who we already know" is tremendous. We have to fight this, to instead steer our time and energy to our perfect prospects, whoever they are. It can be scary reaching out to people you don't know well, but it's also the most direct road to growth. (We'll learn how to do this with *ease* in Chapter 6.)

This goes back to the BD paradox. It's only a paradox if your BD efforts make you too busy with client work to continue doing them. The thing is, what are we busy doing when we're doing business development? Are we spending our limited time wisely, spinning golden thread, or are we simply spinning our wheels?

Let's circle back to the people you know well but aren't very helpful in growing your business. You can still spend time with these folks. You just need to see it for what it is: catching up with old friends. That's fine. Just don't fool yourself into thinking you're doing business development. Or get proactive and share your Target List with these folks who love you. Maybe they can help introduce you to the right person.

Positioning Yourself

You've developed a set of client-targeting criteria. As a result, you have a clear picture of the prospects you're looking for. Moving forward you're going to spend more and more of your time and effort on the relationships with the highest priority according to these criteria. This means investing less time with the people you already know who *aren't* on the top of that list. Most big breakthroughs come from people you don't know well yet, although those you know now may help you get introduced. Once we direct our energy outside our comfort zone, we start to see real growth.

More important, we're starting to create a clear picture of what we actually want out of our clients. As experts, we spend most of our working life serving people. Spending more of our time working with good clients who meet our criteria is one of the most direct routes to a more satisfying and enjoyable career.

Now that we know the kinds of prospects we want to attract, we are ready to begin positioning ourselves and our organizations to do so.

Wait a second, you might be thinking. *I'm happy to bring in more clients. But changing the way I position my business may alienate the clients I already have or drive away new clients that aren't 100 percent ideal. That sounds risky. I can't afford to be so picky. Better to play it safe and keep things vague.*

This is the biggest objection I hear about positioning an organization, practice area, product, or a specific practitioner—branding or "personal branding," as the case may be. People and companies shy away from developing a specific brand because it feels like saying no to work that falls outside of it.

Like it or not, however, specific brands just work better. The more precisely defined the brand, the more impact it will have. If you think of a few of your own favorite brands, you'll see this to be true. It only feels wrong when you're the brand. Think back to the bear on the river. What if in its anxiety to catch fish it wandered back and forth to wherever it last saw a salmon leap? Clearly this would waste valuable time and give other bears the opportunity to carve out premium spots for themselves. The smart bear plants itself in a good spot and waits for dinner.

Luckily we don't need to shift over to a brand-new position overnight. Instead of flipping a switch, think of turning up a dimmer knob. You can still say yes to lucrative work that doesn't fit perfectly in order to keep your pipeline full. Meanwhile, do your *proactive* business development in alignment with your new positioning.

Lead generation, which we will discuss in Chapter 6, is one area where your new positioning will be active in full force. In other areas you can use your judgment and keep it gradual. So if at any point in the positioning process your hackles go up and you decide this is all too scary, remember the dimmer knob.

Long-term profitable growth, check. Short-term pipeline, check.

Crafting Powerful Positioning Statements

Now it's time to position yourself or your organization to attract more of the clients who meet your target criteria. The first way to do this is by creating a positioning statement for your business. The goal of this statement is to answer the *why* for prospects and clients. Why work with you and not some other provider? Why not stay in-house or simply ignore the problem? Your goal when positioning is to create the perception in the client's mind that you are the best solution to the problem, period.

What makes a great positioning statement? Forget for a moment what's in it and ask instead: How long should it be? After all, if a positioning statement is so powerful, wouldn't a positioning paragraph be better and a positioning page a game changer? If I can think of a dozen great reasons to work with me, why not share them all? Let's write the *Moby Dick* of positioning! That'll bring 'em in.

For reasons we'll see, a good positioning statement uses three short, unique concepts to triangulate your position. Let's say you're a freelance web developer. During the targeting process you decide that your ideal clients are too busy running their growing small businesses to learn web design and don't have the staff to handle ongoing updates and maintenance. They just want to be able to devote their limited time to creating lead-generating content and have the budget to afford white-glove support on everything else. You might build a statement around the following three concepts:

+ We provide a turnkey online platform at a custom domain within twenty-four hours.
+ Email us your blog posts, newsletters, and social media updates, and we will edit, format, schedule, publish, and promote them strategically for maximum results.

+ You can upload audio recorded on your phone to a shared folder, and we will edit, produce, and share it as a podcast.

Talking with a potential client, you might say:

+ If you're looking to get up and running with a new, professional-grade website your prospects will love, working with us is as simple as picking a domain name and then emailing us anything you want to share—we'll launch the site, keep it running for you day to day, and help you promote it, all the way to publishing those podcasts you've wanted to do.

This statement reinforces the needs of the client, appeals to different thinking styles, implies superior performance, and includes bold but factual statements. For maximum effect try to convey the same concepts using one word or very short phrases for each element. Here's a sequence, simplifying the concepts with each iteration. Bonus points for alliteration:

+ You're busy running your business. We're going to make it *easy* for you to launch your website, we'll keep it running flawlessly *every day*, and we're going to drive *engagement* with prospects and clients.
+ Easy launch. Everyday reliability. Engagement with prospects and customers.
+ Easy. Every day. Engagement.

As you may already realize if you've tried to craft a positioning statement before, getting to simple is anything but. That's why you're going to learn a step-by-step process for doing so effectively. But let's begin with what is probably your first question: Why *three*?

Studies have shown that more than three points is just too much to quickly absorb. People cope with this information overload by filtering things out. To "make room" for attribute number four, your prospect is going to subconsciously shuffle through the first three attributes, looking for one or more to ignore. More attributes beyond the fourth only exacerbate the problem. To quote one research paper: "three charms but four alarms."

Focus on the three core strengths, and leave out minor benefits. The key objective of a positioning statement is to be simultaneously convincing and memorable. Prospects and clients must be able to remember your positioning and communicate it to others. And people absorb and remember less than you might think. In an assessment published in *Proceedings of the National Academy of Science,* researchers looked at how many discrete pieces of information we can hold in our memory at once.

You might think that you can hold quite a bit of information in active memory. Think again. We stretch the capacity of working memory by "chunking" related information.

To prevent chunking, participants were asked to remember the color and position of different squares. The difficulty of the task increased as more and more squares were added to the screen. People handled three or four squares just fine. Beyond that, accuracy dropped off quickly. So we can comfortably hold three distinct things in our memory at once, but after that, it gets dicey without chunking or other mnemonic tricks.

So, magically, choosing three concepts is optimal in two ways. Three is both more believable *and* more memorable. (Of course, I'm still looking for a third scientific benefit . . .)

This advice goes against the grain. You are passionate about what you do and what you can offer. Off the top of your head you can probably list a dozen good reasons why clients should choose you. Not mentioning *all* those reasons feels like a cop-out, like you're not making the strongest possible argument for yourself.

But narrowing your positioning forces you to consciously think through why you're the best option for the job. It isn't easy to do, but this exercise will bring much-needed clarity to your value proposition. The impact on your persuasiveness will be undeniable.

The Positioning Model

Let's start working on a positioning statement, whether for you, your product or service, or your entire organization. We want to answer the question: Why should someone choose this option? The answer should include three short concepts that describe your position, concepts that are unique to whatever you are positioning. No one else should be able to match them.

That's easy, you might be thinking. *I know our strengths. I'll just pick the top three.* Resist the temptation to lead with what you consider to be your greatest strengths right now. Remember that you have a set of thinking preferences that might not align with those of your prospects and clients. If you want to create a robust statement that works with different people and in different circumstances, it pays to approach things systematically.

A powerful positioning statement draws its strength from five key areas. If you haven't already, download the **Positioning Statement** worksheet or write out your answers on a sheet of paper:

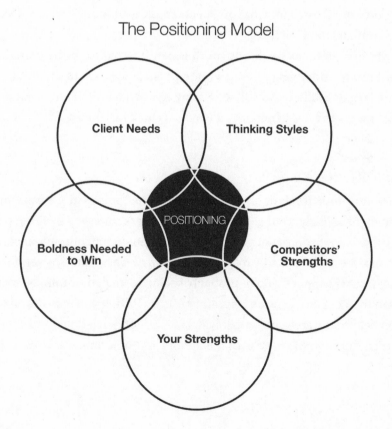

The Positioning Model

Client Needs

There are two parts to this. First, the obvious: What do your clients and prospective clients *say* they need? This is the thing they actually want you to do, like complete a certain task in a certain amount of time within a certain budget. Beneath that, of course, is the true but often unstated reason your client is looking to buy. Our clients are a great example. They might call us simply looking for a BD training session for twenty-two people in Fort Wayne on November 6, but what they *really* need is for those people to do things differently after the event. By asking questions around pre-meeting preparation, the meeting experience, and how we can help with follow-up and reinforcement, we not only differentiate ourselves but are being helpful by broadening the client leader's idea of the impact we can all have together. This flows from our positioning in that we think of ourselves as a behavior change company, not a training company. The point is important: many times what prospects *really* need is different from what they initially think.

It's easy to focus so closely on the client's stated needs that you lose sight of the underlying ones. It's quite possible for a client to have them stated needs fulfilled and still walk away dissatisfied. Why is the client really looking to buy? What does a win *really* look like for them?

Thinking Styles

There are four thinking styles and only three points in a positioning statement. Clearly, your statement will not work for every thinking style equally. Give it some thought: What are the predominant thinking styles among your clients and prospects? If your organization is a vendor of engineering supplies, you're probably selling to analytical thinkers more often than not. So focus on facts and measure ROI. If you're in the education field or the arts, you probably deal with a lot of relational and experimental thinkers: Message with metaphors. Use emotion.

Competitors' Strengths

What are your competitors' most obvious strengths? Can you match them, even roughly? Or would it be better to reframe your offering around a benefit that your competitors don't offer at all? If your competitor is an established national brand, it has trust established, so you might match that trust by offering a no-strings-attached, money-back guarantee. Put yourself in your client's shoes: If you were shopping for this service, what would you consider that competitor's greatest strength? How can you match it or otherwise differentiate your own offering?

Your Strengths

Experts focus myopically in this dimension, creating positioning statements describing their deepest potential impact. Yes, you should highlight your advantages. But just remember that the elements truly differentiating you from your competitors might not be relevant to potential clients. Frame your strengths in terms of *client benefits*. For example, you might have worked very hard to get a particular accreditation. Whereas your education establishes authority, the specific training may be of little interest to a client who wants you to solve their issue today. Keep the focus on what your client needs when highlighting your strengths. How does that accreditation help *them*, using words *they* would use?

Boldness to Win

Are you in first place? If not, what can you change to get there? Do you need to guarantee results? Can you create a positioning that's impossible to say no to? Can you change the decision-making criteria, maybe suggesting that the prospect carve the work up in a way that makes you the obvious choice for a specific portion of it, preferably the beginning? If you're not in the lead—whether you're positioning a service in an industry or a customized solution for a specific deal—get bold in terms of what you're offering or by trying to get the typical purchasing paradigm changed.

Look through each of the five dimensions, then write out your thoughts on each one. The important thing is to come at your position from all five. This will give you greater clarity about how to position yourself so that you become the clear choice for your target clients.

Now it's time to create your statement. Review the inputs, and develop the three concepts. Typically you'll have one concept that matches your competitor's greatest strength as well as two points unique to your business. When done perfectly, no other competitor should be able to match all three.

Next, as suggested above, work and rework the three concepts until they are as simple and memorable as possible. Break out your thesaurus. Is it possible to describe each concept with two words or even one word and still convey your meaning? Can you use alliteration (starting each word with the same sound) or rhyming? We want these as short and snappy as we can make them. Don't rush the process, and don't pound your head against the wall. Just list out on a whiteboard as many different words and phrases that can convey the same meaning, and let your subconscious attack the problem.

Once you have a set of concepts that stick, assemble proof points to bolster your concepts. Make a list of supporting facts—at least three for each concept. For example, one statement might be that your wedding photography business is the fastest. A proof point might be the customized thank-you slide show emailed to every attendee the day after the wedding. Another might be that the complete wedding album is cropped, color corrected, and ready for printing within a week of the ceremony. Be specific and always develop these proof points with your competitors' capacities in mind. Look at their claims, and consider how you might position yours side by side with theirs for maximum advantage.

Once you've created a positioning statement for yourself or your organization, reinforce your positioning in all your communications with clients and prospects, including emails, conversations, on your website, and in marketing materials. It should become your mantra.

Remember: your goal is to create the perception that you understand the client's needs and are the best choice to help them. Your statement should be something clients can communicate to others from memory. Orient yourself toward this goal. If your three concepts are simple and memorable and you communicate them many times throughout your interactions, your clients should easily be able to share them.

Using the positioning process for a service, product, or individual deal follows the same general path. Instead of positioning yourself to reach every ideal prospect you might want to attract, you can fine-tune the elements for a specific deal or client.

The fundamentals of strong positioning remain the same. Likewise, continue to reinforce that service- or deal-specific positioning at every opportunity. Keep it simple, keep it convincing, and keep it memorable.

Positioning is part art, part science. And now that you understand the principles, you can improve steadily over time. It will also take practice until you can target like Annie Oakley, but the discipline of targeting alone can turn a business around.

Know who you're for. Get your positioning right for them and only them. You don't want some other bear eating your salmon.

CHAPTER 4

Get People to Like You (Authentically)

. . .

I can't deny the fact that you like me. Right now. You like me!

—SALLY FIELD, *accepting the Academy Award for Best Actress in 1984*

YOU'VE COME A long way. By *targeting* your ideal clients, you have created a vision for the kind of organizations you want to work with. You've also determined how you're going to position yourself so the leaders there will see you as their best possible option. So many experts spend their careers striving to be everything to everyone and end up treading water. Not you. You're in on the secret: when you identify your ideal clients and position yourself to attract them, *you attract your ideal clients.*

Okay, maybe it isn't a secret, but it might as well be. Most of your competitors don't do it. Knowledge won't suffice; it takes effort and discipline. And here's where it starts to get tough: the more you focus on doing the right things, the more you have to say no to other things. No is hard.

I went through this early on at my company, BIG. When I was just starting out I promoted myself broadly, offering everything from the BD training we do now to executive coaching to strategic consulting for non-profit executive directors. My first website listed seven areas of expertise. Seven! None of them connected to each other either. Looking back, that first website projected a very clear central message: I'll do anything for anyone—just send a check!

(Desperation is a common pitfall, especially early in a career or in the launch of a business or new service. Unchecked, it shines through in your messaging and in your face-to-face interactions with clients. Counterin-tuitively, the more effort you put into targeting and positioning, the more confidence you will feel as a seller-expert. It can seem scary, but less is more powerful and safer.)

Thankfully, I soon found a magical intersection of passion, profit, and demand: business development training. Yet even though the path was clear, I was scared to death about paring my message down, let alone say-ing no to the "old" work. So I took it slow—remember the dimmer switch analogy? *When I took on a new training client, I'd phase out something that wasn't a fit.* Over time I found great alternatives for my ex-clients, which made the transitions easier. If I wasn't the right fit, I'd help them by finding who was.

In case you're wondering, I didn't have the cash flow to make any of this "easy." But I kept up steady pressure, and bit by bit, it worked. The following year was BIG's best. Then things really took off. When I had the courage to do only one thing, the message resonated and the market responded.

So welcome aboard the focus train. At this point the sky is the limit. Or, I should say, *you* are. With ideal clients targeted and positioning clear, the only thing keeping a seller-expert from achieving escape velocity is the ability to connect easily with others and build strong, mutually re-warding relationships. All the lead-generation techniques in the world won't help you if the prospects you meet don't, to put it simply, *like* you.

It can feel weird to study an interpersonal trait like "likeability." This goes back to the old fallacy that some of us have a "natural talent" with people while others don't. Deep down we believe that likeability is fixed. That, like a good joke or a delicate butterfly, it can't be improved or even examined without being destroyed in the process. This simply isn't true: not only has likeability been rigorously studied by scientists, but we actu-ally know a lot about how it works *and* how to get better at it. That's what you'll get in this chapter: the laws of likeability and how you can improve yours.

One of our classes had a participant in the very early stage of his ca-reer. As a nuclear engineer, he was the perfect example of an expert who knew influential things but not influential people. After completing the training, he developed an ambitious monthly plan to put all my principles in action and kept in steady touch with me as he went.

Late one night the engineer left me an urgent voicemail asking me to call him back as soon as I could. I called him early the next morning and learned that he had just been named partner, the youngest in his firm's history. It turns out that his roster of carefully cultivated client relationships had started bringing in more than double what the average partner did. He had fostered great relationships within his firm too. His firm's leadership was excited to promote him, despite his young age. Relationships matter.

Relationship-Driven Business Development

Human beings are remarkably predictable in terms of what they like and what they don't. Although looks and other relatively unchangeable factors play a role, likeability boils down in large part to the way you do or don't do certain things. This means that a handful of research-backed adjustments can go a long way toward turning any self-proclaimed "awkward introvert" into an effective builder of enduring, mutually beneficial professional relationships. What's more, likeability delivers benefits beyond easy smiles and the occasional business-appropriate side-hug—people spend more *time* with people they like.

Why does this matter? For a fast-food restaurant, longer interactions are a bad thing. McDonald's wants customers to scarf their burgers and get back in their cars as quickly as possible to free up tables. The thing is, you're not running a McDonald's. If you're an expert looking to build lasting, mutually beneficial relationships with clients, those clients should want to spend as much time with you as possible.

The more time people spend with us, the stronger the bond. Russ Osmond, PhD, one of the leading experts on motivation, compares a relationship to a rope. At first, people are connected by a few strands of fiber, representing the kismet of a good first encounter. This new connection is fragile, easily snapped by a bad interaction or simply through neglect. Over time and with each positive interaction, however, the rope gets thicker, one strand at a time. Eventually it becomes strong and resilient, proof against the inevitable bad moment or sustained silence.

Thankfully for your business, these ropes can be woven more quickly than you might think. Fibers are added by each positive interaction, so if we're deliberate about the frequency of our interactions and *add value with each and every one*, we can create strong, resilient relationships rapidly.

One more bit about that rope: not only do people spend more time with those they like, but they also spend more money. This is true of that key decision maker whose signature you need in a matter of months.

The money part of all this may feel intuitively correct to you, but at first glance it doesn't make much logical sense. After all, if you need a toilet fixed, it shouldn't really matter whether you "get along" with the plumber. And yet if you're a raving fan of that plumber, it may occur to you as he's packing up his tools that the second bathroom is probably due for a new toilet. And hey, wouldn't now be a good time to install one of those fancy showerheads with ten different spray settings? And how about Dian down the street who was asking for a good plumber? When you really like somebody, you instinctively look for more ways to work together and help each other.

This is the beauty of relationship-oriented business development: when you fill the bleachers with raving fans, all you need to do is select from the opportunities they send your way.

So likeability matters. Big time. What can we do to create more of it?

The Five Drivers of Likeability

Scientists have found dozens of things that correlate to likeability, but not all of them can easily be changed. Five can. Change these five, and expect significant improvements in the ways people respond to you in both professional and personal situations.

Commonality

When attempting to connect with a prospect or client, seek common ground. Shared experiences, hobbies, and beliefs form the foundation of a strong relationship.

A conversation at a networking event or conference is brief by necessity. There are only a few minutes before one of you has to rush off to another panel discussion or keynote. You need to make every second count until it's time to swap business cards.

The problem is that in our hurry to make a good impression quickly, we waste that time _talking_: about our company, our services, ourselves. If you take nothing else away, remember that listening is fundamental to selling. By paying close and careful attention to what the other person is saying, you will learn what they need, which is far more important than what you want to sell them. You will also discover invaluable commonalities that can fan the spark of connection between you.

In one classic study researchers recorded certain basic attributes of both insurance salespeople and their prospects: height, age, income level, political party, and so on. They found that any strong similarities in these areas made customers significantly more likely to buy from that salesperson.

There's no reason being as tall as a perfect stranger should make you any more likely to buy insurance from them. Yet it does. And although being a cigarette smoker might make life insurance a good investment, there's no logical advantage to buying that policy from a fellow smoker. Clearly, this effect is something that occurs below the level of conscious awareness.

Jerry Burger and his colleagues at Santa Clara University took this line of exploration further. In one study they (falsely) told participants that another person shared similar fingerprints. Even this meaningless "similarity" made them more likely to say yes to a request from that person. Although one can argue that a shared religious or political belief might play a role in sound decision making, there is clearly no reason why the random whorls you're always wiping off your iPhone screen should help build a personal connection.

Logical or not, we use commonalities as a _heuristic_, a rule of thumb for saving cognitive effort when making complicated decisions. When meeting someone new, there's simply too much to take in: from age, gender, appearance, and dress to the way they introduce themselves and shake hands. We fall back on heuristics because we instinctively need a quick and easy—if not particularly meaningful—way to decide whether this is a friend or foe. The more we find in common, the safer we feel: Do I like this person? Do I want to continue this conversation?

The less common these commonalities, the better. "You like water too? I think this is the beginning of a beautiful friendship." No. That's why the fingerprint thing works as well as it does. Fingerprints are as unique as snowflakes, so the idea that someone else shares a similar set feels meaningful—even though it totally isn't.

So offering details when you talk pays off. Just the other day, instead of emailing someone to simply say I couldn't talk Thursday at 8 a.m., I specifically mentioned that I'd be at physical therapy at that time thanks to a recent biceps muscle reconstruction. As it turned out, my prospect had had the same procedure performed a few years before. Bingo—connection. On another recent occasion I asked an Australian prospect if he liked the Aussie singer-songwriter Paul Kelly, one of my favorites. Turns out he'd seen him perform the weekend before. We immediately jumped into our favorite albums and songs, a harmonious beginning to our now-deep respect for each other.

Will these rare but powerful connections happen every time? No way. But the more often you're specific instead of vague in conversations and emails, the more real connections will be made and strengthened throughout your career.

Last point: it can be tempting when a conversation isn't humming along to stretch the truth and create commonality where there is none. Remember that you're looking to build client relationships that span years, even your entire career. Maintaining the pretense of a different political belief or the love of a sport you know nothing about will eventually damage the relationship you've worked so hard to build.

I find it useful to record the commonalities I discover. You might keep track in your contact management software. While at a networking event, don't be afraid to step to the side of the room and make a few quick notes on your smartphone or on a person's business card after an interaction. If you're going to talk to more than a couple of people in a row, you're likely to forget important details by the time you're back at your desk.

So remember: listen more than you talk, and be specific when you do talk. Find the uncommon things you have in common with your prospect or client. And always keep it authentic. We'll get even deeper into this when we talk about developing new client relationships. When the rope is fragile, the relationship needs the most attention and care.

Frequency

If you were a fan of the show *Seinfeld*, you might remember George Costanza's advertising-inspired dating strategy:

GEORGE: I'm going out with her tomorrow. She said she had some errands to run.

JERRY: That's a date?

GEORGE: What's the difference? You know the way I work. I'm like a commercial jingle. First, it's a little irritating, then you hear it a few times, you hum it in the shower, by the third date it's "By Mennen!"

Brands have long understood that small but frequent impressions are an effective way to make an impression. You don't think this applies to you as a seller-expert? Tell me if this scenario sounds familiar: You meet someone interesting at a professional event. It turns out that you have a lot in common. The two of you enjoy a good conversation in the limited time available. Then, a week later, you have a short follow-up email exchange. So far, so good.

Now work gets in the way. Three months later it occurs to you that your company has a new service that might be of interest to that person. Or perhaps you conceive of a promising idea for a collaboration. You send them a quick email, expecting a quick and warm response. Instead, a week or two later you receive a tepid one-liner: "Nice to hear from you. Really busy right now, I'll respond later." Then, silence.

We fall into this trap all the time, investing effort in getting a potentially valuable relationship started only to become distracted by work. Sometimes it's possible to get things back on track, but more often the fragile new rope has snapped.

Although the quality of your interactions with a person is important, just as important is the *frequency* of those interactions. A series of small, value-adding interactions is substantially more effective in building a relationship than are one or two big ones spread far apart. Relationships need steady nurturing at first. Behavioral scientists call this the *mere exposure effect*, which has endured in the literature since 1876. (You know research is powerful if it's seen three different centuries.) It turns out that "mere exposure" to something—a concept, a product, a person—has a strong correlation with liking it. The more exposures, the stronger the effect: "By Mennen!"

Admittedly, a series of relatively pointless emails won't magically build a strong connection. Interactions must be frequent, but they must also provide value to the other person to count—quality *and* quantity.

One simple way to handle this is to break up your communications into smaller pieces. Have seven things to follow up on after the meeting? Break them up and spread them out over a week or so. It's easier for the recipient to reply to smaller chunks, and you'll get quality *and* quantity points.

Think about the relationships on your Protemoi List today and ask yourself: Have you been tending to your garden as consistently as you should be?

More on this as it specifically relates to fragile early-stage relationships in Chapter 9.

Mutuality

Relationships thrive on a back-and-forth flow of positive interactions. Clearly, we like it when people do nice things for us. Counterintuitively, we *also* like people more when *we* do things for *them*. It turns out that helping others is enjoyable. So don't be afraid to give *or* to request help— within reason. Think *mutual* benefit.

When interacting with clients and prospects take the time to step back and think about mutuality. What have I done for this person lately? What have I asked this person to do for me?

Adam Grant, a top professor at Wharton, is the worldwide expert on mutually beneficial relationships. Our entire team quotes his research often, and his book *Give and Take* made a big impact on me personally. I asked him about the importance of mutuality specifically as it applies to seller-experts.

"Too many people live in a transactional world," he told me, "where every request means a debt owed and every favor comes with strings attached. In the long run it's better to give unconditionally—that creates a norm of generosity, where people help each other whenever they can. That means when you need something, you can go to anyone in your network, not just the people you've supported in the past or expect to support in the future."

Many times, as the provider of services, we hesitate to ask for help. We should *serve and only serve* the client, we think. But this can limit our relationships, especially for clients we've already served well. If we think of helping as enjoyable, we're inhibiting our relationship growth by *not* asking for help.

There are many meaningful ways to ask for help. You can ask clients for referrals to another part of the organization or to a new one where they know people. You can ask for a client to serve as a reference for prospects. You can ask for advice on a proposal you're making. You can ask for the names of people they think you should meet. We've also had our clients go pretty deep, even asking their clients for advice on their own personal growth plans. It's been extremely successful.

Asking for help provides a new opportunity after you've asked for it: you can express gratitude. "Thank you" is a powerful and underused phrase in the world of business. Simply sending a follow-up email thanking a prospect for meeting with you will already put you ahead of many of your competitors. Thank you for that referral. Thank you for providing feedback on my presentation. Thank you for helping me think through my growth plan. "Please" may be the magic word, but "thank you" is enchanting.

Grant and his colleagues at Wharton have done research on this, looking at the power of gratitude in business relationships. In one part of a study, participants were asked to review a cover letter. After giving their feedback, they were asked to review another. Half received this request only acknowledging the first review. The other half were explicitly thanked for the first review before being requested to do more.

Believe it or not, the rate of follow-through *doubled* in response to a simple thank-you. (How would you like to double the number of prospects you turn into clients?) Grant even tried this outside the lab, measuring the effect of gratitude on the efforts of call center workers. A visit expressing gratitude from the director of annual giving led to a *50 percent increase* in the volume of phone calls made. A little gratitude goes a long way.

One of my favorite clients, Dave Queller, is quite the servant-leader. He has stretched my thinking about expressing gratitude. Shortly after taking over managing thousands of client-facing experts at Express Scripts, a group that manages over $100 billion per year in revenue, Dave personally called every senior client-facing leader. No joke, he made over sixteen hundred personal phone calls in a month, just to say thank you. Here's what he told me about the experience. I started by asking why *this*?

> We had just gone through a huge merger, and our teams were extremely busy, still sorting out their place internally and working double time with clients to migrate systems. I knew people were working very hard, but it would have been easy to get lost, to not feel a connection to this new, $100 billion organization. I wanted to drive a feeling of inclusiveness by telling people they mattered and that what they were doing mattered to *me*. We were all in this together, and I wanted them to know it.

That made sense, but it's *how* Dave pulled things off that truly amazed me—and amazed his people.

> It took me about a month to get to everyone, making fifty to a hundred calls every day but Sunday. I was busy in meetings during the day, so I had to fit this in elsewhere. I had a list, including the people's names, clients they supported, who they reported to, where they lived, and, in many cases, something they had done exceptionally well I could specifically thank them for. That list ruled my life. I wanted to get to

everyone, so I'd come in early. I'd make calls from home before dinner. I'd call people driving to work and on my way home. I'd call people on Saturday mornings. I remember talking with one wonderful person on Christmas Eve morning, catching her sitting in bed with her young daughter. I didn't mean to intrude and offered to reconnect later, but we sat there, all three of us chatting, bonding over what they planned to do on their special day. It was magic. Neither of us will ever forget it, and we now have a common bond over that phone call. I couldn't have planned it that way, but it was the perfect moment to say thank you for all she was doing.

Dave still has people come up to him and thank him for that little gesture. It was a monumental effort, but it opened doors to many relationships, and best of all, those relationships are authentic.

Wow. If Dave, who is on the senior-most team at the twentieth largest public company in America, can make time to call *sixteen hundred* people in a month, surely we can pick up the phone to say thank you a few times a week.

How can you express more gratitude with prospects and clients? Maybe it's a handwritten note. Maybe it's scheduling a cup of coffee. Maybe it's picking up the phone.

Dave said something else interesting to me: "With the rise of electronic communication, we're losing the personalization of business. Just taking the time to pick up the phone and say thank you means so much." I agree. Doing so could be a crucial step in deepening a relationship. Whether it's for a client, strategic partner, or someone inside your organization, a few minutes to show your gratitude is a small thing, but ultimately, it's huge.

We'll cover this topic from a different perspective when we cover lead generation in Chapter 6. These principles can help you expand to new relationships while deepening the ones you already have.

Balance

Frequency of interactions builds strong relationships, but fundamental to that is the *nature* of those interactions. No working relationship among team members or between expert and client is going to be entirely positive or entirely without friction. A great, growing relationship has a little of each: some very positive, fun elements and some elements where one side is pushing the other.

Think of a relationship where the other side is always positive. Every single thing you say or do is awesome, the best thing ever said or done. It's no good. Fake. Sure, we're great, but we're not *that* great! Now think about a relationship where most of the things you say or do are not good enough or simply miss the mark. Too much of that, and you tune out because you can't win. It's no fun. So what's the right balance between sweet and sour for keeping a relationship healthy?

Dr. Marcial Losada and his colleagues at the University of Michigan used profitability, customer satisfaction, and peer evaluations to classify teams of employees as low, medium, and high performing. They found that the ratio of positive to negative interactions among the team members correlated strongly with each team's performance.

For the purpose of the study, a positive interaction was counted when one team member expressed encouragement, support, or appreciation for another—*Great thought, Lisa!* Negative interactions included critical remarks or even suggestions for how the other person might do better— *That's one idea, Mike, but have you thought about trying . . . ?*

High-performing teams had an average of *5.6 positive interactions* for every negative one.* Medium-performing teams had an average of two to one, and low-performing teams displayed more negative interactions than positive ones.

Let those ratios sink in. People work together best when their interactions weigh *heavily* positive relative to the amount of communication about what could be improved.

Think about recent colleague interactions you've had. Were you complimentary and specific about what you liked? Were you honest about what might be improved? What was your ratio? Building in enough positives gives you license to be constructive without being destructive.

---

* All peer-reviewed research is criticized, and Losada's has been criticized more than most. That said, I find the concept of a positive to negative ratio quite valuable and I keep it in mind all the time. The correct ratio will depend on the individuals involved, the situation and many other things. Think of the numbers provided here as a rule of thumb more than an absolute truth.

What I love about this model is it offers a clear metric, something to shoot for. I'm too positive by nature, something rooted in my desire to please. I've had to work to be straightforward and clear about what isn't working and needs to be improved. Thankfully, it comes more easily now. A very senior consultant I worked with had the same issue. He deliberately developed the habit of offering at least one constructive thought in every initial prospect meeting he had. Doing so showed that he wasn't overly eager to please or afraid of being honest. If you're relentlessly positive, try this approach. A little vinegar goes a long way.

Others have the opposite problem. They're quick to point out missteps without offering genuine, positive praise to avoid overdrawing their account. Their prospects, feeling criticized and attacked, stop returning calls. If that sounds familiar, start addressing it by entering every interaction with a positive remark already in mind. Even if you have something constructive to offer, lead with something positive—*and genuine*—instead. Over time and as you see the results, those positive remarks will start to come more naturally, peppering themselves throughout each conversation at comfortable intervals.

Often experts who are relentlessly critical just don't see the utility in saying something if it isn't intended to fix a problem. But being relentlessly critical *is* a problem. Fix it. In your client relationships keep a mental tally of how every exchange is going relative to the "Losada ratio" of 5.6 to 1. High-performing teams instinctively cleave to this ratio. It allows you to add value by being mostly fun and encouraging while also offering actionable insight to help your clients avoid future missteps. Doing so will show your clients, through your actions, that you're helping *them* become high-performing.

Uniqueness

You know the year is nearing its end when the corporate greeting cards start flowing into your mailbox, especially if you're in a position to decide who gets lucrative business. Like clockwork, the companies that consider you a prospect, client, or key decision maker send you their off-the-rack, faith-agnostic, sparkle-encrusted holiday greeting cards wishing you happy holidays and possibly happy New Year for bonus points.

Does this action even register with you anymore? After all, that card isn't about *you*. Every service business keeps a list of clients in Excel on the share drive. Some poor assistant or temp gets tasked with doing a mail merge and then ferrying the stack of cards around the office for each employee's turn at signatures. *David, you're holding up the holiday card pile!* What could be more perfunctory or anonymous?

The same goes for the wine you automatically bring to a dinner or the company-branded pen you bring to a meeting. Sure, it's a nice gesture, but it's also predictable, an expected courtesy, and therefore instantly forgettable. Nowadays we even delude ourselves into thinking that wishing someone happy birthday on a social network is *outreach*. Yeah, us and the 237 other friends, relatives, colleagues, and random high school acquaintances who chose to do so—the moment Facebook or LinkedIn reminded them.

Recently I spoke at a high-profile conference with a friend and client, the CMO of a large professional services firm. We had a great time and had one of the highest-rated sessions amongst dozens. I intended to send him a small thank-you gift right away, but a storm of subsequent client events got in the way. Then a vacation. I didn't get to figuring out what to send him until six weeks later. I felt awful—after all, staying on top of this kind of thing is supposed to be my specialty. Maybe it was simply too late to say thank you for that particular event.

Then it hit me: this might actually be the *best* time to send something. It will be totally unexpected! One thing we've connected on is our love of preparing craft cocktails. I wondered whether there might be a "mixology of the month club" offering monthly deliveries of mixers and recipes. Celebration, creativity, and craft cocktails—what's not to like?

I researched and found a great vendor offering this very thing, and instead of focusing on the one speech, I wrote the thank-you about our entire relationship and how much our team had enjoyed working with his team, all over the world. It was so much more meaningful. The unexpected timing of the gift just made it better.

Spontaneity is the Tabasco of client relationships. Used sparingly but well, it adds a memorable zing to every interaction. Reaching out with an asset or a compliment or a question "out of the blue" delivers a stronger, more memorable experience to the recipient because it is *unexpected*.

From now on, think about the timing of your outreach as it relates to all the other messages people receive. Whenever possible, deliberately break up the rhythm. When it comes to your Protemoi List, you want to contact each person on a monthly basis, but don't allow these interactions to become rote. *Interesting news clipping from Bill—it must be the third Thursday of the month*. Shake it up. Be spontaneous. They'll notice.

We'll discuss spontaneity as it pertains to client planning in a later chapter. Planning out how to surprise and delight clients is a skill every rainmaker should possess.

•

Bill Ruprecht is the former CEO of Sotheby's, the world's largest and most prestigious auction house for fine art, jewelry, autos, and collectibles. It should come as no surprise that he is also a master of business development. He connects with people around their passions like no one I've ever met, and he's a great storyteller to boot. He shared this one with me:

> At Sotheby's I was privileged to know clients in over one hundred countries. When someone contacts me, I get back to them, always, within twenty-four hours. It's a sign of respect. When I became CEO in 2000 I acquired a mentor, the legendary businessman Max Fisher from Detroit, then ninety. Max would call me every day of the week. For years. And once, in that first year, I didn't call Max back. The next day he called again, and I was on the phone. He insisted on holding. When I got on the phone he said, "Bill, I just told the president of the United States I'd call him back because I wanted to talk to you. You didn't call me back yesterday, and I want to know what the hell is the matter with you?" I apologized and asked what was so urgent. He replied, "Bill, what is urgent is that I care about your success, and I call you to hear your voice and to understand what you are thinking about. My time is valuable, young man, and when I call, I expect you to return my call."

When I had been fully dressed down by one of the really grand wise men of the twentieth century, I had a different appreciation for him reaching out to me and the gift of his support. And I always called him back thereafter, from anywhere in the world and at any time, because he deserved it.

In the end my view is that selling is really just figuring out what makes your clients tick and getting them what they need. When you can't get them what they want, tell them. They'll mostly accept that, if it's delivered honestly.

My best clients, the ones with whom I was most successful, have known what they've wanted: to have some fun, get what they need, and work with people they trust.

The study of likeability is a science, but it's not rocket science. In the end we're all human beings. We like it when other people are authentic, positive, and helpful with us—even if we have yet to master those attributes ourselves. As you've seen, the five drivers of likeability don't take much additional work per se. They just require a change of mindset. Likeability makes every aspect of your professional and personal life easier. Isn't it worth changing your mind?

Using Whole Brain® Thinking* to Better Communicate

A big part of getting people to like you is understanding how they prefer to think and communicate. Whole Brain® Thinking allows you to identify the dominant thinking styles of the person you're talking to and then adapt your mode of communication to suit them best. The key to good communication is to shift the emphasis from "expressing yourself" to "being heard."

We want to avoid the common trap of assuming others think the way we do or use the same buying priorities. It's natural—but incorrect—to project our preferences onto others. Instead, we want to listen, come to understand our clients' priorities, and then communicate back using *their* preferences and priorities, not ours.

---

*Whole Brain Thinking,® HBDI,® and Hermann Brain Dominance Instrument® are registered trademarks of Hermann Global, LLC.

Whole Brain® Clues

A. Analytical	D. Experimental
Analyzes	Infers
Quantifies	Imagines
Is logical	Speculates
Is critical	Takes Risks
Is realistic	Is Impetuous
Likes numbers	Breaks Rules
Knows about money	Likes Surprises
Knows how things work	Is Curious / Plays

B. Practical	C. Relational
Takes Preventive Action	Is sensitive to others
Establishes Procedures	Likes to teach
Gets Things Done	Touches a lot
Is Reliable	Is supportive
Organizes	Is expressive
Is Neat	Is emotional
Timely	Talks a lot
Plans	Feels

BASED ON THE FOUR SELVES MODEL AND THE WHOLE BRAIN® MODEL OF HERRMANN GLOBAL LLC.
© 2018 HERRMANN GLOBAL LLC

Once you understand *your own* thinking style preferences, it will become easier to understand how *another person's* preferences can affect how they interpret your words. This connects to how they make buying decisions as well as what they look for in the services you're offering them. With practice you will become able to quickly assess and adapt your communication to their thinking style.

The clues listed above map directly to buying priorities. Here's your magic decoder ring of what to emphasize if you get a lot of clues in a particular area:

+ If analytical, focus on *high value.*
+ If practical, focus on *proven process,* the safe choice.

✦ If relational, focus on *benefits to people* the buyer empathizes with: their customers, their employees, their team, or others.

✦ If experimental, focus on *strategic fit*, breakthrough results, future flexibility, and innovation.

The preceding four bullets are possibly the most important part of this entire book.

Prospects and clients are giving us clues to what's important to them in every interaction. As you start to hear them, you can start to skew how you talk about your solutions using the alignment above. Remember that the vast majority of people have multiple thinking styles and most large

Adapting Techniques

A. Analytical	D. Experimental
• Critical analysis • Facts, no fluff • Technical accuracy • Goal and objectives • Well-articulated ideas • Data, facts, logic • Brevity, clarity, conciseness	• Overview, big picture • Minimal details • Freedom to explore ideas • Metaphors, visuals • New, fun, imaginative • Conceptual framework • Alignment with long term strategy
B. Practical	**C. Relational**
• Detailed time-action agenda • Thorough and with references • Rules and procedures • Step-by-step, linear, sequential • In writing, in advance • Contingency plans • Sticking to the agenda	• Open, informal discussion • Expressive body and voice • Commonalities and conversation • Effect on others • How people feel • Everyone having a chance to contribute • No hidden agendas

BASED ON THE WHOLE BRAIN® MODEL OF HERRMANN GLOBAL LLC. © 2018 HERRMANN GLOBAL LLC

purchases are made by more than one person, so you'll likely need to emphasize multiple benefits.

As you emphasize these priorities, here's a chart you can use to adapt to each thinking style. These are simple ways to dial up the proper communication.

Pay close attention to the areas that seem hard—that's likely where you need to focus the most.

But what happens if you aren't sure of the clues, when there is a large decision-making group, or a buyer seems to be all over the place? That's when you can use a Whole Brain® Walkaround.* This simple technique ensures that you are communicating in all four quadrants. That way your message can be heard no matter what your listeners' preferences. Picking up the clues as I described above is targeted and quite powerful, but it requires a lot of practice.

Here's your hedge. The chart on the following page is called a Whole Brain® Walkaround. It's the process of looking at anything through the lens of *all four* thinking styles. I use this tool every day, for making sure I cover all aspects of thinking on a call or in an email. It works for lunches with clients and dinners with the family, for casual volunteer work at a nonprofit and a high-stakes finalist meeting. Use this to audit anything you do.

Slow down and pay attention to this—it's one of the most important elements of this book. Many of our clients print this off and put it on the wall of their office.

Can you see how looking at something through the lens of all four thinking styles can be powerful? Say we're using it to make sure you're communicating with a prospect effectively on a first-time call. Even if the prospect has a very low preference in one quadrant, communicating in that quadrant can help them by subtly pointing out their blind spots. Personally, I have a low preference for practical thinking, especially as it relates to details around implementation. I always appreciate when someone points out implementation difficulties I wouldn't see. Communicating in all four quadrants is an insurance policy that ensures your message will get across.

Want an easy way to incorporate this in your day-to-day life? Get the **Whole Brain® Walkaround** worksheet, or simply draw a big plus sign on a sheet of paper. Preparing for *anything* gets better when you look at it through the lens of each quadrant.

This approach can be used for nearly any communication—an important email, a lunch meeting, or a formal pitch. The key is to approach

---

* Whole Brain® Thinking, HBDI®, and Herrmann Brain Dominance Instrument® are registered trademarks of Herrmann Global, LLC.

Whole Brain® Walkaround

A. Analytical

Fill in the facts of the Analytical Quadrant.
- The analytical quadrant is represented by presenting facts, financials, logic, and technical specifications.
- It addresses the question: What?
- Examples: What is the current situation? What data supports this? What is the bottom line? What are financial terms/consequences? What is the logic behind this approach/decision? What is the goal or objective?
- Have we included....
  – Clear performance goals, objectives, and measures?
  – Budget or financial issues and outcomes?
  – Data and research to support our goals?
  – Technical aspects?
  – Cost-benefit analyses or ROI statements?

D. Experimental

Write down the concepts of the Experimental Quadrant.
- The experimental quadrant is represented by presenting the big picture, the future state, a holistic view, and/or innovative solutions.
- It addresses the question: Why?
- Examples: Why are we doing this? Why is this important? Why should the listener care? Why is this future state better than the current state?
- Have we included....
  – The big picture and global aspects?
  – A vision of our successful future outcome?
  – A strategy, vision, or mission statement?
  – Our assumptions?
  – Alternative, creative, and innovative new ideas and solutions?

B. Practical

Add the planning details of the Practical Quadrant.
- The practical quadrant is represented by presenting organization, form, structure, plans, and details.
- It addresses the questions: How? and When?
- Examples: How will this be done? How will this be organized? How will this be implemented? How will we reduce risk? When will this start? When will it be finished? How long will it take? How will it be measured?
- Have we included....
  – An agenda, guidelines, and timeline?
  – What steps to take to achieve the goal?
  – A discussion of risks and contingency plans?
  – A proposed action plan and dependencies?
  – Resource requirements?
  – Policies and procedures?
  – Quality guidelines?

C. Relational

Include the personal benefits of the Relational Quadrant.
- The relational quadrant is represented by presenting values, feelings, relationships, and emotions.
- It addresses the question: Who?
- Examples: Who will benefit? Who can use this? Who is involved? Who will resist? Who will be in favor? Who do we need to communicate with? Who is involved? Who is our consumer?
- Have we included....
  – Our feelings about each other?
  – Description of our relationship?
  – Discussion of our shared values?
  – Partnering language (we, us, our, team, mutual, opportunity, sharing, trust, integrity)?
  – Demonstration of listening, empathy, and understanding?
  – Cultural issues?
  – Mutual benefits, concerns, issues?

WHOLE BRAIN® IS A REGISTERED TRADEMARK OF HERRMANN GLOBAL LLC. THE WHOLE BRAIN® MODEL IS A COPYRIGHTED WORK OF HERRMANN GLOBAL LLC. © 2018 HERRMANN GLOBAL LLC.

the topic from each of the four quadrants. Too often we stay stuck in our own preferred quadrants and never consider inputs from the ones where we're less comfortable.

Thinking preferences act like filters for everything you hear, say, and think. That means that the right message delivered the wrong way *for that person* won't be heard. Increased awareness of your own thinking and communication preferences will help you become more aware of how you avoid your least preferred thinking styles and how that can impede your effectiveness when relating to others.

Talking About Yourself

Some of the most important, influential business relationships begin simply. Maybe a friend told you about someone you should meet when you bumped into each other at a coffee shop, or perhaps a casual acquaintance texted you with a quick question related to your expertise. These small, serendipitous moments sometimes set the course of our entire careers— when handled properly, of course. Have you ever walked away from such an encounter wishing you'd handled it differently, without quite knowing what you did wrong? Somehow you can sense that an essential connection failed to spark. But why?

As a seller-expert, talking about yourself is the most vital thing you can do with your time. Does that sound selfish or self-centered? Look, if someone who actually needs help talks to you for several minutes and fails to realize you can help them, *what help are you?*

Even if we're not shy or reticent, we can still be uncomfortable talking about ourselves and what we can do. But again, if people don't know what we can do for them, what use were all those years of training and preparation?

What follows is a simple model for talking about yourself in a way that is both authentic and balanced. Use it, and you will demonstrate confidence and a desire to be helpful that people can recognize and appreciate. The goal is to treat every conversation as an opportunity.

You might think there's something cheesy, manipulative, or cynical about going into every new interaction seeking a business opportunity. But remember that a true rainmaker is authentic—your goal is to be of service. Don't lose sight of that and force the other person to dig information out of you. That doesn't do them any favors. Remember: the other person is probably feeling reticent too. By making yourself more interesting and creating a sense of curiosity, you're making the conversation much easier for them, whether they're going to be a client someday or not.

Let's look at an all-too-typical conversation at a business networking function:

ALEXIS: Hi! I'm Alexis.

JAVIER: Hello. I'm Javier.

ALEXIS: Nice to meet you, Javier. So what do you do?

JAVIER: Oh, I'm a personal coach, I guess, but I hate that term.

ALEXIS [thinking, *Great, sounds like this is going nowhere.*]: Oh really. What do you do as a personal coach?

JAVIER: Well, I help people get better at stuff.

ALEXIS [wondering, *Why is this so difficult?*]: What kinds of "stuff" do you help people get better at?

JAVIER: Mostly finding new jobs that might work better for them.

ALEXIS [thinking, *Oh look, there's a fly on my cocktail weenie.*]: Jobs? What kinds of jobs?

JAVIER: Mostly helping them figure out what kinds of businesses they might be able to start.

ALEXIS [thinking, *That fly is more interesting than this guy. I have to get out of here!*]: Businesses, huh? That sounds great. Listen, would you excuse me? I have to find a flyswatter.

Clearly this conversation wasn't much fun for either of them. Think back to a great conversation you had at a group event—a neighborhood cookout, a professional conference, wherever. What made that interaction so engaging?

Chances are the person you spoke with was both *interesting* and *passionate*. They likely gave you control of the conversation, letting you ask the questions you wanted to ask. They made you curious and then rewarded that curiosity with fascinating information.

A great mystery novel reveals one clue at a time, enticing you to turn the next page. Great conversations work the same way. There's a lively back-and-forth, like a friendly game of ping-pong, each answer leaving an opening for the next.

What to avoid? Dead ends, as in the conversation above. And, on the flip side, monologues. The best answers offer just enough information to create curiosity and naturally spur another line of questioning.

There is an art to conversation. The key to being a master conversationalist is to listen at least as much as you talk and to answer questions with enough detail to continue the flow of ideas.

Let's look at our scene again, after Javier has absorbed the lessons in this chapter. Javier will give Alexis just enough detail to maintain the back-and-forth rhythm of the conversation. He won't talk nonstop, and he won't toss out dry, monosyllabic answers that let the conversation die an uncomfortable death. Remember: ping-pong.

ALEXIS: Hi! I'm Alexis.

JAVIER: Nice to meet you, Alexis. I'm Javier.

ALEXIS: Nice to meet you, Javier. What do you do?

JAVIER: Well, you know how there are a lot of people fed up with the constant challenges of the corporate world? Endless re-orgs. Constant layoffs. [Alexis nods in recognition.] I help people assess if going out on their own and starting their own business makes sense. If it does, I help them get started with a unique, three-step process.

ALEXIS [skeptical but curious]: Oh really? What's unique about it? How does it work?

JAVIER: The first step is really fun. I've developed a method to assess the person's core skills, the things they're truly great at, and measure how passionate they are about each one—being good at something doesn't mean you want to do it for a living. Then we rank and chart out all the skills and match those with viable business options. What's interesting is that most people are anchored on their current role and job. They have no idea how many other things they're really good at, really passionate about, and that offer real value.

ALEXIS [curiosity piqued]: I've heard that most new businesses fail. Does this really work?

JAVIER: All the time. I've got a client getting ready to launch her business next week. She's doing something she never thought she would and loving every minute. I'm so excited for her.

ALEXIS [oblivious to the fly on her cocktail weenie]: Really? What's she going to do? Isn't it scary?

JAVIER: She was in a change-management role at a huge company, but we discovered that her biggest strength and her biggest passion was positioning products and services. She has a natural gift for marketing that she never got to use in her old job. Now she's launching a marketing agency. There's no risk because she's already landed a seven-figure engagement. That's more than she'd make in several years at her old job. She's going to do great because we've orchestrated each step of the process. The beauty of what we do is that our clients only pay for the implementation of steps two and three *if* we find a potential business match in the first step. So it's sort of a no-brainer if someone wants to do the assessment.

ALEXIS: Wow! I've always thought about starting my own business, but I didn't know how. It seems so overwhelming. What are the other steps you put people through . . .

Each time Javier answers a question he's picking up clues about Alexis from the words she uses. If you look closely, you'll see there are procedural thinking clues around process and risk. Javier realizes he is probably dealing with a procedural thinker, someone most interested in a risk-free, proven process. He responds appropriately. He's ready for more questions about timeline, substeps in the process, how to mitigate risk, and even other clients who share a high procedural thinking style to whom he can introduce Alexis.

Each response creates more curiosity thanks both to Javier's obvious enthusiasm for his work and to his results. He's seeded the conversation with multiple things to discuss, including the details of steps two and three, more information about his client and how the heck she landed a seven-figure deal, other clients he's helped, how he got into the business in the first place, and many others. Twenty minutes will go by very quickly. By the end of this exchange Alexis is excited to sign up for Javier's preliminary skill assessment.

The first important thing to notice here is that Javier has not had to push for business or ask Alexis for anything. In some ways he hasn't even talked about himself at all—his focus on his client is establishing his process and credibility. Alexis is asking *him* to deepen the conversation. No boring answers. No filibusters.

The second thing to notice is that this was a productive and enjoyable conversation. Alexis never felt like she was being manipulated or sold to because, well, she wasn't! Javier simply answered her question—"What do you do?"—with enough detail that she could pick up her end of the conversation and keep it moving. It turned out that Javier might be able to help Alexis, but even if that hadn't happened, any number of positive outcomes might have played out; Alexis might have thought of a friend or colleague who would love to meet Javier, for instance.

When you have an opportunity to talk about yourself, start with what I call a *curious introduction*: a short, provocative statement that creates interest and generates questions. It gets a head nod, a buy-in. That little head nod is important—it's an invitation to open the door a little wider. Once you've gotten the nod, listen for clues to the other person's thinking preferences as they respond, and let that understanding guide the conversation. As you refine this technique you can quickly turn a casual introduction into a great opportunity to help someone.

A strong curious introduction feels authentic—it should flow easily and naturally in the context you're in, whether you're at an industry event or just an informal gathering of friends and colleagues. Consider the following curious introduction:

> You know how professionals are under pressure to keep growing their business? I train them to do business development in a helpful way that deepens relationships. We've been hitting high ROI targets because the system is based on over 120 scientific studies and because we use a really tight seventeen-module process. Professionals get excited about business development when they see it as helping their clients instead of selling to them. In a way, we don't teach selling at all—we teach people how to create a buy.

This curious introduction touches all four thinking styles, has several different topics that might strike a chord with the listener, and exudes the excitement and passion of the speaker—me—for his work.

The point is to get the other person talking. Use a curious introduction to spark a meaningful conversation. The faster you can engage the other person in dialogue, the more quickly you will spot clues to their interests, needs, and thinking preferences, leading to an even deeper and more valu-able exchange.

As you talk, keep going back in your mind to thinking style: Are you talking to a practical thinker? If so, talk about how fast, efficient, or well organized your process is. Are you talking to a relational thinker? Don't hold back in expressing your enthusiasm for your work and the joy you take in helping clients. Be authentic. This is about shining a light on those aspects that will most interest and engage the other person.

If you aren't sure how the other person thinks just yet, start with a big-picture, experimental-oriented curious introduction. Then narrow it down from there based on each response.

Obviously, kismet can't be forced. Sometimes you really do just click with somebody, your BFF and/or a "brother from another mother." But most of the time it's perfectly possible to connect with the people you meet in work and in life by getting yourself in tune with human psychol-ogy. Sadly, they don't teach you this stuff in school.

•

In this chapter I've given you some research-backed, time-tested tools for improving at the business of people. Some of these behaviors may already be second nature for you, but chances are that many of them won't come naturally. Be patient with yourself as you learn. Likeability is incredibly self-reinforcing. When you start to see how a few small changes can trans-form your interactions, you'll be increasingly motivated to master every element in this chapter.

In the next chapter we're going to start looking at lead-generation strategies. That's right: you will need to design and implement a true strat-egy, not just collect a few tips and tactics, if you want to fill a pipeline with promising new prospects.

I'm also going to introduce you to one of the foundational compo-nents of the system: the *give-to-get*. No exaggeration: it's going to trans-form the way you turn prospects into clients. You know how sometimes it's hard to create demand for your services? Well, in the next chapter I'll show you the missing piece of the puzzle.

CHAPTER 5

Turning Prospects into Clients

• • •

WITH STEADY PRACTICE the tools in the previous chapter will help you develop the capacity to communicate and connect with other people, from prospects and clients to friends and family. In this chapter we turn to the task of attracting the attention of other people in the first place. People skills won't do you any good if you're sitting alone in a room and waiting for the phone to ring. Your prospects are dim without, well, prospects.

A *lead* is created when an individual or business shows interest in your services and provides contact information. Even if you've been operating in your business for years, the source of new leads may still feel mysterious. If you don't keep careful track of your lead-generation efforts, it can feel like new ones arrive out of the blue, unexpectedly and unpredictably—or, worse, that they barely arrive at all. Many seller-experts feel like the flow of leads is essentially out of their control, like the stock market or the weather.

Whether your leads feel out of the blue or out of control, you can do better, though it hasn't always been easy to figure out how. There is very little written on lead generation as a practice. What you do find is old school: smile-and-dial cold-calling techniques. The idea with these is that you call a lot of people you don't know and leave a message asking them to call you back. Then you send an email asking if they got your voicemail. Then you send an email every two days asking if they got your email asking if they got your voicemail. "It's a numbers game," sales gurus say. "Just keep at it, and you can achieve a 5 percent success rate, if you're lucky. You can do it!"

I can't do it. First, a 5 percent success rate means we're teaching 95 percent of the people we call that we're weirdo pests who are desperate for business. (And if you weren't feeling desperate when you started cold calling, you will by the time you're done.) Second, if we do get a person on the phone, we automatically need to overcome an initial negative perception. Even if this technique did work in terms of keeping businesses alive, most people still wouldn't do it. It feels uncomfortable. Certainly not authentic.

I've found that most seller-experts just defer to doing what their mentor or first boss did or maybe what they themselves tried last year regardless of whether it worked: speaking at the same conference, guest posting on the same blog, and on and on, without any clear sense of what's making an impact and what isn't.

Let's change that. I'm going to outline a series of techniques that will work for you. They have worked consistently for the thousands of seller-experts I've trained over the last decade across industries and professions. The best part? They all attract leads with *value*, not by begging. Nothing inauthentic, uncomfortable, or weird involved.

When you design your technique around something people want, something that would be helpful to them, something only you have, they'll be glad you reached out and excited to meet you. Our litmus test for this value is that prospects bend their schedules to meet with you instead of the other way around.

Let me be bold for a second: you cannot have too many leads. This idea can stir folks up a bit. Deep down many of us fear an abundance of leads. It can feel like too much work, too many emails, endless follow-up: "I'm busy already! How would I cope if I had even more to do?"

Here's what you'll do. You'll find more of the work you love. You'll say no to the less valuable, more commoditized work you don't. You'll further refine your unique brand. You'll be happier because you can choose the work you want to take on. You'll raise your rates. You'll make more money. You'll hire people to handle the excess or maybe just refer it out to others—whatever works for you. Hiring people grows your group.

Referring work out means more people will refer the work you want back to you. Did I mention you'll raise your rates? What's not to love?

What's the worst-case scenario? That a truly terrific prospect comes along and you don't have the bandwidth to take on the work? Let's play the tape forward: you refer the prospect along to a strategic partner with a pang of regret. Yet even here you win. The lucky recipient of the referral owes you big time for a great new client. The prospect's first impression of you is that you're highly in demand—you can bet they'll be curious to work with you next time around. This, right here, is the biggest downside of too many leads. And it's pretty great.

A steady flow of leads makes every other aspect of business development "magically" easier, from targeting your ideal clients to negotiating the appropriate rates for your services. Selling becomes easier when you don't feel like your entire month, quarter, or even year depends on any one prospect signing on the dotted line. The benefits of steady lead flow will astonish you. In order to get there, though, we need to open the floodgates.

Before we dive into creating the right lead-generation strategy for you and your business, you'll need one of the most powerful tools in your new BD arsenal, one that *creates* demand: the give-to-get.

Give-to-Get

Show me you're willing to invest in us. Do your homework and come with a gift of knowledge or something that demonstrates that you value my time and the relationship.

Heed the words of this Fortune 100 C-level leader, someone I've worked with for over fifteen years. After many years spent on the receiving end of "sales efforts" she has no patience for being sold to. What she wants is an individual willing to invest in the relationship and give her company something of value that will help them solve real problems.

Don't make the common mistake of trying to close a deal in the first meeting. (This "now or never" mentality is often driven by an insufficient flow of leads. Back to that problem shortly.) Most seller-experts stick to a two-step process for closing deals: One, get prospect. Two, grab project. "Me, Tarzan! You, client!"

Regardless of whether this blunt-force approach is effective in the short term, it damages the *relationship* at its most vulnerable stage. We don't want buyer's remorse; we want raving fans. So what do we do instead?

When it comes to true business development, you need to give *before* you receive. In our model you *give* something of value to the prospect strategically designed to *get* your relationship to the point where a deal becomes the obvious next step. Trying to close immediately feels like trying to force something. A good sales process feels as inevitable as a ball rolling downhill.

There are four steps along the way:

1. introductory meeting
2. give-to-get
3. small project
4. big project

Let's look at each step in order.

The Introductory Meeting

This is the first one-on-one or small-group introduction. Maybe a prospect gave you their card after hearing you speak at a conference. Maybe a client in one area of a company introduced you to a colleague in another area.

However it happens, this is your first interaction with a qualified prospect and, as such, represents a *critical* juncture in what might become a valuable relationship. A good introductory meeting should not feel like business development; it should feel like colleagues solving problems together.

Your goal in the introductory meeting is *not* to close a deal; it's to get to the next step. Usually all you can hope to do in first meetings is help the prospect see if there's a fit. *You* already know there's a good fit because you've used your targeting criteria. *They* don't know that yet. So help them see: ask questions, figure out where their needs are, and describe your unique positioning in *their words* and *their thinking style*. Look for ways to be helpful.

What's the next step? A give-to-get, described below. Yes, sometimes you can skip that step and go straight to a small project, even a big project, but usually that's the result of an urgent need combined with a killer referral. It's rare, but if it happens, seize the opportunity.

Even if it seems clear that this particular prospect isn't going to turn into a client anytime soon, look for ways to be of service in the meantime. Things change quickly. Needs pop up all the time. You will often be surprised by where things lead. The key is *showing* the client what you do, not *talking* about what you do.

The Give-to-Get

This is a service or product you offer the prospect with the goal of getting to a small project. Give-to-gets are not token gifts—they represent actual value for the prospect. They offer a taste of what it's like to work with you. To be effective, a give-to-get must:

+ be easy for you to create and execute,
+ offer genuine value to the prospect, and
+ lead to paid work.

Often a give-to-get takes the form of a diagnostic, something that offers value to the client by tracing symptoms back to the source of the problem and identifying possible solutions—without actually solving the entire problem. Remember: the goal of the give-to-get is to get to the next step—paid work. A chiropractor might offer a screening that identifies the possible source of someone's chronic pain. A management consultant might offer a team profile that identifies interpersonal bottlenecks hindering collaboration and innovation. In both cases the prospect can't help but wonder, *Can you help me solve this?* More on designing effective give-to-gets in a moment.

The Small Project

This is a small-scale first project. The client is willing to invest in you because (1) you have something of value they want, (2) they are curious about something you say you can do, or (3) they want to experience your service on a small project before risking it on a large one.

The bridge to cross here is getting the client to pay for something. Many of our clients call this a "paid selling effort" because you're actually getting paid to grow the relationship. What's important, above all, is psychological: people pay attention to what they pay for.

The first project also helps reduce friction for future work by getting you into their system as a vendor, getting the initial legal requirements signed, and otherwise clearing logistical hurdles. They also create a subtle shift in the mind of the buyer: you're not a person selling to them anymore—you're on the team. However you look at it, small projects are a big deal.

The Big Project

This is always the goal, but you must *earn* the right to go after this through the successful completion of give-to-gets and small projects.

•

This path is all about momentum. Each step has a single goal: getting to the next. Use this model to create momentum with all your prospects as well as to rapidly expand the *number* of opportunities you have with a single target client, creating multiple paths to large projects. Depending on the nature of your service and the client in question, you might have multiple give-to-gets and small projects going concurrently, each with the goal of getting to the next step.

Although the path to a big project has four steps, in practice the evolving relationship between you and a prospect will look more like the branches of a tree. Inevitably some possibilities will dwindle while others flourish beyond your expectations. You need to continually and intentionally shape your give-to-gets and small projects to move toward more substantial work.

Designing the Perfect Give-to-Get

The science behind give-to-gets amazes me. We've taught this technique to thousands of students across hundreds of clients in dozens of industries. It always works. Why? The psychology of influence.

Robert Cialdini, PhD, has done more work on this subject than anyone. His book *Influence* has sold more than three million copies and been translated into over thirty languages. Cialdini took his own research, synthesized it with the latest work in the field, and isolated six core factors that drive influence. Give-to-gets are the only BD technique I've seen that utilize every single one.

Reciprocity

People tend to return a favor. Starting your relationship with a gift of your expertise builds goodwill that's usually returned in multiples. Investing in give-to-gets pays.

Commitment and Consistency

People tend to continue down a path they've begun. Making the next step easy, without the hurdle of a contract, gets things moving smoothly. Give-to-gets get your prospects working with you fast, providing a simple step on a path to purchasing.

Social Proof

People like the safety of doing what they can see others are doing. Inviting several key people to a give-to-get session builds "social proof" inside the organization. A properly designed give-to-get impacts multiple decision makers at once.

Authority

People tend to trust experts. Transitioning from "talking about what you do" to "doing what you do" provides an important experience for your prospect. Give-to-gets let you demonstrate your expertise and prove your value by solving a client's problems alongside them.

Liking

People do more business with those they like. Working with a client to solve their problems will give you dozens of shared interests and other commonalities to help build a connection. Give-to-gets establish a personal connection between expert and client.

Scarcity

Scarcity creates demand. Your time is valuable. You can't give away your expertise or products endlessly. It's appropriate for you to point out how many give-to-gets of a certain kind you can offer to help the client understand that not everyone gets one. It's a big deal for them and for you.

•

There's no doubt give-to-gets make an impact. But my favorite part is that they *feel* great—to both seller-experts and prospects. Recently I was talking through our methodology with a prospect. The concept of give-to-gets came up. They loved the idea. Near the end of the call I offered to have them audit one of our public training classes on our dime if they'd send at least two key decision makers and if we could have a call afterward to discuss possible next steps.

"Hey, is that a give-to-get?"

"Yes!" I replied. "Doesn't it feel great?"

"It sure does. Sign us up."

Leading a team of over four hundred client-facing professionals for Aetna's National Accounts group, Ross Sanders knows a bit about the effectiveness of give-to-gets. I talked to him about their give-to-get initiative, and this is what he told me.

We offered select customers free HBDI® Assessment sessions, which tied to our offering to assist with drafting a three-year benefits strategy. These sessions were not designed to market our products or services but to assist in developing a long-term strategy for success.

This give-to-get initiative increased customer retention, elevated our customer relationships to include C-suite executives, allowed us to better understand our customers and tailor future offerings to suit, boosted sales, and drove referrals to other prospects. Give-to-gets create the opportunity to get in front of our customers and prospects with value and consulting while our competitors are out pushing product. This differentiates us in the market.

The criteria that make for an effective give-to-get are simple enough: it needs to be easy for you to do *and* of real value to the prospect, all while leading directly to paid work.

So how do you build a give-to-get that works for your business and with the resources you have available? Work backward. Design your offering based on the project you're trying to win and, as always, keep the thinking preferences of your prospect in mind. Follow these three steps for success.

Determine the Big Project You Want

This step is usually easy. The key is being strategic about your choice and not anchoring on the kinds of things you already do. Pick the kind of thing you'd *like* to do for the client, factoring in the reality of what you're known for doing now.

Design a Small Project That
Leads to That Big Project

For an ad agency it might be a conceptual design for a campaign along with a draft timeline and steps. For a graphic designer it might be new graphic identity guidelines along with an analysis of everything that needs to be changed to adopt the guideline. Note that both of these small projects (a) add a lot of value and (b) clearly demonstrate the *tremendous amount of work and expertise* it will take to perform the big project. A small project gives the client the seed of the big project but makes clear how difficult it will be, either in effort or expertise. One last pro tip: start with a price that is easy for the decision maker to approve without a burdensome approval process. Then build the scope around the price.

Design the Give-to-Get to Lead to the Small Project

Remember the criteria: easy for you, valuable for them, and leading to the next step. Sometimes it's as simple as: What are the first couple of hours of the small project? If there's value in that, carve it off and give it away. Whatever you decide to offer, make sure it appeals to all four thinking preferences. Sure, it can bias to one, but make sure *something* in your offer appeals to thinkers dominant in any.

Examples are helpful for bringing the give-to-get concept to life. Here are some that might inspire you.

Specific Application of a Key Topic

I start with this give-to-get because we see it often and it's usually effective. Key topics are anything many people would be interested in hearing about. Depending on your expertise, this could be a new way of connecting with customers (marketing), a new technology (software, programming, outsourcing), a new regulation (law), a new business approach (consulting), or even an overview of a new approach to wellness (healthcare). It can also be a new approach to an existing process. Anything of interest to clients can work.

This approach includes two pieces: (a) an introduction to the topic by the expert and (b) a discussion of how the client could apply this knowledge. The first part should be insightful and brief. The magic occurs when the expert applies this knowledge *to the client's unique situation*. At first, people bias to the first piece—look how smart we are!—and don't leave enough time for the second. Get to the discussion part quickly.

One of our clients creates marketing automation software. They offer a give-to-get where they (a) review the trendiest components of marketing automation and (b) conduct a lively interactive session using posters, Post-it Notes, voting, and brainstorming to guide their clients through a process of diagnosing their current automation approach and selecting the elements to tackle next.

Their process skewed experimental (brainstorming) and relational (interactivity), with time left at the end for practical thinking around next steps. So they added budgets and metrics to embed analytical thinking as well. The sessions are designed not only to spark new ideas but also to get consensus on what to prioritize in the future.

Guess what question is nearly always asked at the end of each session? "Can you help us with these priorities?"

Strategic Planning Session

The process above can also be used to lead a strategic planning session for a client's team. We've seen this work all the way up to the C-suite. Use the process above, but instead of covering a key topic, look at the priorities of the department or business.

This give-to-get should be aligned with the small project of creating a detailed strategic plan for the team. You can give the first session away, but charge for the rest. It's valuable: you're helping your client immensely and learning about where they're headed in the future while you're at it.

Analysis

This technique is perfect for large software deployments, outsourcing, healthcare providers, consulting, and anywhere else a business case needs to be made before even the possibility of embarking on a big project.

Although it biases to analytical thinking, the best tap the other three modes too. The key is to scale the size of your analysis so that it gives a cursory overview and keeps the process moving forward while ending early enough that you can charge for a more detailed one.

As always, start with the big project you want to create demand for. From there pull back and ask yourself: What does a business case need to show to get people to say yes to this? That's the analysis you should get paid to do as a small project. What is the cursory-level analysis that would lead into that one? That's your give-to-get.

One of our consulting-firm clients gives away an industry analysis as a give-to-get, with the key piece being the results of an annual survey on how other industry leaders are investing in their major physical plant assets. The companies in this industry are so large that most don't have a great catalog of their assets. So this give-to-get provides a lot of value, then begs the question: What are *we* doing?

The answer is usually hiring the consultant to figure it out. And when they get paid to do this small project, they include a cost analysis of their major assets, benchmarked against the industry (analytical), some brief executive interviews on what they *should* invest in (relational), how their current investments align with their business strategy (experimental), and recommended next steps with a Gantt chart (practical). Their clients love this analysis. Can you guess what usually happens next?

Project Planning

If an analysis helps determine whether a project is worthwhile, this method proves that you are necessary for implementation. Because the priorities are already set, this method skews heavily practical with a sprinkling of the other three.

Many times your clients already have initiatives under way but don't realize the expertise they'll need or the sheer bandwidth it will take to eventually succeed. In these cases start with some interviews or a data request. Dig into what the client is trying to accomplish and how it connects to the business strategy. Identify the important milestones, the costs, the team involved, and the intended impact. Cover every thinking style.

With this information, compile a report. Start by reiterating why this is important to the business. Repeat back what you've heard, and add your own perspective. Then show the numbers. ROI. Impact on the business if it's on time, compared to running late by a day, a week, or a month. Show your assumptions. Lay out the technical expertise needed to do this well. Then emphasize again the positive or negative impact if the project is on time or late.

Sprinkle in quotes from stakeholders about where the project stands and the pitfalls they see along the way. With your case made for the importance of flawless execution in an experimental, relational, and analytical sense, close with a practical look at timeline and steps, preferably with a Gantt chart. This is a valuable and no-nonsense way to prove why you're needed in the process.

Introductions to Peers

If you do most of your work with clients facing the same issues, you probably know many people in similar roles. The give-to-get with the greatest delta between effort for you (almost none) and value to your prospect (potentially huge) is to offer introductions to their peers.

Offer to connect your prospect with other people who have a similar role or grapple with similar business problems. This is especially powerful when you can connect a prospect with one of your raving fans, one who has already worked with you to deal with the issue at hand.

Set up a call or meal for the three of you. This lets you add value to both people by chiming in with your expertise. This method skews relational, but you can weave in the other three quadrants during the conversation. The introduction preemptively connects your prospect to your best references, further establishing your reputation and credibility. These meetings almost always start with the prospect asking, "So how do you know _____?" Get ready for your client to rave about you.

Training Session

Training sessions are nearly always a winner. The topic might be anything from new technology or legislation relevant in the industry to a trendy new management approach along with a case study.

This give-to-get allows you to demonstrate your expertise and passion for a topic in front of key decision makers and influencers. It can be designed to appeal to all four thinking preferences. As you help prospects learn, you will be well positioned to influence their own strategy for dealing with this new information (one likely to include a small project with you).

The key is picking the right topic (something you're not currently hired to do but that the client needs) and having the right people attend (decision makers who are not your day-to-day contacts). Don't settle for the first topic the client suggests.

Once you invest the time in researching and preparing the session, you can deliver it to as many prospects as may find it relevant. You can also record the session for sharing or deliver it live as a webinar. This onetime investment of time and effort can be leveraged over and over again.

·

I want to share two important tips on give-to-get offers.

First, the best way to get a yes for these is to create an example output, a generic version of the report, analysis, or plan. If you perform interactive sessions, show photos of the flipcharts and Post-its from an example session, complete with smiling clients. *Showing* the outputs or process of the give-to-get helps prospects say yes. Without examples of what they'll get, the offer is too vague.

Second, it's entirely appropriate for you to ask the prospect to do some work. This might mean submitting data or inviting certain high-ranking people to the meeting or something else. By definition you're providing something valuable, and as we'll see later, there's a lot of science behind people buying into what they help create. If you make it *too* easy on the prospect, they might not be buying in and won't be excited to get the output. Said differently, if they're not willing to invest a little time getting some value at no charge, they weren't going to buy anything anyway. Better to get a no early than to invest your time with little chance of success, wasting everyone's time.

Building Your Give-to-Get Toolkit

The give-to-gets I've covered represent a fraction of the many ways an expert can assist a prospect with an appropriate investment of effort and time. Always look for new ways that your external perspective, professional network, expertise, experience, and focus might be useful to your prospects without a great deal of effort on your end. Remember: these are people who are usually stuck in one vantage point at a single company and are very limited in terms of time and autonomy.

Different industries and different types of businesses will be better suited to some give-to-gets than to others. What follows are some examples of good, better, and best options in several very different industries— the possibilities are limitless.

The three criteria for a give-to-get are easy to understand but sometimes hard to apply. Like the rules of chess, you can quickly understand how the game works, but it can take a long time to become an effective player. When starting with give-to-gets people tend to give away the wrong things (those that don't lead to the next step) or too much (effectively performing a small project for free). Don't worry if the industries below aren't yours—that's not the point. These examples will help you see the subtle differences that can ratchet your give-to-get from good to best.

Presentation Coaching

Good: one-hour overview of methodology to create a meaningful presentation.

Better: same as good, but shorten the overview to thirty minutes, then spend thirty minutes *evaluating an existing presentation*.

Best: same as better, but alter timing to include ten minutes at the end covering the steps and time needed to perfect the existing presentation.

Software

Good: review technology goals of the prospect in the area your software performs, then conduct a software demo that highlights the areas where you might be able to improve their efficiency.

Better: same as good, but show examples of other software deployments that have been customized to meet similar needs.

Best: same as better, but conduct a demo of a cutting-edge new software that few people have seen and aligns with prospect needs. Have the attendees sign a nondisclosure agreement (NDA) beforehand, and leave time at the end to ask for feedback and to describe how the new software fits with their business processes.

Marketing Agency

Good: half-day creative brainstorming workshop on the marketing of a new product, including follow-up of three conceptual logos, a style guide, and a marketing plan.

Better: same as good, but *less*, where the workshop exposes the client to the conceptual logos (without finalizing them), and a rough framework of a marketing plan.

Best: same as better, but with a follow-up call a week after the in-person workshop with documentation for the vast amount of work needed to launch the marketing plan along with the skill sets required to be successful.

Law

Good: continuing legal education (CLE) session on a topic you already work on with people you already know.

Better: same as good, but the session is on a topic you *don't* currently work on but would love to.

Best: same as better, but attendees now include *new relationships* that control the external workflow of the new topical area.

Large Services Contract or Outsourcing

Good: analysis of client data that evaluates the cost savings of additional services. The analysis takes 120 people-hours and the readout meeting uses static, printed data and is conducted with normal, day-to-day contacts.

Better: same as good, but the analysis takes 80 people-hours and the readout meeting uses a dynamic Excel modeling tool in which the client can adjust assumptions and see the results immediately, driving much more interaction and engagement.

Best: same as better, but the meeting is conducted with all major decision makers, including C-suite executives you rarely work with.

Your give-to-gets will be a major component of your BD repertoire. Handling them in a casual, off-the-cuff manner is a surefire way to scatter your efforts and end up doing a lot of work for free. Instead, retain a strategic focus: offer them only where they are most likely to turn into small projects, not as a one-size-fits-all gesture to give new relationships a boost.

When you settle into a rhythm of using give-to-gets with a prospect, you are not only earning the right to do business with them but also teaching them what to expect from you during paid work. We've discussed how behavioral science tells us that frequency and consistency can turn a behavior into a habit for us. It works for our relationships too—get your prospects hooked on you. In the beginning of a seller-prospect relationship, quantity counts as much as quality. You need both, but emphasize the number of interactions you have with your prospects for the first several weeks so you stay top of mind and comfort and trust can grow. Break up larger communications into smaller ones. Spread them out over time. Add value. Become the habit.

Many of our clients have taken the concept to the next level, building give-to-gets that scale. These are built to be used again and again across the entire organization. Sometimes give-to-gets should be customized to a client's specific needs, but often they can be built to scale this way. This might take a little more work up front, but they can then be used with dozens or even hundreds of prospects. Giving your seller-experts a tool to use over and over again can generate demand across an entire organization.

Now it's time to develop an approach to give-to-gets that works for you and your business. Get the **Give-to-Get Brainstorming** worksheet, or simply draw two four-quadrant squares on a piece of blank paper.

In one square brainstorm specific give-to-gets you can deliver to prospects right away, broken out by thinking style. This perspective is on what you have *now*, what you have sitting around that, with a little polish, could be used many times. For example, you might be able to do an analytical-oriented evaluation or facilitate a practical-oriented project planning session without much additional effort.

In the other square write down give-to-get ideas you might be able to create with a little development work. This perspective is from your prospects: What would they love to *receive* as a give-to-get? What would they quickly say yes to? These might be any of the examples we've talked through or something else. Think with empathy from the position of the perfect prospect you mapped out in Chapter 3.

Remember that a great give-to-get will pull through all four thinking styles, so feel free to write down an idea in the middle of the four quadrants if it equally covers all four or, slightly off center, if it incorporates a couple of thinking styles more than others. No give-to-get should be limited to only one quadrant—even the CFO cares about more than getting the financials reported accurately.

Now you have work to do. Look at the active prospects in front of you today, and match their thinking styles to give-to-gets you can deliver immediately. Again, when selecting and designing a give-to-get for a prospect, begin with the end in mind. Start with the big project you want to do, and then work backward from there to the small project and from that to the ideal give-to-gets that might spark the process.

Now set up a call or a meeting and offer a give-to-get to a prospect. See how it goes. The best way I've found to offer one is to say, "Would it be helpful if we . . . ?" I've found that much more successful than "Would you like us to . . . ?" You'll get a higher rate of acceptance with the first phrasing. The first sounds like a genuine offer, the second like the prospect is asking too much of you.

Once you've delivered on a few give-to-gets and even turned one into a small project, you'll have a much better sense of how this method works in practice. The experience will inspire new, better give-to-get possibilities tailored to your strengths, ones that are very easy for you while being highly valuable for your prospects.

Give-to-gets demonstrate your willingness to invest in your relationship with a client. That relationship needs to go both ways: the client should be willing to invest time and effort in the give-to-get as well. Make sure you keep them involved throughout the planning and execution.

When your give-to-gets consistently fail to lead to more engagement from a particular client, they've become what one of our clients jokingly called *give-to-gives*. This is a clear indicator that you are dealing with someone who is not going to hire you for a big project—invest in somebody else. This is another way that the work you put into a give-to-get translates into less wasted effort overall. It's important to keep those gains in mind as you weigh time spent on business development against time spent in other areas of your business.

Most of our clients pitch their give-to-gets more informally—over lunch, for example—but there are times when putting it down on paper makes sense. When the stakes are high or you need to be a bit formal with a prospect, it helps to offer a one-page overview of your commitment to helping them. Personalize it with content unique and specific to them to show your sincerity.

This one-pager includes:

+ a brief overview of your company, using your positioning;
+ areas you are willing to invest in, where your expertise aligns with the prospect's current problem, and with the possibility for a bigger project; and
+ a list of possible give-to-gets that you would be willing to deliver.

Once you've created your one-pager, you can use it as a guide for the conversation during the introductory meeting. Be sure to practice what you will say and how you will present your give-to-get strategy during that meeting.

Offering to actually invest in a client and give something away without charging can strike prospects as unusual—that is, something to be turned down reflexively. Be sincere and authentic when you describe why you have chosen to invest one of your limited give-to-get opportunities in this client; for example, explain why they are a good fit for your business model, specifically using the targeting criteria you developed in Chapter 3. Let them know this is how you grow your business. Make clear what you are willing to do, helping them with a choice of, say, three give-to-get options, and what you hope the outcome will be if you perform well—that is, the next stage of the relationship.

Don't forget that last part. That's your get. Without it, you'll get great at providing something entirely different: give-to-gives.

•

One more thing: the opportunity to be authentic and useful can come unexpectedly. You aren't always going to have a custom-designed one-pager on hand when you meet a potential prospect. When serendipity does appear, be prepared with a Magic Bag of Ideas. This is a collection of items demonstrating your work and expertise that you always carry with you, either in your bag or as a set of digital files you can immediately email along to a new acquaintance. Examples include:

+ a copy of a give-to-get analysis you did for a client
+ a listing of new services you have in development
+ samples of your small and big projects
+ articles on topics relevant to your prospects and clients

If, during a conversation, a topic comes up that aligns with one of the items in your Magic Bag, you now have an opportunity to provide value and help move things along to the next step in the BD process. That's the beauty of being prepared. What would be helpful for you to have on hand in your own Magic Bag of Ideas?

Designing Your Lead-Generation Strategy

Steady demand for your services begins with a solid plan for generating interest from people and businesses who could use your help—if they only knew. Lead generation is the start and heart of acquiring new clients.

Lead generation is the task of creating interest in your services. It establishes a connection with those who might be interested in those services. A thoughtful lead-generation strategy focuses your efforts on attracting new clients within a well-defined target audience, as defined in Chapter 3.

Quality leads get you to the next step with the least effort on both sides. For example, when the prospect has already registered an interest in your firm or in your services, you'll find far less friction in establishing an introductory meeting and progressing from there. But quantity of leads is also vital. A professional with a small list of top-quality leads still won't win every single one. Even if you execute perfectly, budgets dry up, priorities change, and projects get canceled at the last minute. A broader approach may need more filtering, but it can also deliver good prospects you would never have found another way, something that can save the day when a highly qualified lead leads nowhere. We want a strategy that makes the right trade-off between quality and quantity to boost your overall odds of success.

Every lead-generation tool in the next chapter offers a trade-off between quantity and quality. Some tend to bring in one or two highly qualified prospects; others create a flow of less likely possibilities to winnow through. Relying on either type of approach alone won't suffice. Diversifying your techniques is critical. Here we look at assembling the best portfolio of techniques for your business. Our goal is to establish the deal flow you need with the time and resources you have available to invest in growth.

There are a lot of ways to get leads. All of them should be focused on getting introductory meetings established, with give-to-gets as the next step from there. The right recipe for you may not be a successful allocation of techniques for someone else's business. Your personal portfolio depends on these factors:

+ the time you can invest
+ the skills you and your team possess
+ how long you can wait to see results
+ your position in the marketplace
+ the amount of leads you need
+ the number of potential new clients in the space
+ whether you can get to these prospects through your existing network

Every situation is unique. On the extreme of one spectrum, a software company focused on one industry niche may only have six or seven potential corporate clients worldwide. On another, a tax controversy attorney might have thousands of potential clients out there each year but will have no idea which specific taxpayers will get audited. That's why simply imitating lead-generation tactics used by other businesses, even superficially similar ones, is a bad idea. You need to think through the unique needs of your own business to create the mix that's right for you.

In the following table the lead-generation tactics in this book are broken out along two spectrums: scope and personal connection.

Lead Generation Strategies

	Targeted Focused on finding a specific organization/person	**Targeted with Potential for Broad Reach** Mixture of direct targeting specific organization/person and broader sources	**Broad Reach** Focused on finding multiple leads from broader sources
Warm High flow through rates and some personal component	Turning friends into clients	Forums	Speaking
Mixed Warm-Cold	Specific referrals	Strategic Partners	Webinars
Cold Low flow through rates and lowest personal connection	Cold Marketing	Event Attendance	Writing

In the following chapters I will introduce you to each of these lead-generation tactics in detail along with examples of how they might be adapted for businesses of different scales and in different industries. Before we get there, however, let's look at the big picture. Ask yourself:

How many hours are you willing to invest in lead-generation efforts of any kind each year?

If you're just getting your business off the ground and haven't gotten your pipeline flowing yet, this could be a very large amount. Twenty hours a week—or roughly a thousand hours a year—is perfectly reasonable if you need a large number of quality leads to start flowing in order for your business to achieve takeoff velocity. Conversely, if your work involves a handful of steady clients and you're already busy, you might only be able to spare a couple of hours each week to drive new business to replace those clients who phase out for one reason or another. Your business probably falls somewhere in between, from a hundred to a thousand hours in the coming year.

Once you have a concrete sense of how much time you're planning to invest, you'll be much better able to allocate this resource between different tactics. Your goal is a robust, well-diversified strategy. For instance, if you're only going to spend a hundred hours on generating leads each year, can you really afford to spend thirty of those hours on Twitter? After all, when has tweeting ever translated into a paying client for you? If that does strike you as a poor investment, look at how you can reduce the time you spend on Twitter through automation or delegation—or simply by deleting your account—to free up more hours for a tactic that will deliver more bang for the buck.

Tactic diversity is also important because lead generation isn't an exact science. As you transition from a haphazard approach to a systematic one, your understanding of what works for your business will remain imperfect for some time. You'll want to hedge your bets—you don't want to put all your energy into a single tactic that turns out to be ineffective.

Now make a list of all the activities you currently engage in to drive new leads, from social media and blogging to attending conferences and so on. As you go through each of the lead-generation tactics that follow, add the promising ones to your master list until you have a complete array of every single one that might be of use to you.

Next, select the three to five tactics that strike you as the most promising based on the needs of your business and the criteria already mentioned—skills you have on your team, time until results are needed, and so on. Decide on the percentage of time you plan to invest in each of those tactics, and calculate the hours available. Get the **Lead Generation** worksheet, or just map it out on a piece of paper.

For example, if you have 250 hours to invest in lead generation each year, and you decide to allocate 20 percent of that time to email marketing, that gives you 50 hours, or about an hour a week, to spend on your newsletter. If that isn't enough time to write, edit, and send something valuable, let alone work on building your list, could you do something with less time, like assembling a handful of links each week that might be useful for your prospects? Could you invest in an outside writer or engage a member of your team to share editing duties or to help with growing the list?

One last thing to keep in mind: track your results. If you're like most seller-experts, you've always treated lead generation as an afterthought. Although you may have been diligent, even zealous, when getting yourself off the ground, you've probably become lax about generating new leads as you've gotten busy with client work. As discussed at the beginning of the book, this feast-or-famine mentality forces you to scramble whenever things quiet down and also keeps you from being selective about the clients you take on.

From now on, you're going to treat lead generation as an investment of your most precious resource: time. That means you need to take note of what works and what works even better. Although you may be guessing at how much time you've spent in the past or at the specific allotments, if you track the time you spend on generating leads over the coming year and the results that each approach delivers, 365 days from now you'll be far better able to create a new strategy that delivers tremendous results with minimal time invested. So start a spreadsheet now, and start tracking.

Buyers, Influencers, and Gatekeepers

Before you can qualify your prospects, you need to distinguish between buyers, influencers, and gatekeepers. Buyers have budgetary authority, positional authority, and a direct connection to the project you will eventually seek to win. In short, they're the ones who actually turn on that green light. Influencers, however, may have a strong relationship with the buyer. They might be direct reports, project team members, external advisors, and so on. Gatekeepers are those who have access to or control over the buyers' and influencers' schedules, sometimes through an admin (always a good person to know).

Once you start to think about your prospects in terms of these categories, many of the odd mechanics of trying to connect with them will become clear. For example, a gatekeeper seeking an internal promotion might keep you at arm's length from the buyer with green-light authority in order to get the credit for bringing you in. (Now it's clear why that long-promised phone call with the buyer never seems to come together.)

Poorly qualified projects will rarely lead to the next step in the cycle. Qualifying leads properly may mean some short-term delays and disappointments, but it will save you endless hours over time. With these definitions in mind, let's look at the qualifying process. Use your targeting criteria to determine the organizations to focus on. Then use this cheeky but easy-to-remember mnemonic for finding the right people to talk to within those organizations:

Is There $ in the ATM?

$. Does your client have or can they get *money* to spend on this project?

Authority. Does your client have the *authority* to make the decision to move forward on this project? Are you talking to the real decision maker?

Timing. Does your client believe this is the right *time* to proceed with this project? Does your client have the *time* to invest in the project and give it its full due?

Motivation. Given their busy lives, is the client truly *motivated* to push this forward?

The more preparation and planning you do and the more selective you are up front, the more polished, productive, and profitable your BD efforts will be. It's easy to think of rainmakers as King Midas, turning everything they touch into gold. In fact, true rainmakers are *picky*. They only bother touching golden things.

•

We've made major strides in this chapter. Simply changing your approach from "Me, Tarzan. You, client!" to the step-by-step path to a big project creates a tectonic shift in how you interact with prospects and clients. Meanwhile the give-to-get is usually the biggest "aha" moment for the professionals in my training sessions. No longer do you need to drive relentlessly toward the first paid engagement, doing who knows what harm to the relationship with the prospect along the way; instead, you now create momentum in the selling process with something of genuine value to prospects and clients. This tool alone has the potential to dramatically improve the way both sides feel along the way.

Now that you've given some thought to a robust, diverse, and systematic lead-generation strategy, it's time to dig into specific tactics. Every business's needs will be different, but I feel confident that you will discover a set of lead-generation tactics in Chapter 6 that will be effective for you. There are many leading indicators correlated to your future success, and the most important is generating qualified leads.

CHAPTER 6

Lead Tactics

• • •

THIS AREA IS where *everyone* gets stuck. Whether you're a new freelancer or a high-end investment banker, you can't have too much of one thing: leads. More leads means more options, more flexibility, and more control.

In the following pages I'm going to introduce you to the most powerful lead-generation tactics, period. You'll select a handful to form the cornerstone of your lead-generation strategy using the approach in Chapter 5. In the end you'll have a concrete action plan suited to the skills you possess, the time you have available, and the resources you can draw upon.

Planning and preparation spell the difference between success and failure for *any* tactic. We helped one professional evaluate a conference he had gone to four years in a row. He had never gotten a good lead despite the event being filled with targeted prospects. Worse, it took him about thirty-two hours to travel to and attend the two-and-a-half-day conference. Rather than letting him skip that year's event, we added about three hours of prep to his process using the conference techniques in this chapter so he could finally make the most of his time. Voilà! He brought twelve commitments for a give-to-get meeting back to the office. Same conference. Correct approach. High ROI.

Some techniques ask you to step outside your comfort zone. For example, you might consider yourself too shy or self-conscious for public speaking. Or perhaps you find writing intimidating. Often these fears are ungrounded. If a technique seems like the right fit for your BD needs, give it a whirl with an open mind—you'll be surprised at how quickly your apprehension goes away when you see the subsequent flow of qualified prospects. To help guide you, *all* these techniques have their own worksheets at **mobunnell.com/worksheets**.

Buckle up. This chapter is the most challenging in the book but has the potential to match. With the right lead-generation tactics in play, you'll never again need to wonder where your next client is going to come from.

Turning Friends into Clients

You probably already know a number of potential clients personally. Often these friends or acquaintances are well on their way to raving fan status. After all, they know you, your character and reputation. They may not, however, have connected the dots between what you can do and what they need done. This friend might be in a decision-making position at a company you have in your sights, never even suspecting that your expertise could help them clear an important hurdle.

As with selling and business development, most professionals hold bewildering beliefs around working with friends. Many mistakenly think that they need to establish a wall between personal and business relationships, despite countless successful examples to the contrary everywhere you look. Of course, it's also possible they're afraid to broach the subject. Perhaps the acquaintance isn't even aware that their friend possesses their sought-after expertise. One way or the other, experts usually hesitate to cross this bridge because they fear it might put the personal relationship in jeopardy.

This hesitation cracks me up. Say you start working with a new client, a total stranger, and things go well to the point that you do a lot of work together. At this time most of the professionals I teach want to deepen the relationship by doing things outside of work like entertaining, getting spouses together, and the like. In other words, when we start with work, we try to broaden the relationship to a genuine friendship. So why wouldn't we want to start with people we already like and try to broaden the relationship to work?

Remember: your purpose is to help people. That's the reason you spent all that time learning. When we go into the selling process with the idea that we're going to get one up on someone else, well, of course we wouldn't want to sell to a friend. But when we sell with the *authentic desire to be helpful,* turning a friend into a client suddenly feels like the most natural thing in the world.

If you're a top-notch tax accountant and an old college buddy mentions his big tax obligation due to a unique situation, are you going to tell him to find an accountant on craigslist or, worse, stay silent out of a misguided sense of integrity while he pays more than the law requires? Of course not. If you're good at what you do, you will suggest working together to get his taxes lower.

Once you accept that selling is being of service, all you really need is a simple methodology to turn friends into clients. These are the easiest leads to generate—you've already established a rapport. Once you start working with a friend, you'll be shocked at how quickly they reach raving fan status. If you have a lot of people in your network who fit your target profile, this might be your core strategy for kick-starting your client base.

The key to making this work is the right give-to-get. A give-to-get provides the ideal way to introduce the idea of working together. For each friend on your list, select the perfect give-to-get to offer for their thinking style (and determining that should be easy, as you know them so well). If you know your friend is a strong analytical thinker, focus on your success metrics with similar clients and on the fact that the give-to-get will be of high value and cost absolutely nothing. If she's primarily experimental, paint a picture of how creative and fun it would be to work together. Brainstorming together—yippee! What type of project would your friend be most interested in trying?

Now, draw four quadrants on a piece of paper, and carefully craft an initial message to suggest the give-to-gets you're willing to offer. Write down points that will resonate with all thinking preferences, but make sure you have some whammies to appeal to your friend's strongest area. Then develop those points into a pitch. If you work on behalf of a company, it's important to make clear in your message that this give-to-get is an investment on behalf of the entire organization, not you personally. Expand the conversation and transcend the two-person relationship. Let's say you're at a marketing agency and a friend of yours is at a company whose new product is flailing in the marketplace. You could say something like,

> We should do dinner more often. I like how we play off each other's ideas. In fact, I had a thought. As a partner at my firm, I get to influence where we direct resources. I've been able to grow our business by investing in companies that are a perfect fit for us, with no expectation of being hired. We do this because our clients need to see us work to understand how valuable we are, seeing our ideas and thinking applied to someone's real-life problem. We can't tell—we can only show. I would love to invest in your company and your new product. Like I said, no expectation of anything in return. I'm sure something good will come of it. If you like that idea, I've got an idea for a half-day meeting format we've used that has been proven to boost product sales quickly. It involves our expert in . . .

Even if you're a solo practitioner, the idea is to use the give-to-get offer to quickly and seamlessly step beyond the personal relationship and into the professional sphere. As always, mention scarcity: authentically let them know how infrequently you can offer this give-to-get. This helps the friend feel special. With the offer on the table, expect the same questions or objections you'd get from any prospect. Be ready to overcome the obstacles that come your way, and don't take any of it personally. After all, you're the one who initiated a professional conversation—you should see it through on those terms.

Keep your focus on the goal: a win-win for you and for your friend. Even if it's not the right time to help your friend in a paid or unpaid way, they'll know more about how to help you in the future, and you'll learn more about how you can help your friend. They'll also be better equipped to refer others your way. When you do this right, you can't lose.

Specific Referrals

Raving fans are your fastest path to new clients through referrals. Also, remember that loyal clients are usually ready to become raving fans—typically they only need a request for a testimonial or a reference to make the leap. Both groups trust you. Their desire for you to succeed will come across to every lead they refer. These clients *want* to help you win. All you need to do is tell them what works best for your business. That means you need to spend time with them to ensure they understand how you do business and the types of clients you want to serve. You need to explicitly ask for their help.

Your raving fans should feel like you are giving them a gift, not handing them a task. Asking for referrals has a bad rap because most people do it the wrong way. You may have experienced this yourself. A service provider says, "You know, Mo, I grow my business based on referrals. If you'll give me the names of five people to call, I'd really appreciate it." To me this sounds like, "You know, Mo, I'm going to lean on you to give me the names of five people. Then I'll harass the heck out of them, begging them to meet with me by using your name, and completely embarrass you in the process." This method leads with begging, not value. We'll do the opposite, giving value to our best clients. I will show you a four-step process that drives referrals while protecting the existing relationship.

To begin, prioritize a list of each raving fan (and those close to becoming one) with those who have the strongest, largest network of target clients on top. Then meet with or call the first one on the list.

Frame the Referral

You've invested a great deal of effort in defining your target client criteria. Unfortunately you're the only one who knows what they are. We've all been sent referrals that are wildly off the mark by enthusiastic friends and clients. It can be frustrating, but we need to remember: these people are just trying to help us.

You need to help your raving fans understand how best to help you, and that takes time and effort. Begin by explaining that you are working on growing your business and that referrals are a key component of your strategy. Ask them if they'd be willing to help you by referring people they know who are a fit for your target-client profile.

Here's the key element: explain your give-to-get strategy and how much you're willing to invest in the *right* prospect. It's easier for people to refer potential clients when they can see the value that will be delivered to those people before they spend a single dollar. You're effectively giving your raving fans a gift—the give-to-get—that they can then offer to people they know. It's a big deal and should be positioned that way.

If your client is enthusiastic about helping you and giving this gift to others, share your target client criteria you developed in Chapter 3 with them and, critically, the types of clients you are *not* targeting. This will help avoid confusion and wasted effort down the road.

Open Ask

Next, ask an open-ended question such as, "Do you know anyone who matches this profile who might be interested in discussing my company helping them, on our dime?" The emphasis here is on the meeting and on receiving the give-to-get, *not* on "buying X, Y, or Z" or "that I could sell A, B, or C to." You just want your raving fan to start matching the people they know against your target criteria. Give them plenty of time to think about this without interrupting them. This open-ended ask is important because they may have great ideas for introductions you haven't thought of.

Specific Ask

Depending on the size and nature of your industry, you can follow up the open ask with a specific ask. Show the client your current Target List you created in Chapter 3. The goal here is to see if they can make connections to any of your previously targeted prospects.

Be sure to wait until you've given them sufficient time to process the open ask *before* you bring up the specific ask. Many times the open ask will spark creative connections and unexpected ideas—*if* the client is given a moment to noodle on it. That's why we use this order.

The specific ask is important because the person you're talking to might not be thinking of some obvious connections they have. I've been amazed at how sparks can fly when someone is given a list accompanying the specific ask. The specificity is what makes it powerful: *Oh! That company's CFO is my neighbor! She's great. I'll see her Sunday and can talk to her then.*

Build the Referral Together

Now that you've worked together to identify people your client would be willing to send your way, it's time to build the referral together. This works in a very similar way to building a proposal together with a client because the goal is the same: to create an approach that fits, where the client has a vested interest in the outcome. To get the raving fan even more excited, work together on developing a meaningful give-to-get for the new contact, with an eye toward addressing his or her most pressing needs.

You can have an idea for what would work best, but be sure to solicit their input. They can see both sides. This way your client will be excited that they were able to help their contact get something of value. You can also help your client write the script for introducing you, one that frames the referral as a gift from them to their contact:

> Hey, you've got to meet Andy. He's known as one of the best financial planners in town, and he's got something I think would benefit you. He'll do a complete analysis of your investments and make recommendations for how to increase your monthly cash flow without dipping into your savings. No charge, no obligation. He only has time to do this for two new potential clients each quarter, and I know he has one slot left this quarter. The typical charge for this type of analysis is $2,000, but you'd get it for free because you're coming through me. I went through it myself and found . . .

Raving fan relationships can be some of your most important channels for creating new leads. These people are looking for ways to help you. *They want you to succeed, and you're letting them down when you don't ask for help.* Raving fans have already demonstrated a desire to help you grow your business. And the fastest way to turn a loyal client into a raving fan is to ask for a specific referral this way.

Frame the referral as a gift to your client. Make it fun and enjoyable by building everything together in a spirit of collaboration. By doing this you'll not only create more leads but will also deepen your existing relationship.

Cold Marketing

Sometimes your network can't get you there fast enough. If you're relatively new to a market or don't have a clear path into your targeted companies, cold marketing may be your only viable approach. Conventional wisdom says that this form of lead generation is inefficient, maybe even a complete waste of time. That's wrong. Although it's often easier to rely on word of mouth or referrals from raving fans, cold marketing works when it's done correctly. In fact, cold marketing can be an extremely robust form of lead generation in certain cases.

Many professionals successfully pitch their services to people they've never met. The best cold marketing incorporates a personal touch. At a time when people are bombarded by pitches via email and even social media, a phone call is an extremely personal and effective way of making contact. Another personal approach is a handwritten note accompanied by materials that might be of interest, like a book or white paper. With proper preparation and research, cold marketing packs a punch, especially when paired with unique marketing or a distinct insight.

This can work for any type of business. I'll give you an easy example from my own. When we moved into our current space, an office building in midtown Atlanta, I researched the other tenants to see if any of my neighbors fit my target client criteria. I wrote the head of each matching organization a handwritten letter and attached it to one of our training binders. I made a point to draw personal connections between me and them and made a joke out of how getting together would be the easiest commute I've ever had.

Most important, I told them that we'd be willing to invest in them and why they fit our perfect client criteria. I offered a specific, customized give-to-get offer to each leader. As I walked into each office to deliver the package, wearing my suit and tie, the receptionists probably assumed I was Atlanta's best-dressed bicycle messenger. Within a couple of days I'd heard back from each recipient. They all wanted to meet, and one wanted to meet right away.

That's how cold marketing works when you work it the right way: more time upfront in customization, but a much higher hit rate.

Do Your Homework

Start with your Target List. If you're targeting a company, research as many potential points of entry as you can find. You're looking for someone with lots of commonality who meets the qualification criteria in the prior chapter (remember $ in the ATM?), Once you've selected the specific person you intend to reach, double-check social media and your contact list to confirm that you don't know anyone who could offer you a direct introduction. Once you're sure that a cold approach is the only one available, do your research. Cold marketing calls for legwork to compensate for the implicit trust and credibility that come with a direct referral.

Read everything you can to educate yourself on the company. Hunt down all the information you can on the specific person you're going to contact—career history, awards, memberships, and affiliations. Look for points of connection. Perhaps you went to the same college or once spoke at the same conference. A small similarity is better than none. At minimum it shows that you invested time and energy in doing your homework.

Company websites contain a wealth of information. Press releases can give you up-to-date information on recent developments. Using LinkedIn and other tools can help you look at a prospect's work history, professional interests, published articles, and other key info. Even if you don't know anyone in common, chances are you'll find at least some common elements.

Special Delivery

Select a physical asset relevant to your services and expertise. Make it valuable and make it professional. Then, think through the delivery mechanism. Hand delivery signifies extreme importance. Overnight delivery is right behind it, usually getting opened right away. Below that, snail mail, now much more unique than maybe the lowest delivery mechanism, email. The *way* you send your package sends a message about how important it is. One way or the other, send something *before* calling. A handwritten note accompanying a well-considered package makes a great first impression.

Make the Call

After the package has arrived, there's one more step before you pick up the phone. Write out what you're going to say. Then rewrite it to make it shorter. No one is going to see this; the purpose is to think through the pitch so it's as concise and clear as you can make it. Outline what your company has to offer and the connections you share with the prospect. Once you've crafted this on paper, you'll be more than ready to handle the conversation. You don't want to get on the phone after all this effort and ramble.

Now, make the call. If you aren't connected directly, leave a message asking if the package was received. After that, switch to email to continue following up regularly. Find new ways to add value by sharing valuable information or assets in every email. The benchmark I use here is seven outreaches, but it sometimes takes more. You'll need to be consistent and patient, always adding and offering more value. In general, if you're not getting a call back, you're not adding enough value.

Once you're on the phone, keep the conversation brief and precise—a few minutes at most. Your goal isn't to talk about your full service; it's to talk through the give-to-get and set up a meeting or call to discuss how it would work. Focus on getting to the next step. Immediately upon hanging up, send an email and an invitation to connect on LinkedIn.

It takes confidence to call someone you don't know. Lead-generation techniques take us out of our comfort zone. It helps to think of this call in your own mind as a gift to the prospect. If you've done your prep work and have a clear idea of what you can offer, this is truly the case.

Cold marketing gets its bad reputation from the fact that thoughtless and disreputable sellers default to it. They know few people—and few people want to know them. What you're doing here is authentic, generous, and personal. The results will speak for themselves.

Forums

Value is at the heart of effective lead generation. The more value you can offer your prospects, the more open they will be to an introductory meeting. Real-life experiences shape our opinions more profoundly than reading marketing materials or website testimonials, so one way to make a lasting impact with prospects is to stage a forum. *Forums* are an ideal opportunity to connect with people and deepen multiple relationships at once.

Forums are not about self-promotion—they're an opportunity to deliver real value at scale. You can afford to invest more in a forum than you might in other lead-generation techniques because it gives you the opportunity to connect with a dozen or more of your best prospects in one evening.

You might bring in a top-tier speaker whose presentation is specifically relevant to your industry, or you could select a topic of discussion pertinent to your expertise and the types of problems you help solve. A forum can be a book launch, a research unveiling, or something equally interesting to your prospects. You might offer attendees the opportunity to "beta test" a new offering or service and offer feedback—experimental thinkers love this approach. (Don't forget to get everyone to sign an NDA.) The event can even take the form of a complimentary group training session. Forums can spell the difference between telling your prospects about the benefits of working with you and letting them experience it for themselves.

Forums are anything but turnkey. To work, they require targeted planning and a real investment of time. The payoff is that they can deliver genuine value to prospects while giving you the opportunity to connect with many in a single event. Being the organizer of a forum also establishes a certain credibility for you with attendees and those who hear about the event. By giving your prospects an opportunity to interact with you and members of your team or company in a memorable way, you create a strong emotional tie, laying the groundwork for the next step in strengthening the relationship. As always, make sure to follow up with each attendee in the weeks following the event.

Here's what you need to do.

Target Group

Write down the perfect target group. Do you want people with a certain role, like CFOs? Do you need people from within a particular geographic area? It helps to select a group or affiliation in which people will benefit from networking with each other and no one else is already bringing the same folks together. Find a niche you can own.

Value

Define a specific thing this group will want. Networking? Insights? Be very intentional about deciding what these people want most and then build your forum around that. Use your understanding of positioning to decide on three unique elements to make the forum stand out. Make sure to test the concept with others. Is anyone else providing this value to the target group?

Strategic Partners

Who else might be interested in meeting people in your target group? Find partners who can add value and don't compete with your services. Ideally, they should be able to bring their own clients and prospects to the event as well. The partners you choose will send a strong signal about the quality of the forum. Choose wisely and with an open mind: in addition to other companies, consider not-for-profit organizations, schools and universities, and even state and local government entities. Once you have a list of options, stick with no more than three—this is typically enough to cover your target marketplace and provide the necessary perspectives.

Cornerstone Clients

This step is key: to build momentum, bring your marquee clients on board first. You'll do this because the first question everyone asks is: "Who else will be there?" If you can get a couple of well-known clients to commit, you'll have a great answer to that question. Once you've created your strategic partnerships, think of the best cornerstone clients across all your relationships. Think about which of the clients in the target group would be most influential with the rest. Decide on three to sign up first—their participation will greatly influence the rest. To get them to buy in, involve them in the planning process. Let them tweak the concept, format, and even the date of the event. They may even be willing to host it for you or help sign up their peers.

Build a One-Pager

This document summarizes the target group, the purpose of the forum, and other specifics. Distribute the one-pager to potential partners and cornerstone clients to get the ball rolling.

Plan and Implement

Lay out the action steps and the timetable for hosting the forum. Pull in other experts from your organization to help. Make it a company-wide initiative if you can. Forums provide a tremendous amount of leads and access so everyone involved will benefit.

Depending on the type of presentation, forums can be any size, from a happy hour to a full-scale conference. Whether large, medium, or small, focus on inviting the right people and selecting a fantastic value anchor that will be a draw for those you invite. Even for people who don't attend, the marketing for your event can make an impact: *I can't make the event, but could I talk to you about your approach?* Draw a crowd and wow it, and everyone will go home extremely likely to tell others about their experience, building even more credibility for the next event.

As you've seen, forums take real effort to do well. Many companies think people will just show up if they send an e-invitation to everyone on the mailing list. They won't. You need to work for every attendee. Prospects need to have a specific sense of the networking value they'll get, over and above the value of the actual presentation. Bring that value down to a personal level: *I spoke with Jane—she is really looking forward to meeting you at the event!* Communicating this personal value will ensure that you get the minimum number of cancellations.

Make sure your team members reserve time to make calls to get people to attend and that every confirmed attendee is called a couple of days prior to see if they'd like to be introduced to anyone else planning to attend. It's great to send out an email blast letting people know about the event, but it will take one-on-one calls to get people to sign up and show up.

If you have the resources and the time to create a high-quality event and personally invite and follow up with all the attendees, a forum might be the most worthwhile investment you ever make in lead generation. It offers an unparalleled opportunity to genuinely connect with large groups of prospects. You can't beat it for efficiency—if you're willing to do the legwork.

Informal Meet-Ups

Depending on the nature of your service and your target prospects, a formal, carefully planned, and staged event like this may not be necessary or even appropriate. A lighter approach can be as simple as inviting an important expert to your town to meet with key clients and prospects or simply coordinating around a visit that expert had already planned to make.

For example, if a well-known author with a new book relevant to your industry is coming to your area to promote his work, you might reach out to that author or the book's publicist about a group dinner. This kind of small event can be valuable for authors looking to connect with business leaders, entrepreneurs, and influencers—often they're stuck in an unfamiliar town with nothing to do after completing their primary publicity obligations. Once your invitation is accepted, email key prospects and clients explaining that the author will be in town on a certain evening and inviting them to a discussion of the book. This approach can work with any relevant expert, of course, even someone inside your organization.

This approach builds your credibility by associating you with an expert and doesn't require the preparation a forum does. An invitation to an event like this can have a very high response rate to boot. The best part? People will see you as well connected and, thus, valuable to know.

Strategic Partners

Depending on the nature of your work, there are almost certainly a number of practitioners and companies that work with the same clients you do but provide a complementary service. Partnering with these can be a terrific win-win.

Strategic partners want to know the people you know and vice versa. You can even establish formal agreements to work together to generate leads—through a forum, for example—or simply by making personal introductions for each other. A talent consultant and a compensation consultant might call on the same human resources leaders. If they pool their resources, they could host a larger, more impressive lead-generation event than either could manage alone. Or they could systematically make personal introductions between their clients and the other partner. Each can easily drive highly qualified leads to their partner on an ongoing basis. Strategic partners are referral annuities. (Actuaries love annuities.)

It's best to think of strategic partners as matchmakers. Their responsibility ends at a referral—the path to raving fan is still up to you. Keep your expectations for any such partnership realistic. Do you have the willingness, availability, and connections to make successful introductions? That's what it takes to be an effective strategic partner.

You can partner with individuals or organizations. Either way, show them how they'll benefit from the relationship. Stay ahead by providing more value than you receive. Some partnerships are so important that it's best to have a formal agreement, maybe even including a commission. You might even establish goals on the metrics—number of introductions, volume of work sold, and so on. I usually recommend starting slow, with two or three introductions in each direction.

As with a new hire, some partner relationships will work out and some won't. Focus on the most valuable ones and invest in them. Meet frequently with your partners to make sure you're communicating well. Keep them apprised of new developments in your business, and listen to what's going on with them. These tactical conversations will spark ideas for new connections and new projects.

When it comes to establishing strategic partners, you can stick to the same format you use for your Protemoi List. Write down all the potential partners you can think of and then simply think of a "deal" as a "referral"— that's the point at which you turn a prospective partner into an active one. Now work on deepening these relationships as you would with any other key relationship for your business until all your strategic partners are raving fans to boot.

This is one of my favorite ways to generate leads. I have many strategic partners on my Protemoi List—some of them provide so many leads and so much value that they're more important to our business than many of our paying clients.

Event Attendance

Large onetime or annual events like group meetings, conferences, and the like represent opportunities for lead generation, but using them properly requires discipline. When you approach an event with business development in mind, you should keep your focus entirely on how you can increase your network and connections. Simply showing up, attending a few requisite sessions, and then hiding in a corner to answer emails or chatting with people you already know isn't going to develop anything other than your thumb and jaw muscles.

Many professionals are intimidated by the thought of networking in a throng of new people. By using these four Cs to map out a strategy for an event, you will be able to seize the moment in a focused and fun way. You'll also want to open a spreadsheet or similar app to track the prospects you'd like to meet and the subsequent results. Here are the four Cs.

Clarify

What are your goals for the conference? Above all, *who* do you want to meet? List the specific people, companies, and roles that would be the most valuable for your business. Write these names down.

Connect

Don't wait until you're on the conference center floor. Think of creative ways to approach each prospect beforehand. Do you have mutual connections who might be willing to introduce you over email in anticipation of the two of you meeting at the event? Can your strategic partners help? Do you happen to follow each other on Twitter? Do your best to connect with a prospect before you arrive to set a time to meet, and if you can't, get creative while you're at the event.

Converse

Think in advance about the questions you plan to ask prospects. Use the gravitas model we discuss in Chapter 7. How can you smoothly bring up a mutual affiliation or connection? Entering each conversation prepared with multiple possible points of connection will help make the process a lot less stressful. Turn what could be cold into something warm.

Commit

Decide on a valuable give-to-get for each prospect. Remember to think backward: What kind of big project would you like to take on for this prospect? Start there, and rewind to an appropriate give-to-get that is relatively easy for you, valuable for the prospect, and likely to lead where you want to go. Also, think ahead to see if there might be a good time to set your follow-up meeting. Perhaps you'll be in their city soon or you'll be at another event of mutual interest. Otherwise, simply set up a call. Remember the magic phrase: "Would it be helpful if . . . ?"

This last step is imperative. Research out of Cornell University and Canada's Western University found that a face-to-face ask resulted in a yes thirty-four times more often than the same request sent via email. Ever go to a conference, have a great conversation with someone, and then get no response to your emailed follow-up? This is why. *Get the yes in person.*

Speaking

Talk about getting out of your comfort zone. It's said that some fear public speaking more than death itself. Whether or not that's actually true, it's definitely the case that speaking is a skill that needs to be developed if you want to practice it professionally. If you line up an opportunity to get in front of a crowd of qualified prospects, the last thing you want to do is wing it.

If you already know your way around the stage, great. If not, and if you think this would be an effective lead-generation approach for your business, it's time to develop your skill set. Find a great speaking coach. Invest in some of the many excellent books and courses on public speaking. Best of all, get in front of a crowd. Toastmasters is an organization with regular meetings around the world. It offers an unparalleled opportunity to develop and present speeches on various topics in front of a receptive audience of like-minded people working on their own speaking skills. If that doesn't work, you might work with your peers to create an internal speaking group to help develop your chops.

Once you know how to speak effectively, the next question is: Where? There are thousands of speaking opportunities out there, many of which are outside of large conferences. Frequently, smaller groups meet on a regular basis around role-based or development-oriented topics. It could be anything—top ad agency execs, HR professionals, start-up founders.

These groups can be great opportunities for you if they contain a critical mass of potential prospects. Of course, large conferences are usually a part of the picture too. Sometimes you need to pay to speak, sometimes you can speak for free, and sometimes they'll even pay you.

One of our clients generates most of their leads through conferences. They consult in a business area with several dedicated conferences. Because they want to be seen as market leaders, they are happy to pay for the privilege of speaking at these events. They pick their conferences well and carefully track results to ensure they are putting their efforts into the events with the highest return on investment. They can trace some of their largest clients all the way back to meeting them at speaking engagements years ago.

Here are the steps to develop your strategy:

Target Prospects and Conferences

Begin with the people you want to meet. Look at your target criteria, and figure out which roles are the perfect entry points for the organizations you want to reach. Research the conferences these people attend. Often conferences draw people a level or two below the ones you actually want to meet, so focus helps. Think about smaller groups and narrower conferences that will give you a higher density of appropriate prospects. We find the role of the attendee to be the key to success.

Pick a Valuable Topic

Brainstorm unique topics suited to each conference you've identified. This is best done as a group activity—work with your peers and clients to zero in on the topics that resonate most in your industry and market.

Find Copresenters

Would your topic be more valuable if you copresented with a top client? You can accomplish more and establish greater credibility with the right client at your side, and it's a great way to move that client along the path to raving fan. When you're speaking alone, attendees tend to expect a pitch. When you're speaking with a client, attendees expect value.

Plan and Implement

Speaking at certain events can involve a certain amount of hassle. Do you need to submit a formal proposal to speak or just make a quick pitch to the organizers? Document these steps for each of the events you have in mind.

Make an Offer

People rush out of conference rooms to make the next session or to grab that cup of coffee before the out-of-hotel event. A good speech is nice for brand awareness, but it won't result in leads—leads happen through one-on-one conversations. Give attendees a reason to ask for one. Offer to email a unique, valuable asset to the folks who give you their business card. Offer a give-to-get for people who match certain criteria. This call to action is the number-one thing missing from most speeches.

Webinars

This tool shares elements with speaking and forums. The web makes it astonishingly easy to deliver a high-quality, interactive presentation to prospects all over the world. Webinars are typically onetime events, though you may deliver several each year. As with similar tools, the key to success is delivering tremendous value to your audience and ending on a specific call to action.

A sense of urgency helps. Pick a topic that is time sensitive. Maybe a new piece of legislation will have a sweeping impact on your clients or you have some newly completed research you can finally share, such as a well-executed case study or a short training module. You can deliver the webinar yourself or bring in a client to copresent.

Once you've selected your topic and possibly recruited a copresenter, decide on a call to action. This is typically a give-to-get or small project offered at the end of the webinar. Many experts miss this step and waste a valuable opportunity. The thing to remember is that webinars are generally open to the public, so the give-to-get should require a low level of commitment from you. You'll want to qualify these prospects before offering anything too substantial. You might offer a one-page assessment, a half-hour call to further explain the research topic, and so on. Once you get the initial give-to-get organized, you can decide whether to offer more for a highly qualified prospect: a half-day session on the topic, for example. To woo on webinars, follow these steps.

Establish Goals and Set Metrics

Always begin with a goal for the webinar. Are you looking to drive the right people to a specific service? If that's the case, choose metrics that will help track your success in meeting this goal. Decide on a specific, realistic number of leads you'd like to generate. How many total attendees would need to attend to translate into this many qualified leads? (This calculation will get easier after you've hosted a few.) Webinars can work with remarkable consistency, so start measuring and optimizing your approach from the first one.

Craft the Marketing

Now it's time to package your service and expertise in a way that will be compelling enough to draw a large audience. Think carefully about how you will spread the message about the webinar—think back to what you've already learned about positioning. What can you present that is interesting, relevant, and urgent enough to drive significant attendance?

Decide on Presenters

Now that your goals and positioning are clear, decide on the ideal presenter for your message. Of course, everyone on the webinar will need strong speaking skills. Ideally, whoever participates will also have name recognition in the industry and a great story. This is where copresenting with a raving-fan client can help—and clients are typically happy to have an opportunity to promote their hard work. Meanwhile the client or client company's name-recognition level will factor heavily in your overall attendance. Your prospects judge you by the company you keep—if they see a genuine player in the industry allied with you in a webinar, it will go a long way to changing their perception of your company.

Plan and Implement

Planning a webinar is similar to planning a live event, but with an added technological twist. In addition to scheduling the various milestones, including planning meetings with the internal team, meetings with potential copresenters, and so on, you'll need to decide on an appropriate platform for the presentation. There are many factors to consider when choosing one, such as features like real-time voting, ease of use, and reliability.

Make an Offer

Similar to speaking, you need to make an offer to transition from this one-to-many conversation to a one-on-one. Without it, you're marketing, but you're not generating leads. Create an offer for people in need of your services to connect with you on some kind of give-to-get session. That's your key to success. You might want to create scarcity if you're worried about too many people asking. Mention that you can only do a certain number of these and that you'll perform it for the first X number of people who contact you. (You can always make exceptions later.)

Writing

Yes, they still make paper. But even if people end up reading what you've written digitally, more traditional periodicals can still be a great lead generator. Few techniques build credibility like writing. However, simply writing a few articles a year will not send droves of ideal prospects through the door. Without a strategy, experts often end up publishing these articles in publications read by their *peers* but not their *clients*.

The key to making writing a successful part of your lead-generation strategy is to target the right periodicals and to write thought-provoking content that will spur prospects to reach out. The odds of any single reader turning into a client are relatively low, so targeting the right publications with a large readership among your target market will maximize your chances of success.

Also, don't confuse writing to establish credibility with writing to generate leads. There is some overlap, but each kind of writing works best with that goal in mind.

So how do you write right? Start with research. What periodicals or websites do your clients read regularly? If you can, talk to your clients about their reading habits. You might ask them if an article or blog post recently captured their attention and even drove them to take action in some way. These anecdotes can be illustrative.

If you can't talk to clients, look at the themes you see resonating in your industry. You might aim your topics to appeal to a particular thinking preference. This approach can drive a more focused, memorable article. For example, writing about the success of your consulting business in general isn't nearly as compelling as offering an in-depth analysis—accompanied by lots of graphs—of how you helped a single client company reduce overhead by 12.3 percent. That article may not be to everyone's taste, but if your ideal prospects are analytical-leaning CFOs, you can expect it to make waves. Meanwhile using the same case but with the focus on the new six-step management process that helped drive the reduction might help steer your article toward practical COOs.

One of our clients is a tax controversy attorney. He wrote an article about what to do when facing IRS scrutiny and placed it in a periodical read by accountants, his primary referral sources. (The periodicals *he* reads are mostly read by other attorneys.) He then forwarded the article to accountants with a give-to-get offer: a "lunch and learn" on the topic for their partners. This successfully drew many qualified leads.

Most professionals see publishing a piece of writing as the finish line, but I view the publishing as the *starting line*. The magic comes from you or a third party sending the piece to others with a genuine offer to help them. This uses the published piece to build credibility and pairs it with a powerful give-to-get. Here's the full sequence of steps.

Identify Target Publications

As always, go back to your Target List. Be sure to identify not only the function of your perfect prospects but the specific level of role as well. Is the treasurer the ideal entry point, or the CFO? Once you've defined this, it will be much easier to identify the right publications to reach those readers.

Empathize

What insights can you offer to help solve an issue for these readers? What topics are people in these roles deeply concerned with? What skills do they need to improve? What specific upcoming events in their industry or marketplace are relevant? Once you're thinking in terms of their problems, you'll be better able to frame how your services can help.

Find the Technical Angle

How can you blend your expertise with the topic to make a specific, compelling point? Is there an insight you can offer based on your unique perspective? Do you have a case study that might apply? What results can you share?

Plan and Implement

Now generate the steps of your plan to get your article written and placed. This might include initial meetings and introductions with publication editors, approaching clients to cowrite, or researching submission guidelines.

Make an Offer

Notice a trend? You have to figure out a way to go from one-to-many to one-on-one. The way to do this with writing is to send out your published piece to specific targets with an offer for a give-to-get. The writing gives you credibility and an asset. In larger organizations you might enlist other partners or account managers to send this out. They can say nicer things about you than you can and are able to make the offer of your assistance.

Interviews

Writing to generate leads offers another, parallel opportunity: people love to be interviewed. Of course, the need for an interview needs to be authentic—an article, white paper, or blog post is just the opportunity to create that authentic need. A conversation with the right person can add insight or opinion to your own message and bring the entire piece to life.

Meanwhile the initial interview, review of drafts, and the eventual publication of the article provide multiple opportunities to bring your interviewee along the path to raving fan. This is a terrific way to build a relationship with an influencer, key prospect, or important client.

•

Generating leads generates success. You can't have too many, and having an abundance of leads makes everything easier, the snowball rolling downhill toward your goals. When there are too few leads, everything else has to be perfect—you have no margin for error. This creates stress. Stress creates "selling"—in the bad way.

Now that leads are coming in—or will be shortly—it's time to figure out how to efficiently turn those leads into happy clients.

CHAPTER 7

Turning Leads into Clients

● ● ●

CONGRATULATIONS! YOU'VE SUCCESSFULLY turned on the spigot. Leads are flowing, and life is good.

Now that you have more than enough prospective clients to choose from, prosperity should be just around the corner. Have fun buying that new yacht—I bet you'll have some great tips for their sales team.

Just kidding.

Whether you generate one new lead or one hundred, what you do next is critical. Believe me, I've seen it all. The ways people handle—or mishandle—new opportunities boggles the mind. Some seller-experts routinely close only one in a hundred opportunities, with this sorry conversion rate shrinking with the more time they actually spend talking with any one prospect. A rare few, however, bring in relatively few opportunities but manage to close nearly all of them, with the odds getting better over time. What could account for such a disparity?

I hear this all the time: "Mo, can you help Phil with his opportunities? He surfaces dozens, hundreds. He just has a little trouble closing them." *Oh, Phil,* I think to myself. *I can tell you right now that you're deep-sixing your odds of closing long before the close.*

How you handle each lead is the key to your success. Ultimately this is where you succeed or fail. This is where you learn to love or hate selling, where you dance the happy dance after a call or wonder, after weeks without a response, *what did I do wrong?*

Let's start with how to do it right. Talking to prospects should be efficient, for them and for you. It should also be both exciting and easy; everyone should look forward to it. If prospects are willing to invest their precious time with you, there needs to be a spark of interest to kindle. So do it. Make it fun. Talking to prospects should never become a tired routine—although you should stick to a process, always leave room to be creative, responsive, and *present* when talking to *this* prospect, *this* person.

Remember the idea that when someone's buying something, it should feel like it's their birthday? This is where business development becomes fun for us too. This is a moment when we can replace *selling* with *problem solving* and let our big brains shine, serving up the fruits of our hard-earned expertise and experience and making somebody else's day.

In this chapter we're going to learn how to take all the incoming interest we've created and manage it in a sustainable, effective, and fun way. As with every other element of business development, this challenge demands a systematic approach as a baseline.

Building Opportunities Step-by-Step

Rainmakers follow a step-by-step process. They have to. Anyone with a little luck can get lightning to strike once—it has to strike somewhere. Getting lightning to strike regularly demands acres of well-maintained lightning rods. If someone in your organization or industry steadily brings in qualified prospects and turns them into clients and raving fans over and over again, you'd better believe they're using a process.

The question then is: What is the most effective process for turning a prospect into a long-term client and raving fan? In popular culture wooing a prospect like a pro is straightforward. Take them to a fancy restaurant—seriously fancy, the kind with leather banquettes. Split a few bottles of good wine, tell some funny stories, and then hand them a really expensive pen so they can sign on the dotted line. Done deal.

In real life this approach usually ends in failure, even if you did spring for *two* orders of the molten chocolate cake. Nobody likes being wheeled and dealed. Even if you do somehow get to a paying project, you've done so at the cost of damaging the long-term relationship.

The proven approach that follows is linear and sequential, meaning it goes through the same stages in the same order each time. Sometimes the cadence is different, and sometimes you'll repeat a step. Sometimes there are multiple ways to tackle the same step. The important thing is to *see the path from the buyer's perspective.* If you look at the buying process through the eyes of the prospect instead of your own—what you want and what you need—the correct next move always becomes clear.

Most organizations are stuck in *their* perspective. From the buyer's side I can tell you it's truly awful. Here's how *not* to turn a prospect into a long-term client.

Talk about yourself, a lot. Use PowerPoint to accentuate how tedious this will be. Include a slide that says, "Mission and Values" because the best way to let people know you have integrity is to announce it loudly. Oh, and can you show a slide of your client logos with some of them pixelated because you snagged them from a company website an hour before the meeting without permission? Also, make sure to forget to change the footer so it still features the name of the last prospect you pitched.

Create boredom. Use lots of jargon so you sound just like everyone else. Don't ask questions about me. I might enjoy talking about myself or the problems I need to solve. We don't want that. If you do ask about me, please use generic questions so I know you didn't do any homework, like "What keeps you up at night?" Never heard that one before.

Send a proposal. At this point I might ask for a proposal just to get you to go away. Please make it both generic, so my unimportance to you is clear, and formally designed, so that it's clear I shouldn't even consider suggesting any changes. Make sure that the only way I can add value is to pick apart your set-in-stone approach.

Pester me endlessly. Keep on sending the same email. "Mo, did you get my email following up on my other seven emails and three texts that followed up on my proposal you didn't like? Mo? Mo? Mo?" *Sorry, Mo isn't here right now. He moved to the San Juan Islands and accidentally on purpose dropped his phone into the mouth of a killer whale.*

This is an exaggeration, but I've sat through many meetings as a buyer myself that skirted unbelievably close. Whether or not you've been through an ordeal like this, I hope I've made my point: the buyer's experience comes first. Focus on that, and you can't go far astray.

Here are the same four steps done right.

Listen and learn. Give the client or prospect plenty of opportunity to talk about themselves and the problems they're facing. Ask thoughtful questions based on your research that establish your expertise and interest while building your likability.

Create curiosity. Turn the spotlight on yourself—specifically, explain how you can help the client or prospect solve these problems. Use *their* words, reflecting *their* situation in their words instead of falling back on generic industry lingo. Be helpful and suggest the next incremental interaction.

Build everything together. Make it easy for the prospect to collaborate in designing the approach. This is a four-step process that lines up neatly with the four thinking styles: (1) craft the goals, (2) create the plan, (3) pick the teams, and (4) agree on terms. This order feels good to the buyer and sustains momentum toward the next step. Depending on the scope, this can be accomplished over a period of months or over the course of a single meeting.

Gain approval. Thanks to the psychology behind this process, the final sign-off should be the easiest and fastest step. After all, you've built incremental buy-in during the preceding steps, with potentially dozens of incremental "approvals" along the way. This is just the final one. You might ask that a contract be signed by Friday to meet the agreed-upon timeline. If this stage doesn't move smoothly, either a previous step was skipped—meaning the buy-in didn't really occur—or something on the client's end has changed. Sometimes a new decision maker has entered the conversation or budgets have tightened. These things happen. Rest assured, we'll talk about how to handle them.

At each step be helpful, act in the best interests of your client, and align your actions to drive incremental advancement. Don't try to push too far, too fast. When people fail, it's usually because they're trying to hurry things or skip steps, like asking for approval on a contract when the client hasn't even agreed to the various deal components. To the client this reads as being pushy. When you're only asking for the next incremental step and your request makes clear how that step will help them, the client sees it as helpful.

I'll explain the first two steps in depth in this chapter and get into the rest later on. Every opportunity on your plate will be at one of these steps. Your primary goal at each step is to move the opportunity along to the next. In this way the process serves to direct and organize your BD efforts in a way that's easy to track and sustain. Without this path, momentum stalls.

The Opportunity List

Let's try it from where you stand today. It's time to create your first Opportunity List, using the **Opportunity List** worksheet, a blank page, or project management software. Moving forward, this is where you are going to keep track of any and every situation in which you need a yes from someone to move forward. This could be a contract you're negotiating for a consulting gig, the chance to speak at an industry conference, or a shot at meeting with a highly connected potential source of referrals. Closing a deal can refer to a lot more than just getting hired for a single piece of client work.

For each opportunity you're fielding, write down the current and next step in the process. If you've just connected with a new prospect and you've set up an initial call, you're at *listen and learn*. If you're waiting for a prospect to sign off on an engagement, you're at *gain approval*. And so on. Go ahead and categorize each of your opportunities this way.

Once you've categorized your Opportunity List, you have clarity: you know where you are now and where you're trying to go across the full spectrum of your BD efforts. Knowing your next proactive step—from the client's perspective—is the key to success. As you progress, make sure to update this list so you can always see at a glance how your business development is going and where your valuable time should be invested next.

Here are some examples from one person's actual Opportunity List, including the stage and next step.

Speak at industry conference (create curiosity). Send Bill the written summary for each of the three speech topic examples we picked as our favorites and ask for his improvement ideas. Include open times for a call to pick his favorite and flesh out details.

Current State Analysis (gain approval). Send article Gabby just published summarizing her approach to Jim and ask him if they still want results for the board meeting (if so, we need to have the contract signed by Tuesday!).

Initial meeting with new decision maker, Josie (listen and learn). Call Josie to let her know Becky's schedule has changed and that she *will* now be coming to town. Would it be helpful if we did the overview meeting in person? I think it would help her better acclimate to the role—if she agrees, it would need to be on May 12.

Craft solution for Spencer (build everything together). Email Spencer the agenda for our meeting to design the approach—goals, plan, team, rough budget numbers. Ask for his improvement ideas, and remember to ask who should be included from his side. Send dates we could fly in for the meeting.

Notice the themes: incrementally moving forward, being helpful, framed from the client's perspective.

Let's dig into the first two of the four steps. We'll cover the others in the next chapter.

Listen and Learn

Few burdens can't be lightened by sharing. Listening, carefully and patiently, is one of the fundamental human gifts we can give each other. No matter how bad things get, just unloading a few worries off our chest with someone who can quietly sympathize *before* responding provides relief.

Yet as simple as it is to sit still and listen, few do it well. The moment someone starts talking, we can't help but start crafting responses. If someone has a problem, we try to think of a time when we had a bigger one. If someone has a success, we look for ways to match it or at least puncture it. And this is with our *friends*.

Think of how frustrating it is when you try to talk to someone about what's bothering you or what you're excited about and all they want to do is top it. We love to be heard, so we cherish those with the rare capacity to zip their lips and let us have our say in full. Yet when it's our turn to listen, we still open our big mouths.

What's true with our friends and loved ones is doubly true in business. Seller-experts fail at this stage more than at any other, which is ironic considering that of all the tickets, meals, and other perks we lavish on important clients, offering an ear is both the most affordable and the most appreciated gift. Instead, in a rush to move the conversation straight to the deal (and avoid uncomfortable silences), experts talk and talk and talk—about what they know, what they've achieved, whom they've worked with, and what they can do. Meanwhile the prospect starts wondering whether to just get the problem solved in-house or perhaps ignore it until it goes away.

Give your clients the spotlight. Diana Tamir, a professor of psychology at Princeton, found that sharing your personal opinions activates the pleasure center of the brain. That's right: talking about your own ideas and beliefs lights up the same region of gray matter as eating a great meal or—I'm just quoting the research here—having sex.

This means you can give clients a high simply by putting them on a soapbox. Ask them to share their perspective on what's going on with their business or in the industry at large. Ask them their opinion on how these problems might be solved. You'll walk away with a better understanding of what they're facing, and they'll like you more to boot.

Beyond the fact that the listen-and-learn step leads prospects and clients to like you more and want to spend more time with you, it also serves a critical purpose in the step-by-step BD process. That's right: the *learning* part.

Often we're so eager to launch into our pitch that we only let the client give us the barest sketch of their problem before diving in. If we're only willing to sit with our discomfort and let the client get it *all* out, however slowly and indirectly, we may see the potential for a larger and deeper engagement than the one springing immediately to mind. Instead of offering answers, ask questions. Get to the bottom of it. Then, find other "its" to get to the bottom of. Keep asking, keep digging. Sometimes the problem on the table is just a symptom of a larger, undiagnosed one. Being able to hear and respond to a deeper problem is one of the most compelling demonstrations of experience and expertise. It won't happen if you're busy proving how smart you are, though.

Great, you may be thinking. *This technique is free, makes clients like me, and translates into larger, more lucrative engagements. I'm going to start listening to and learning from all my clients from now on.* Not so fast. Letting clients talk about themselves seems easy on paper, but it can be surprisingly hard to do in practice. After all, *we* want to get the high by talking about ourselves too. Worse, research by Dr. Victor Ottati, a professor of psychology at Loyola University, reveals that experts become increasingly closed-minded when it comes to their own subject of expertise. That means we naturally tend to ask fewer questions as the topic of discussion aligns with what we know.

Above all, experts have a deeply engrained habit of relying on their mouths to convince others and make the sale. In fact, being know-it-alls has often gotten us good results in life, starting way back in elementary school. We like it. It takes months or even years of deliberate practice to fully cultivate the habit of listening, especially in moments when time is short or the pressure is high. Experts crave the spotlight—fight that craving. Instead, make this about the client. Give them the birthday experience. You'll get the chance to show off in the next two steps as you progress into helping the prospect solve their problems.

Listen and Learn in Practice

Here's a simple way to start making the most of this step: Take out a Post-it Note and write "Listen and Learn" on it. Now stick it on your monitor. (If you're the type to have lots of little Post-it Notes all over your desk, feel free to crumple those up and stick them in a drawer. You want to focus on this one.)

From now on, every time you get on the phone with a prospect or client (or spouse, friend—anyone, really), look at that Post-it, take a deep breath, and let it out. Then listen. Really listen, without an agenda, until the other person has had their say. If you feel a lot of ideas bubbling up, write them down for later and go back to listening. Then ask questions that reflect that you were *actually listening* and go deeper. Whether or not *you* find the topic important or relevant, give it the same degree of careful attention you'd expect when reporting a theft to a police detective. (Don't be weird about it, Sherlock. Just be empathic and interested.) You'll be astonished by the results.

This doesn't just apply to phone calls. Take a good look at that Post-it before heading out to lunch with a client or to an evening networking event. Make "Listen and Learn" your new mantra.

Beyond this there are a number of other tactics that work together toward advancing a new prospect along to the next step of the process, creating curiosity:

Proactively reach out to clients with something of value. Part of becoming more comfortable with selling is understanding that people may not realize (a) there is a solution to their problem, (b) you have the expertise to provide it, or even (c) that they don't have the capacity and time to solve it alone. To listen, you need to get people talking, and that means actively approaching clients with valuable ideas and information that might spark curiosity on their end. Don't be shy, whether with fresh leads or with clients you haven't approached in a while.

Add value in every interaction. In this first stage of the process look for ways to add value with every email, every instant message, every phone call, every meeting. Remember: our primary goal in this step is to get to the next step, create curiosity. We have no time to waste. Even a quick scheduling email can be an opportunity to suggest a solution or offer a relevant link. When people realize how useful it is to communicate with you, they become much more responsive. Value can be added in simple ways. The easiest way to add value is to be upbeat and add humor. It draws people toward you.

Customize messages. One of the best ways to make someone feel insignificant is to communicate in a way that feels rote or even automated. It's funny how often a hand-typed email can still read like spam when it doesn't include specifics. Why waste an opportunity to make it clear that *you* are the one doing the communicating and are paying attention to the person you're communicating with? The more we listen, the better we are able to tailor every communication with the recipient. This applies to the entire spectrum of information: from the fact that an upcoming merger is keeping the prospect's firm super-busy, to remembering that Samuel prefers to go by Sam, to just asking if your client's daughter is still looking for that escaped hamster, Hamtaro. The p.s. in an email is a great place to personalize. Everyone reads the p.s.

Listen for needs and interests. The best way to zero in on the largest and deepest possible engagement is to open your ears and engage all four thinking styles. Pay attention not only to the problem as stated but also to all the other issues that get hinted at during a conversation with any prospect. The gravitas model later in this chapter helps here. Look for experimental information about the client's vision for the future, analytical information about the client's revenue and other metrics, and so on. If you get good at this, you'll start spotting the seeds of other opportunities.

Vary delivery methods. Try new channels of communication if you feel like you've gotten into a rut. If you've communicated primarily by email, switch things up with a call. Go retro: snail-mail a printed article with a handwritten note—it feels special these days. If you're going to be in the same area, offer to buy them a cup of coffee. Varying the delivery method helps avoid the client-side feeling that you're an automated, value-generating robot programmed to email a TED Talk every third Thursday.

Monitor frequency and timing of interactions. Don't leave the flow of communication to chance. If you don't set up a system for regular follow-up, it's far too easy to lose track of whose court the ball is in. Make sure to remind yourself when to check in after sending a message to a client, and be sure to respond promptly as well. This is vital, especially during the first few weeks of the relationship. It may feel mechanical at first, but you'll soon wonder how you got by any other way.

Ask provocative questions about the ideas the client likes. People pay experts for their expertise. If they already knew what you knew, they wouldn't be talking to you. Although it may feel polite or supportive to let the client lead the conversation, it can also read as passivity or ignorance. If you're really paying attention, and if you're really an expert on the subject, you should be able to ask pointed questions, ones that may even fly in the face of the client's assumptions and beliefs. Don't hold back. Few things demonstrate expertise like asking the right questions.

As you can see, listening is important, but it's just the start. In reading this you may already have some fresh insight into why you've had trouble with prospects in the past. As clients ourselves, we tend to expect this level of treatment and take it for granted, but as you can see, it calls for a degree of attention, preparation, and thoughtfulness from the expert. Nothing automatic about it. The results more than make up for the effort, of course. You need to listen to truly be heard.

A number of tools in the system play a part in the first step of the process. We'll get to one tool, the gravitas model, later in this chapter. But first, on to the second step.

Create Curiosity

Depending on the scope, the listen-and-learn step can last all of one phone call or it can stretch out among calls, emails, and meetings for weeks or even months. You might need to meet with multiple leaders or even multiple teams at a client organization to get the full picture of the problem and for all of them to get a sense of who you are and where you're coming from.

Eventually, however, the goal is always to get to this step: create curiosity, where you get the prospect excited about what you can do for them. It should be obvious by now why you can't do this effectively without listening first. Once you've listened, however, it's time to reflect on what you've learned. When the client sees that you genuinely understand their problem *in its entirety*, they will immediately become eager to hear what you have to say about it.

As always, your goal during creating curiosity is to move the opportunity to the next step. One sign of this transition point is the moment when the client pauses and then says, "Great, so what's the next step to work together?" When you hear that, you know you're ready to build everything together.

So how do we get from listening to building?

Create Curiosity in Practice

We all get hooked now and then. You're going about your business, guard up, and then suddenly something catches your eye and you instantly want to know more. Ever been out with friends at a bar and someone declares a fact that another immediately challenges? *There's no way Bob Gibson's ERA was below 1.20 in 1968!* Or maybe the group can't remember something. *Who was Will Ferrell's love interest in* Elf? Curiosity compels us to pull out our phones for answers in situations like this, betting a round of beer on answers like "1.12," and "Zooey Deschanel."

All of us experience this sense of curiosity, but only a few know how to instill it in others and get them hanging on every word. It's the gift of the natural storyteller—or so many think. It should come as no surprise to you by this point that there's no such thing as a natural storyteller. Creating curiosity in others is not an inborn talent; it's a skill, and one that can be learned.

Dr. Jacqueline Gottlieb, a professor of neuroscience at Columbia, has shown that curiosity is one of our most powerful intrinsic motivators. If you can instill curiosity in clients, they will want to meet with you again and again. Other research by Dr. Matthias Gruber at UC Davis found that people remember more facts when they are curious about the subject at hand.

The art of arousing curiosity lies in the careful use of suspense. A good mystery novelist doesn't say whodunit in the third chapter; curiosity needs time and space to grow. As the research shows, this isn't a "trick" to hook people—it is quite enjoyable and helps them learn.

Creating curiosity can be very simple when talking to a prospect. For example, you might answer a client's question in general terms while suggesting they meet with your peer, who happens to be the foremost expert on that particular subject. Now the prospect wants to meet this expert—they're hooked.

The problem is, we often feel pressure to move quickly: "I need to close this deal to get promoted" or "I need to have this meeting go well to make my targets." The fastest way to develop a client relationship, however, is to slow things down and give the story time to unfold.

Using your storytelling skills, you will assemble all the characters and places and props and plot devices (everything you've learned from listening in the previous step) into a compelling narrative, a whole-brained vision of the future. Your client's future: *This is what it would be like to work with me.* The more effectively you tell this story, the more likely the prospect will want to experience it in real life.

So how do we do this? It's a process, of course:

When an idea sticks, focus on creating curiosity, not pushing. Resist the temptation to tell the prospect what they should hire you for too quickly. Instead, offer some give-to-get options aligned with the prospect's thinking preference to build interest: *I know a decent amount about this issue, but our expert on this type of engineering is Stella. I'm sure she'd have an interesting perspective on this, as she's just concluded some really interesting and relevant research. It's hot off the presses—I haven't even seen it yet. Should we set up a call with her?* You don't need to have all the answers, but you can tee up other experts to offer to them or find them yourself once you have more time.

Suggest a meeting to discuss how the concept could work. Now that the prospect's interest is piqued, suggest a meeting so you can discuss implementing the give-to-get. Or sometimes you won't need a give-to-get. You might be able to suggest a meeting to discuss what it would be like to work together. Whatever the next step is, ask for it: *Would it be helpful if I described a two-hour, interactive meeting we've facilitated that makes it easy to get started? The meeting ends with a perfect work plan for going through a change like this. It gives clients a jump-start in a very short period of time. We're happy to do it on our dime, just so we can introduce you to our change-management practice leader and our comprehensive process.*

Make it extremely easy to select a date. Don't introduce friction at this crucial point. Offer multiple days and times in a clear format so the prospect's team can easily coordinate among themselves. And, of course, leave enough time for your team to prepare. *How about we pull out our phones while we're here in person and select a tentative date? I've found agreeing on one in person is a lot easier than kicking around dates with eleven people over email, don't you? It saves time and a lot of headache.*

Pull in the best resources from your company. Don't hesitate to bring in your company's senior leaders for this meeting. This is an unmistakable sign that you value the relationship. If you're going to speak about a subject that lies outside your own area, make sure the specialist is in the room to answer questions. *We've got a couple of experts who target this topic, but I'm going to shoot for our best, Aleisha. She'll have to fly in from the Dallas office for the meeting, but I'm sure she'd be happy to do it. We don't call her Awesome Aleisha for nothing.*

Spend an adequate amount of time preparing. Do your homework. Use Whole Brain® Thinking* to anticipate questions and ideas from every possible angle. A prospect who prefers connection-oriented relational thinking might still come prepared with a long list of concerns from their analytical team member.

Once you've really knocked a prospect's socks off this way, you're going to wonder how you ever signed a new client the old way, rushed and semiprepared. Throwing spaghetti at the wall to see what sticks might be fun for a three-year-old, but it's no fun for a seller-expert who needs to clean up his own mess.

Now, instead of having to drag the deal over the finish line, your prospects will be the ones pushing to go to contract and get work started. With the seeds of curiosity planted, they're going to want to go to this new world you've described right away. The sooner, the better.

Creating strong interest in the prospect will eventually get you to where *they* ask about working together on a paid engagement. At that point you're ready to move to the next step: build everything together. I'll get to that in the next chapter. Before we get there I will show you a key tool that will broaden and deepen your capacity to communicate and connect at any step of the process.

Use Gravitas to Expand Your Comfort Zone

Ah, the vaunted "comfort zone." That term gets tossed around a lot when people are nervous about doing something they know they should. "I'm

---

*Whole Brain Thinking,® HBDI,® and Hermann Brain Dominance Instrument® are registered trademarks of Hermann Global, LLC.

not sure if I can—that's a little outside my comfort zone." What exactly are we picturing when we talk about this mythical place? For me it might be my broken-in Eames chair. Once a year or so we run out of Red Bulls in the fridge, and I end up taking an amazing afternoon nap in that chair. It's one comfortable zone.

Everyone has a comfort zone that defines the behaviors, emotions, and environments where they're most at ease. It's the state of operating without anxiety, sticking to a limited set of behaviors to deliver steady performance without a sense of risk. The truth is, there's nothing comfortable about the comfort zone at all. In a way, you're trapped there. You know what to do and you know you should do it, but you can't because it's outside your zone. Your comfort zone isn't a cozy lounge chair—it's a padded cell.

Everyone's comfort zone is different, depending on their life experiences, thinking preferences, degree of extroversion or introversion, and so on. One person might be perfectly happy delivering a talk to a large crowd but deeply uncomfortable with the intimacy of a face-to-face conversation. Another might only want to juggle spreadsheets at a desk and resist pretty much every other aspect of the job, especially if it involves talking to another human.

As a seller-expert, you advanced to where you are today primarily through developing and exercising your subject matter expertise. Maybe you picked up this book because this is the first time you've ever had to win your own clients. Then again, maybe not. Some experts who have been responsible for filling their own pipelines for *years* strenuously avoid certain BD activities until desperation forces their hand. Have you ever skipped a networking event out of social anxiety or spent the requisite five minutes in the corner at a conference mixer before skulking back to your hotel room? *I have a lot of emails to answer*, you say to yourself. The fact is, our jobs are always more than our primary expertise—our role might also call on us to make an important pitch, speak to large crowds, or even— *gasp*—talk to a human being with a C in their title.

We all have areas of the job that lie outside our comfort zone. To succeed in business development and become a genuine rainmaker, you need to navigate through some of these uncomfortable areas. For one thing, you may be expected to help drive business in areas outside your own area of expertise. Experts become experts because they're paranoid about not knowing all the answers. There are few ways to make one more uncomfortable than to drop them in unfamiliar waters. The impact of avoiding discomfort, however, is potentially enormous, in terms of both your company's success and your own personal and professional development.

An example: Joe gets promoted to partner at his firm because of his outstanding expertise in a specific area of insurance litigation. He knows this area better than anyone in the industry. As partner, he is tasked with expanding the firm's business in twenty-nine other practice areas, areas Joe knows relatively little about beyond the basics.

Uncomfortable, Joe spends most of his time expanding the litigation area only. He wants to rack up impressive results for the upcoming partner reviews and doesn't have the appetite to try anything new at this critical juncture. By resorting to behaviors he knows will be relatively successful, he reduces his risk, but he also learns nothing about the other practice areas. He rarely cross-promotes with other partners in different practices who have different subject matter expertise, and his impact on his firm—and his own career—never grows.

No one is an expert at everything. And, as Dr. Ottati's research showed us earlier in the chapter, more expertise can correlate with more closed-mindedness. Rainmakers learn to be comfortable in unfamiliar waters. One of the most effective ways to achieve this is through *gravitas*.

Creating Gravitas

Gravitas is a quality of substance, of depth of personality. It was one of the virtues expected of every citizen of ancient Rome, along with duty, dignity, and justice. You don't have to wear a toga to recognize it, though: Have you ever known someone with the capacity to dramatically change the course of a discussion or the energy in a room? Someone who asks the most revealing questions and makes bold, insightful observations that stick with you long after the conversation is over? Have you ever met the kind of person who adds value to every conversation, making connections between seemingly unrelated topics and helping the other person see problems they didn't even know they had?

This is gravitas at work. It's the ability to go *deep*, to have a dialogue with substance, add value on any topic, and encourage others to let you help them. Sometimes it's the ability to point out the obvious or, as Patrick Lencioni calls it, "getting naked." His book of the same title made an impact on me. He advises you to ask questions, even the "dumb" ones everyone else is too afraid to ask. Sometimes the most powerful questions are the ones that challenge the accepted or "obvious" answers.

You might not solve someone's problem completely, but you can bring in an expert, conduct an analysis, or take other actions to advance the BD process to the next step. Using the following gravitas model will be invaluable as you listen and learn and create curiosity.

The Gravitas Model

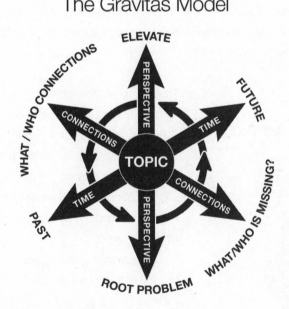

To cultivate gravitas your goal is to converse across one or all of the dimensions in this model. As you talk, think through each of these axes to draw unexpected connections and ask penetrating questions that open up new lines of thought. Let's explore each axis in detail.

Time Axis

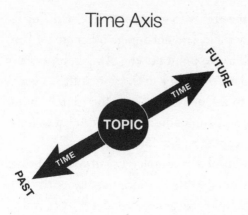

Time. Looking at the past provides input for current and future decisions: What's the most important experience you've had that got you to this role? Why do you think the prior leadership emphasized that area? What would you have done differently? What historical data do you think we could use to benchmark the potential improvements we're talking about?

Looking to the future, however, spurs creative thinking: What do you think this would look like if it were working well? What are your future plans for this? How would you say the process needs to change? What do you think the industry will be like in a year?

Perspective Axis

Perspective. Sometimes you can't see the forest for the trees. At the elevated end of the axis, you adopt a ten-thousand-foot view of the problem: How does your CEO see this fitting in with your overall strategy? What are the most important performance metrics, and how does this issue impact them?

Meanwhile generalities alone can often miss a critical detail. To unearth the root problem, get granular: What do you think your customers would say about your current onboarding process? Are you spending the right amount of money on this issue to make it work? What are the steps your employees really care about? How do you know if this works?

Connections Axis

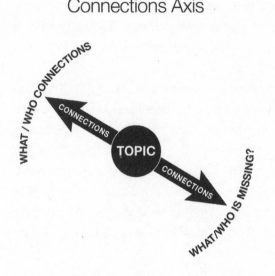

Connections. Now it's time to approach the subject holistically by drawing connections. On one end of this axis, you seek to discover the people and activities already associated with the topic: Who are the most critical people on your team? What skills do they have and need to improve? Who else is involved? What other projects are they working on, and what would they say about their priorities?

On the other end, you explore the connections that haven't yet been made: Who else should be on this project? Who else should weigh in on our direction? What other data would help? What facts are missing? What additional steps should be taken?

•

As you can see, none of these questions require specific subject matter expertise to be useful. Even better, notice how they would light up the pleasure center of the prospect's brain. These questions aren't facts and figures you can grab off a website—they dig into the client's own views and priorities. Even if the client doesn't mention it, you're helping them by asking questions. You're helping them see around corners.

Used systematically, the gravitas model broadens and deepens a conversation in a way that people will immediately notice. Often we're only comfortable conversing along one or two of these axes. As a result, our conversations end up in the same ruts. Once you learn to integrate the gravitas model into every interaction, you'll see how much richer and more rewarding all your communication can be.

This is one of my favorite tools. It gives me a rush to shine a light on my prospects and be helpful in my questions. The depth of questions shows my expertise and allows me to generate curiosity. For example, I recently had breakfast with the CEO of a healthcare company. Coincidentally, it turns out that we'd been neighbors for about a year when he first moved with his family to town.

We'd met in front of his home on one of Atlanta's rare snow days, and later that year we'd had a watershed relationship event. I was in the yard practicing softball with my two young daughters. Suddenly their jaws both dropped, their faces turned red, and they silently pointed. Standing up out of my catching stance, I turned to see my neighbor's sons, two and four, in the picture window right behind me, buck naked. Before I could react, it got worse. They started dancing. My friend and his wife got there about thirty seconds too late. By that time both girls had covered their eyes with their softball mitts.

(Patrick Lencioni, if you're reading this, this story might take "getting naked" to a new level.)

Fast-forward ten years, and we still keep in touch. When my friend reached out to me recently he'd realized his company needed help with their sales and account-management skills. We met for breakfast, relived the old stories, and got down to business. We talked for over an hour before we talked about any specific things my company could do. We dug into how they'd gotten where they are. Which things could be changed quickly and which would take time. Which processes were working and which were broken. Which quick wins he could create and which sacred cows couldn't be touched.

Then we dug into his strategic planning process, including where they are and what should happen next. I seeded curiosity by mentioning that we'd solved problems just like these with unique tools and that we'd measured specific behaviors in a way he could use with his teams. By the time our food was cleared and the coffee was refilled, he had a dozen questions for me. By letting him lead the conversation, I made it possible for him to prioritize the topics in an order that made sense to him. Meanwhile I could answer his questions within the context of his own strategic planning. We had a great meal, and now BIG is helping his company solve its problems.

Use the gravitas model to help engage with prospects and clients by adding substance, identifying opportunities, and moving the BD process to the next step. It's useful when you meet someone new, when you're preparing tough questions for clients, or just to inject life into any conversation that seems to be getting dull. Dull means we're not lighting up the other person's pleasure center!

Of course, if you're responsible for business development in other areas of a larger company, you can't rely on gravitas alone. Get a degree of familiarity with the major solutions your organization provides. White papers, one-pagers, lunch-and-learns, internal networking, staff meetings—even the company website can be a useful way to brush up on what the rest of your organization is doing. For your area of expertise you'll know the answer to nearly everything. For other areas, take the pressure off: you just need to know enough to get through a client's croissant and coffee.

Combining Gravitas and Give-to-Gets to Expand Outside Your Comfort Zone

Now it's time to pull two key concepts together. You've seen how powerful a give-to-get can be in securing a meeting. You now know how to use gravitas to add value in areas that are not your strong suit. Using these two techniques in parallel, you can swiftly grow business outside your comfort zone.

Once you've built trust with a prospect or client, all you need to do is listen and proactively suggest a valuable give-to-get that involves a subject matter expert in that area. Once everyone is in the same room, you can be the bridge between the client's issues, which you've taken the time to learn, and the expert's solutions. You are the key to success here. Gravitas will allow you to shape the conversation so it's valuable and, ideally, leads to another give-to-get or even a small project.

Whatever you do, don't let yourself off the hook for setting up and attending meetings outside your comfort zone—much of the leverage in growing a client relationship lies outside of it. People often tell me they're "too busy" to stretch this way. Perhaps they're busy with other client work—they can't spend time introducing someone new to "their" client. Even if you're fully booked, why can't you introduce others at your organization to a client? Don't you look even more important when you're booked? Won't the client value your effort even more if you're really busy?

Helping others when you're busy makes much more of an impact than doing it when you're actively looking for work.

Look at it this way: if you spend the next six months setting up powerful give-to-gets between your best clients and subject matter experts in other areas, what's the worst that could happen? You would dramatically grow your company's business. You would deepen your relationship with your clients by providing value, racing them along the path to raving fan. Your clients would start to see you as a strategic advisor instead of simply a service provider in one area. You'd begin learning about unfamiliar areas by participating in real conversations with those experts. And your company would start to see you as a rainmaker. Worth the risk?

Rainmakers don't just have a tiny storm cloud over their own head like Daffy Duck in an old cartoon; they make it rain across the organization and across their social networks. Rainmakers are ceaseless turbines of serendipity, creating value for everyone they know.

•

You can now see how a systematic, step-by-step approach is the most effective way to create a buying experience that works and delights your prospects. You know how to use an Opportunity List to ferry every opportunity on your plate along to fruition without letting anything slip through the cracks. You've learned how to tackle the first two steps in the process—listen and learn and create curiosity—and how to capitalize on even the most challenging interactions using the gravitas model.

Now it's time to finally understand the inner workings of that mysterious but pivotal event: *the close*.

CHAPTER 8

Closing the Book on Closing the Deal

• • •

"Great. So what would it look like to work together?"

There are few sweeter sentences for the hardworking seller-expert. You've now seen how much careful planning and deliberate effort goes into properly generating lots of leads, sifting through them for your ideal prospects, and gradually building those relationships from the ground up. These magic words are a clear signal that all the effort is about to turn into an actual, living project. Time to do your thing. Exciting, right? I never get tired of it.

To get here you *listened and learned*. You *created curiosity*. The prospect is ready—even eager—to work with you on solving their problem. The deal is about to close. This is the easy part, isn't it? After all, you've teed everything up beautifully with your new BD skills.

Can you believe that people get all the way to this point and still manage to let things go sideways? After all the botched approaches we've seen so far, you probably can.

I've had it happen to me. Early in my career, when I had just been promoted to managing consultant at Hewitt, I got a call. *The* call: a key client asking me for help. We did a lot of work for this client—one of the largest hospital chains in the country—but this would involve a new, strategically important area for them and for us. They wanted to build a talent development program for their COOs, including individual assessments, competency development, rotational programs, engagement monitoring, and training.

It was a big deal. I was excited. It was just the kind of project our talent and organizational development practice was actively seeking. Our communications practice might be involved too. I rallied the troops and led over a dozen internal meetings. At over a million dollars, the project got the attention of several practice leaders and our office manager. We invested at least a hundred people-hours in preparing the longest, most beautiful proposal you could imagine. We even broke Hewitt's graphic identity guidelines in the process of snazzing it up. I was a rebel!

I suddenly felt like all my relationship building had finally paid off. People were asking me how I'd surfaced such a big opportunity. I emailed the proposal in and tagged my calendar to check in with the decision maker in a few days.

Then, nothing. No one called me. I'd had a great relationship with the head of talent. Couldn't get him to call me back. I loved spending time with his boss, the head of HR. He wouldn't call me back either. Days went by, then weeks. Internally people asked me when we'd start work. Winning was a foregone conclusion with such an all-star team and such a killer proposal.

Weeks later I had the opportunity to talk to the head of HR at the end of a group call scheduled to discuss other projects. I asked him if I could call him when we were all finished. I hung up and dialed him directly, nervous, sweat rolling down my sides. Hesitantly, I asked him how things were looking with that big proposal, what the other people on his team thought. He sounded a little shocked, almost like he'd forgotten all about it. *Oh, that! Man, what were you guys smoking when you wrote that—a million dollars? We were thinking $30K, maybe. We just wanted some help designing it. We saw your proposal and figured you didn't understand what we wanted, so we just did it ourselves.*

I can't even remember what I said in response. I must have apologized and hung up. It's possible I'm still fuzzy from the concussion I got when my head hit the desk.

Building the proposal *without any input from the client* was exactly the wrong thing to do. It's a lesson I'll never forget. I thought I was saving them time. I thought I knew what they wanted. I thought I knew what they needed. I thought wrong, wasting everyone's time and harming our relationship with the client in the process. I had personally led the team right into this mess, one overly optimistic internal meeting after another. It's been twenty years and I *still* feel the pain.

Here's the good news: you don't have to repeat my mistake. This chapter will show you every aspect of getting deals across the goal line—how to close.

When a sales expert out of the "smile and a shoeshine" era tells you to close the deal, it usually involves holding out a pen and letting a dramatic silence compel the prospect to submit and sign on the dotted line. Closing like this inevitably takes a toll on the relationship you've so carefully cultivated up until this point. That may be fine if you're trying to sell a patch of Florida swampland, but for a seller-expert, *the relationship is paramount.*

Relationships *are* your business. Can you imagine a factory owner saying, "Well, we broke all the equipment doing it, but the important thing is we met this month's production quota." One deal will neither make you nor break you, but one well-placed raving fan relationship can transform your entire career. We want our clients to feel thrilled they're working with us, like they've won the lottery. Closing the deal with silence and a pen won't cut it.

And yet we *do* need a signature on that dotted line. So how do we get there in a way that is *authentic* and *balanced*, a way that breeds *confidence* in both sides and is fueled by our *desire* to overcome obstacles and help the client? A-B-C-D. These traits are the hallmarks of a rainmaker.

In the previous chapter I laid out the four stages of the selling process and explained the first two. You may have noticed that the stage after listen and learn and create curiosity isn't close the deal but *build everything together*. Although the ends may be the same, the means are very different.

Build Everything Together

Ask any seller-expert to name the most frustrating part of their job, and they'll probably say, "It takes too long to get to the signature." This is true for business development in nearly every industry and service. Even as it adds steps, the collaborative, incremental approach to closing the deal described here will go a long way toward collapsing the time it takes to get to yes and boosting your success rate through the roof.

This means working together with your prospect every step of the way. The closer you stay to your prospect, the faster you'll get to the close. Your goal is to get and keep the prospect actively engaged so they have just as much of an investment in a positive outcome as you do.

It's far too easy to derail a relationship when it's time to propose a paid project. Often we act like mind readers. In our haste to propose and close, we make all kinds of assumptions about the prospect's understanding of our offering, their level of commitment, their expectations about our service, and so on. We do our song and dance, get them curious, go away, and come back a week later with the specifics of what we'd like to do, drawn up in full. To our chagrin, we're sometimes met by surprise from their side, even confusion: *What were you smoking?*

We discover that, between the initial conversation and the creation of the proposal, a gap in understanding somehow opened up. Bringing the proposal to the table in its finished form like Moses with his stone tablets, we make that gap plain to all, to the acute discomfort of both prospect and seller and to the detriment of the relationship moving forward. Even if you get things back on track, that damage is done.

There's another way: to speed things up, slow down.

Michael Norton, Daniel Mochon, and Dan Ariely identified what they dub the "IKEA effect" after the Swedish furniture giant. This is one of my favorite findings ever: their study showed that people who assemble IKEA's flat-pack furniture themselves negotiate higher prices when selling that furniture to others than people who were given the furniture fully assembled. Folks couldn't help but attach more value to a MALM dresser or BILLY bookshelf they'd painstakingly put together with their very own hands.

It might seem logical to "make it easy for the client" by designing the approach or writing the proposal without their involvement. After all, busy people value convenience. Doing all the work, however, fails to build commitment on the client's end of things. Hand them a deal that's already constructed, and they can only add value in one way: by finding problems with it.

People value what they help create. When I suggest this approach, however, the counterargument I often hear is: "Our clients don't have time to help write our proposals. They would flip out if we asked them to do this."

I get it. But there's a way to make it easy for them while securing their input and buy-in. Here are four simple steps you can use.

Goals. Write draft goals for the project based on what you learned at the listen-and-learn stage. Let the client know these will only be 60 to 80 percent right and invite their edits. There's no way you'll understand all the nuance even if you've asked all the right questions. Be sure to incorporate your unique positioning here. If you're not unique, you're a commodity. Get buy-in on this before moving on. Without agreement here, you won't be sure if they want the quick-and-dirty or Cadillac approach. (Or, should I say, the $30K or million-dollar approach? The pain is real!)

Process. With goals agreed upon, you can map a process. Here's where you'll write down who does what and by when. Work backward, for example, from the board meeting where they'll need to show results. Incorporate the face-to-face meetings they already have with their team. Even incorporate the time it takes to finish the contract process with you. Build the plan, let them know it's a draft, and see what they think. Try to get this decided on before you move to the next step.

Team. Now that you've agreed on both the goals and the process, you'll be able to suggest a team, both on your side and theirs. Who will lead? Who will support? Who needs to chime in? Who could be a part of this to learn? The prior two steps will tell you if they need your A-team's attention or if you can get by with lower-level resources. Nail this down, as it could have a big impact on moving things forward.

Terms. With the prior three steps identified, you can build pricing and other terms. One benefit of doing things in this order is that you eliminate the tendency for clients to "jump to the pricing first" before understanding the underlying effort and value. Doing things in this order lets you establish and perfect the effort and value while positioning yourself as the best choice. That helps the client understand your pricing and helps you avoid unnecessary negotiation.

Now, let's address the fear that your clients won't have time to provide input on a draft proposal. In practice it's all about how you frame it. Make it clear to the client that this process will save them both time and energy as well as ensure they get exactly what they need—no more, no less. Instead of going back to your office and typing up a proposal that might be 50 percent right, you can walk them through four basic steps that require only slight editing on their side, quickly arrive on the same page, and formalize a proposal with hand-in-glove fit. One and done. My clients have seen great success doing it this way.

You might feel less comfortable suggesting this multistep process to your busiest and most important clients, but often these are the ones who most appreciate a good process for getting things done right the first time. Here's an example I experienced a few years ago. A strategic partner collaborated with us on a major opportunity—they would do some organizational design work while we handled the training and ongoing reinforcement. The client was a large public company with offices all over the world, and we both wanted to work together on this meaty, high-profile work.

The initial meeting with the client's C-suite went well, and though they'd made it clear repeatedly that time was of the essence and that their board was breathing down their necks, I suggested this process. We'd summarize the goals, process, and team in a one-pager, get their reaction, then price things out based on the scope and value.

On the ride to the airport my partner firm's leader turned to me: "There's no way they'll edit the one-pager. These guys are just too busy."

Busy or not, they edited it. Heavily, in fact. They told us later that they held multiple meetings considering every word—even the order of the bullet points. If the issue is important, if there's a reason to retain you, the client will engage. The CEO will make time, glad for the opportunity to get things sorted properly at the start instead of heavy course correction later on.

One last thought: this process also helps you deal with prospects who *don't* engage. When clients say, "send me a proposal on that," you don't know whether they're serious. It might take fifty people-hours to pull a team together, craft a plan, price it, and get it produced. In other businesses it can take two hundred hours or more. Are you going to put that kind of work into what might be a halfhearted whim on the part of the prospect? To gauge their true level of interest, ask the prospect to do something.

This is where the initial step of getting the prospect's input on the goals will help you immensely. It can be done in a simple email, with the goals written in bullets in the body of the email. Because you've already gone through the listen-and-learn stage, it'll only take you fifteen minutes. If they write back with edits, *great!* You know they're engaged. Thank them and start building out the process. If they go dark, never answering your email, *great!* You got out with fifteen minutes invested instead of two hundred hours.

Each time your prospect agrees to do something, think of it as another small close in a series of closes. In this way you will be *constantly closing*. The more times the prospect says yes to small requests, the more likely they will say yes to larger ones.

Building everything together ensures there will be no surprises and your prospect will help push things forward. Everyone wins.

Where and How to Build Everything Together

You can build everything together right from the beginning. For the introductory meeting create the agenda together. Ask the client to invite other key stakeholders. By inviting them, your prospect is implicitly endorsing you. Likewise, a give-to-get works best when you work together with your prospect to develop the goals and objectives.

In this way, by the time you're ready to tackle the small and big projects, the prospect will already feel more like a collaborator, less like a customer being pressured to buy something. Whenever possible, walk down the path hand in hand with the client.

For simpler engagements you can walk through the four steps on a phone call or in person. For more complicated ones do it in person in front of a whiteboard over the course of a few hours. Or space four conversations out over a series of calls. We've even seen clients implement the framework with online meeting software, collaborating with a client on the other side of the world by writing the answers to the four areas on WebEx, with the client editing as the seller-expert types.

Hybrids exist too. One of our clients uses a thirty-minute, in-person meeting to get agreement on the goals and to collect high-level input on the process and team. Then they go back to their shop and use Gantt software to fill in the details, reviewing them with the client online as they explain their logic, with both teams jointly agreeing to any changes. A verbal discussion of fees follows, and it's all over. Everyone is excited and ready to move forward.

One professional implemented this process after going through our training. A consultant who works with finance executives, he was used to facing endless pressure on pricing. In one week he built everything together with a key client at a Fortune 50 company and agreed to meet him at 7 a.m. in his office to sign the contract.

The consultant walked into his client's office, coffee in hand, ready for a final rejection. *There's no way this could work out*, he thought. After all, this was a seven-figure contract with a marquee client, and it had happened in a *week*. Instead of an objection, his client blurted out, "Mike, this is the best contract I've ever read!" Mike replied, "You *should* love it—you wrote half of it!"

Happy client. Happy consultant. Happy me.

So back to the prospect's question, the one that began the chapter. "Great. So what would it look like to work together?" Your answer is: "Let's look at that together. I've got a process that will save you time and build the perfect plan. Here's what I'd suggest . . ."

Resolving Objections

Obstacles can show up at any time during the BD cycle. The best professionals are proactive about them. They anticipate problems and do what they can to remove or overcome them before the problems bog down the process, sapping it of its hard-won momentum.

Rainmakers focus on solutions, not obstacles. With experience they find that most hurdles that come up during the closing process look bigger or harder than they really are. A few basic problem-solving approaches are sufficient to get you through just about anything.

As you work through building the deal with your client, look for obstacles in your path by asking the prospect for input. This overcomes objections before they occur. Use Marshall Goldsmith's concept of "Feed-Forward": *What's the number-one thing we should do in the next step to be successful?* It's rare that anyone asks this question, so it may take a little thought on the prospect's part before they realize that something's been bugging them or that there's a problem lurking right around the corner. Remember: listen and learn. Zip your lip and give them time to think it through.

Let's say an objection pops up you didn't foresee. No problem—it happens. But there are two things to keep in mind when it does. The first is to have the right mindset. The last thing you want to think is, *Oh no, not someone bringing up our pricing again.* Your prospect will sense that frustration right away. Instead, embrace their objections. *Learn to love them.* Thank the prospect for bringing up the issue. If the prospect didn't want to work with you or didn't value your relationship in some way, they'd avoid the conversation. They'd hide. If they're bringing up an objection, there's at least part of them that wants to find a way to work with you, now or in the future. Thank them for bringing an issue up. Make this *easy.*

The second thing to keep in mind? Surprise, surprise: it's a process . . .

Resolving Objections Process

As you develop the capacity to anticipate and resolve objections during the closing process, you're going to start noticing some patterns. Although some objections will be totally unprecedented one-offs requiring brainstorming, the vast majority will become familiar to you. Buyers of a particular service in a particular industry tend to share many of the same concerns.

Instead of reinventing the wheel each time, get the **Resolving Objections List** worksheet or put four columns on a blank page: Objection,

Question, Underlying Issues, and Resolutions. From now on, when you resolve a new objection, add the particulars to this list. The most important thing is the question you ask in response. Over time you'll build up a useful array of questions and resolutions to common objections.

Here's how it works in practice. Let's say the prospect points out that the pricing "seems high." Consulting your list, you see that this objection's corresponding question is, "Can you tell me what you were expecting in terms of the cost?" Responding to an objection with a question does several things: it flips you from feeling defensive to problem solving, gives you time to think, and, importantly, shows the prospect what it's like to work with you.

The underlying issue and the resolution both depend on thinking preferences, so you'll want to divide each one in four to be prepared to come at this from the right angle. If, for example, the prospect replies in an analytical way—"Your fees are 13.2 percent higher than the next competitor's"—you'll have an appropriately analytical response in the fourth column: "How about we take a look at everything to see if we can find a way to change our process and team so that our fees can be where you need them to be? What's your target cost?"

Or the prospect may reply with an experimental preference: "I just don't see the value for this high of a price and how it would be a priority for our strategy." Consulting the resolution column, you might reply, "What price would make this a priority? Or is there an element of this project that would be a priority?"

Often prospects are reluctant to share their true objection. It's hard to be the bringer of bad news. Or perhaps what's obvious to them isn't obvious to you. For whatever reason, they won't fully explain themselves. As we can see from the price objection above, the same stated obstacle—"Your price seems high"—can have different underlying meanings, from a value issue to a fair price that the prospect is afraid to take to their boss because of a faulty apples-and-oranges comparison. Ask questions. Diagnose the true problem rather than wasting time addressing symptoms.

Think of the power of having a well-developed Resolving Objections List shared across your whole team. This has been a deal-closing magic wand for many of the teams we've trained as well as a vital onboarding tool for new hires.

Asking for the Advance

I'm convinced this is the number-one way to speed up your process. And as a recovering actuary, I don't rank things lightly. Number one! There can be only one number one.

We've all heard so-called research quoting the exact number of interactions a sales rep needs with a prospect to close a deal. The idea of taking these numbers as religious truths, as many sellers do, cracks me up. The number of calls necessary will vary depending on the skill of the expert, industry, strength of the endorsement going in, intensity of the need, budgetary authority of the initial person you meet, and many other factors.

That said, these figures do help clarify things in one sense. I've heard numbers like five, seven, even fourteen. Yet the typical salesperson makes two. Whatever the "right" number is, it isn't two.

Still, anything we can do to speed up the process helps. By always asking for the next step and collecting small commitments, we accelerate.

In a groundbreaking study on commitment, Jonathan Freedman and Scott Fraser at Stanford found that people were much more likely to say yes to large commitments after they had agreed to small commitments directionally aligned with the bigger ones. In a related vein, Anthony Greenwald and his research team at Ohio State found that people were more likely to follow up on things they told others they planned to do.

Method matters. As mentioned, researchers found that a face-to-face ask was *thirty-four times* more likely to get a yes than an email one. (Anecdotally, asking over the phone seems to deliver results closer to face-to-face than to email.)

Little asks make a big difference. Here's an example from my own business: A while ago we were having an off quarter. Looking back, there were lots of reasons for it, but as I reviewed my leading and lagging indicators, I got mad: *How did this happen?* We already had a great client base and thousands of raving fans. Somehow I'd let my flywheel slow down.

Thinking things through, I realized I needed a new focus. I'd never measured asks for the advance before. Why not? After all, they were completely under my control. They looked like the perfect leading indicator to get my flywheel spinning again.

I estimated that I had asked for the advance six times that week. I was dead set on beating that going forward. In my weekly planning session I thought of a dozen or more ways I could ask for the next step, always framing it in the best interests of my clients. In some I'd ask for something specific, like getting the statement of work signed or to setting a meeting to build everything together. In others I asked more vaguely, like ending a delivery-based email with, "What else can we do to be helpful?"

The results blew me away. I couldn't believe how many opportunities I'd been letting pass me by without an ask. The next week I had twenty-six, and twenty-seven the week after that. Then fourteen, thirty-one, twenty, twenty-nine. I could *feel* the flywheel starting to move again.

Then we had a significant article published on a Monday night. I decided to take the time to email the article around to clients and prospects with a customized note for each pointing out the areas where they would get value. At the end of each note I asked for a different next step.

It was a lot of hard work, but it felt great. At the end of that Wednesday I messaged my COO, Darla, with exciting news. I'd hit thirty-two asks for the week! My mind was numb. Time to kick back and celebrate the win. As I was heading away from my desk Darla messaged back: "Why don't you go for fifty? It's only Wednesday—you have two more days to think about this."

Fifty? Didn't she understand how hard this was? Didn't she see the sweat I'd put into every single outreach?

That night, while talking it over with my wife, Becky, I decided that I *would* go for fifty. And as usual, Darla gave me sage advice, even though it wasn't what I wanted to hear at first. Darla was right. I could do this. (By the way, if you don't have someone like Darla in your life, start looking.)

As 5 p.m. rolled around that Friday, I sent my fifty-first ask. Like a first-time marathoner falling across the finish line, I finished the week exhausted but happy.

Here's the best part. Within two months our pipeline had more than doubled. My new leading indicator, ask for the advance, turned out to correlate beautifully with my most important lagging indicators. Opportunities started coming out of the woodwork.

Asks can take many forms. Making them work means (1) always framing the ask in terms of value to the prospect and (2) using language that will resonate with them.

Here are some examples for a wide range of scenarios:

+ Should we set up a call to plan the kickoff meeting?
+ How about I work with the team to draw up three options for how that could work? We find that the path reveals itself quickly when our clients see three broad-ranging options.
+ Have you had a chance to review the proposal? We'll need the signature by Friday to book our flights cost-effectively.
+ What should we do together next?

The idea is to slice the process up into small pieces and tackle each one on its own. Every advance is a win. By proactively asking for it, you're speeding things up.

One of the biggest things our clients hear from their clients is the desire for them to be *proactive*. Asking for the advance helps you and, done properly, your clients as well.

The last stage of the buying process is to gain approval. As you'll see, when you're in the habit of asking for the advance every step of the way, this once-looming hurdle will suddenly feel like just another ask, not all that different from any of the others.

The Seven Pricing Principles

When it comes to objections during the closing process, price is usually obstacle numero uno. After all, this is *business*.

Before we talk about money, let's talk about talking about money. Most people avoid the topic. Maybe they were taught that discussing money isn't polite. Maybe, deep down, they're afraid they're not worth their rates. Maybe they had a bad experience talking about money in the past. If this is you, get over it. Right now. Money talk is a part of any healthy client relationship.

Mike Duffy is one of the leading experts at talking about money with clients. He's head of pricing at King & Spalding, one of the top global law firms. One of the main measures of the success of a law firm is profitable growth. King & Spalding has rocketed up the charts in the last decade in growth, breaking the $1 billion revenue barrier in 2015. Mike's internal coaching and external client discussions are a big part of that success. He was also a longtime partner at EY, one of the largest accounting and advisory firms. Between top-tier accounting and law, he's coached partners on this subject for over twenty years.

"Many professionals are great advocates for their clients, but not for themselves or their firm," Mike told me. "Ignoring or postponing discussions of money harms the relationship. The great ones pair the negotiation of fees with a discussion of the value being provided, usually starting with the value. These conversations are *tremendously* important to the relationship and, when done well, deepen and strengthen it, with each side getting the best result."

Mike added, "I often conduct loss debriefs with clients for matters we don't win. Internally it's easy to say we lost on price. But, in my experience, 95 percent of the time we lose, it has very little to do with price. Focus on your value and why they should hire you besides price, but bring up pricing early and often. Make it easy for the prospect to see that you're worth what you charge, easy to work with, and easy to hire. Your competition is likely avoiding talking about money. If you make that part of the conversation easy, it can be a tremendous advantage, a meaningful differentiator."

More often than not, objections around price have less to do with dollars and cents and more with psychology: the *way* both sides talk about money. In the end your prospect wants to feel good about what they're paying for. They want it to be the "right" amount.

Maria Cronley of Miami University collaborated with four other researchers at the Universities of Rochester and Cincinnati. They found that people rely heavily on price as a predictor of quality *and* that the relationship strongly impacts the purchasing decision. According to the study, price matters. It matters more for complex purchases, when the purchase is important to the client and when time is of the essence. The more these three elements are elevated, the more pricing matters.

Does this sound like what you do?

The following seven pricing principles will help you arrive at the right price for both you and your clients.

Embrace Pricing and Don't Self-Negotiate

Rainmakers don't flinch at a pricing discussion. They think of money as the quantification of the scope of work to be performed and the level of the team that's needed, that's all. It represents the client's perception of the value they will receive from that work.

Why is this important? Your goal is to make the conversation about money as easy, effortless, and enjoyable as the rest of the buying process. Shed the heaviness of the dreaded money discussion. Make jokes, lighten the tone. Research has shown that people even negotiate less when a joke is made to kick off a financial conversation. Think of being helpful to the client—they might be dreading the money conversation too. If you make it easy—even *fun*—to talk money, they'll take your lead. Remember: it's just another incremental step in being of service and building a relationship.

When should you bring up pricing? Early and often. Start with broad ranges if necessary. That way you won't box yourself in. If you're too expensive, *great!* Find out early and refer the prospect to someone cheaper. You've just saved a lot of time and effort for yourself and for your client. If you're a pricing fit, *great!* Fine-tune your pricing as you learn more. The worst-case scenario only occurs if you leave pricing to the end, wasting a massive amount of time on both sides only to end up frustrating everyone.

Resist the urge to self-negotiate. Don't second-guess your pricing. I was training a group of managers from a global consulting firm when some real-life self-negotiation intruded on this very portion of the training. As we went on a break a senior leader shouted, "Wait, everyone! I just got this email from one of our consultants. It says, 'I think we should lower our price on this project from $75,000 to $49,000 but do the same work. There's *no way* she can pay $75,000.'" He added, "I *guarantee* we haven't asked the client if she can pay $75,000. We're self-negotiating!"

(He then jokingly asked if I thought there would be a market for a training class on self-negotiation. He figured they were so good at it that they could teach others.)

Here's how to avoid this: Begin with the prospect. If it's true, position your fees early by letting the prospect know that "we're sometimes a little higher than others, but we're worth it." This seeds the perception that your higher fees correlate with the value you will deliver. Then use these words: "About how much are you looking to spend?" Don't ask what their budget is. Budgeting processes are fraught with pain—there's no reason to bring that into the conversation. Also, they may not have a budget yet or might be able to get more. Start with what they're looking to spend. Budgets will come up if needed after that, and in the right context.

If the client's answer is higher than you expected, tell them you'll likely cost less. They'll be pleased. You can offer additional services that would make up the difference and add a lot more value if they're interested. If the answer is lower than you expected, reset their expectations by explaining what they can expect to get for the lower amount. Show them in concrete terms the impact before committing to that number.

Anchor on Value

Here's a simple demonstration of anchoring: pick a number, anything, like five, six, or seven. Got one? Great!

I've done this in hundreds of groups. Nearly every time, when I ask someone what they chose, it's six or seven, occasionally eight for the rebels. It's rarely above ten. It's never something like 1,569,234. Despite the completely open-ended directive to pick any number in the universe, 99 percent cluster around the numbers I mentioned. That's the power of anchoring. Once a number is in someone's mind, every subsequent number they think of will relate to that anchor.

Anchoring is, well, anchored in science. It's one of the most powerful behavioral science principles, and it impacts thought processes ranging from decision making to negotiation.

So what number is most helpful for your prospect to anchor on? The *value* of your services. We can get there, for example, by asking the prospect how far they think we can move the needle through our work with them. Let them come up with the assumptions themselves. For my business, if we can train people and increase revenue 1 percent for a $1 billion company, that's a $10 million value. All of a sudden our fees don't seem very high by comparison. How could you quantify your value?

If you discuss some work that you have calculated will save the client $500,000 a year, anchor on that number. Every reference to money in the pricing discussion should be placed next to it:

+ You'll only need to spend X to save $500,000.
+ You'll recover your investment X times over the next five years.
+ You'll save X times more than you'll spend in the first year alone.

Don't rely on your prospects to calculate your value. Some will, but most won't. It's easier for them to compare your pricing to other options. If you don't give the prospect a relevant number to anchor on, they could be using anything to judge it, regardless of how poor the comparison. Anchoring establishes the intrinsic value of the service at the outset. Whether you charge $50,000 for an analysis (1 percent of the first year's savings) or $500,000 for a full implementation (you'll save ten times more than you'll spend in the first year alone), there is a clear basis for your numbers. Once you've established a logical value anchor, your fees will suddenly seem much more reasonable.

Avoid discounting. If you reduce your fees during the negotiation, it suggests that the initial price was arbitrary, leaving the prospect wondering how much more of the fee is open to discussion. That's why I strongly encourage standard pricing across all clients. We switched to this model years ago, and although it was hard at the beginning, it has been fantastic since making the transition. Those clients who have adopted it on our advice agree.

It helps to know that, according to research by Malia Mason and her team at Columbia, specific prices get much less pushback than rounded ones. For services, people typically calculate their price *and then round it to a general number*, which, ironically, drives prospects to negotiate harder because a round number seems arbitrary. Stick to the more accurate original numbers, and your clients will try to negotiate them less often.

What Costs More Is Worth More

Because it's so difficult to estimate the value of something you haven't experienced yet, your brain uses a heuristic, a shortcut: what costs more is worth more. Because our brains find this typically true, we use it as our starting point.

You go ring shopping with your fiancée. One stone is $3,500. The other is $7,000.

Now, before you do any research: Which one will you assume is higher quality? Be honest. That's everyone's starting point.

We like to think that we're completely rational when it comes to spending money, but when making large purchases under stress, instinct plays an enormous role.

Services are even more difficult to gauge than products, which might have detailed specifications at the ready. Most people will say the price of a service comes down to the provider's background, experience, qualifications, training, notable successes and failures, relationships with clients, references, whether they've worked together before, and various other factors. Intangibles, mostly. Regardless of what you point at, the price of a service is still very much a crafted thing. Although a diamond ring's price is at least in some way dependent on the price of the diamond and the gold, the price of a service is mostly an invention. And how to compare two services? It's even more difficult than simple products. This leaves buyers with one concrete data point: price.

This doesn't mean clients want to pay more or that they always will, but there is no question that a higher price creates the perception of greater value. If Consultant A charges $675 an hour and Consultant B charges $200 an hour, the prospect will start from the assumption that Consultant

A has more experience, knowledge, skills, and so on. The pricing disparity alone will convey to the prospect that Consultant A delivers more value. Even if the prospect decides to move forward with Consultant B, there will always be some curiosity about what the more expensive provider might have delivered.

Of course, the cheaper service might be a lot better—but it will take other proof points to overcome the bias.

This is only one of the messy, subjective aspects of pricing that make it such a headache for seller-experts and prospects alike.

Remember this: the positioning you learned in Chapter 3 is key. If you're seen as unique in the mind of the client, you can command a premium. If you're seen as an indistinguishable commodity, you're in a race to the bottom.

Make Everything Cost Something

The price should reflect every significant value change as you build everything together. Remember: money is simply a quantification of the scope, the team, and the client's perception of your value. If the scope changes, the price *must* change. Otherwise you end up minimizing your perceived value, even damaging the relationship.

Let's say your client calls up: "Jim, I love the project we've been talking about. Your price is 7 percent higher than another group. Can you do the same work for 7 percent less?" You acquiesce and hang up, thinking you pleased Jim. Did you? He hangs up the phone and starts thinking, *Jim was going to charge me 7 percent more than he had to! Maybe I should have asked for 10!*

When you don't ask for something in return, you create more problems for yourself. The client's already figuring out how to ask for more later, to see where your bottom price is. *You're training them to ask for a discount next time.* Not good.

Pricing changes should only be given for something in return. This can mean lower pricing for more volume, faster payment, or a longer term. But intangibles (below) are also good ways to provide the discount needed to win and seed the client for future growth. Here are some examples of intangibles you can ask for in return for a concession to help the client:

+ Set up introductory meetings to leadership, other lines of business, specific individuals, industry groups, and so on.
+ Craft mutual press releases.
+ Agree to the client giving a testimonial on your website or LinkedIn.

You can change the entire conversation by asking for tangible or intangible concessions in return for client request. Like so:

"Jim, I love the project we've been talking about. Your price is 7 percent higher than another group. Can you do the same work for 7 percent less?"

"Phil, I'd love to do this project too, but we're flat-out busy right now, and it would be difficult for me to reduce our pricing without sacrificing quality by using a different team who doesn't know your industry as well. We did anticipate that you might ask for a discount with the price of oil where it is. What if we did the project for 3 percent less in return for two things: First, streamline by having your team handle step 2a, saving us some time. Second, if the project goes as well as we all think it will, take me to lunch with your CFO to celebrate. There's value to us in meeting her because she could potentially provide introductions to the other lines of business we're perfectly suited to work for. We'll make you look like a hero, of course. What do you think of that trade? Easy for you, valuable to us, and it'll save you 3 percent."

This conversation is completely different. When Phil agrees and hangs up, he'll feel like he's working with someone who's quite good—and quite busy!—and that he's made a deal that's great for everyone. Everything needs to cost something. When it does, things make sense.

Build Everything Together, Looking for Mutual Wins

As you work with your client, look for trades that help both sides. The best trades are the ones that are easier for you to give and of tremendous value to the client.

Keep asking questions. Keep checking to see if your trades resonate with the client. If something changes with the goals, process, or team, make the appropriate change in pricing, clearly labeling and identifying that you're changing X price because Y changed. We find labeling trades helps the other side clearly see what is changing.

The key to this principle is *mindset*. Don't focus on the mindset of a hostage negotiator; instead, just be a proactive, helpful problem solver. You're displaying the mindset of what it will be like to work together after you gain approval.

Make money conversations easy.

Make Buying More a Better Deal

Buying more should always be the smart choice. Insurance is cheaper if you bundle your life, car, and homeowner's insurance. Cable is cheaper if you bundle internet, TV, and VOIP phone. Simply *buying more of the same thing* fits this mental shortcut too. The large box of Cheerios is cheaper per Cheerio. Costco has made an entire business model out of bulk purchasing: *Look! I got a great deal on this pack of fifty toothbrushes!* Larger purchases save you money per item. It just makes sense.

Bundling services can help you increase the size of your deals. One way is to provide three options: the classic good, better, and best framework. This can show the prospect the value of spending more with you. It helps you (fewer buying processes to manage), and it helps them (a better deal). Win-win. And proactively helpful.

Be Willing to Concede One Last Thing

One last thing about that one last thing that always comes up at the end of a negotiation. Plan ahead for this final request by deciding in advance— instead of in the heat of the moment—on a concession you would be willing to make in order to close the deal and a request you might make in return. This curious phenomenon is so common, it's worthy of its own principle.

Here's the deal: the final concession should *never* be on price. No last-minute discounts—what could send a worse message? Instead, think of another valuable, nonmonetary concession you could make that would give the prospect that small but satisfying victory at the close of the deal. Have it in your back pocket for when you hear the magic words, "one last thing."

This concession might be the location where the work will be performed, an acceleration of the delivery schedule, an increase in the frequency of project reviews, or any other modification that would be valuable to your prospect. If the client *does* ask for a price reduction, think of one last small request you can ask of them. Make it easy, but again, everything has to cost something. No freebies, even at the end.

Be ready to handle that "one last thing." It's a psychological hurdle to close the deal and begin the project on a good note. It helps stave off buyer's remorse and gives the new client the reassuring sense that they've selected the right option at the right price.

●

Now you understand how to build everything together, resolving objections as you ask for the advances until you're ready to close at a price that both sides can happily agree on. Whew! There's a whole chapter in that sentence. Here's the main point: if you do the things in this chapter, gaining approval is easy. Do it the right way, and *your client* will be asking you to send the contract over.

If you're having trouble gaining approval, you're farther along than your client is. Circle back to them to see where you're really at, then start over from there.

For a seller-expert the deal—any deal—always comes second to the relationship. Developing client relationships to the fullest will deliver far more value over time than any pricing option or positioning statement. In the next chapter we're going to learn how to turn every new client into a raving fan.

CHAPTER 9

Strategic Client Planning for
Long-Term Success

• • •

NOW IT'S TIME to zoom in on planning for client interactions. Your success depends on two areas: individual client meetings and targeted client planning. Short term and long term—next week and next year. These two frames are where the action happens and your future is shaped.

First, meetings. People make decisions in meetings. Meetings make; they create movement. Emails and voicemails have their place, but big decisions happen when people actually talk to each other. The big advances happen in conversation.

How you plan for these client meetings determines how you'll perform in them. Like an athlete on the field, you'll play how you practice. If you wing your preparation, you'll get haphazard results. I'll show you how to prepare for client meetings that generate engagement and energy and end with concrete next steps.

Second, client planning. Good BD habits will improve results for you across the board, but ultimately your success is built on one client and one relationship at a time. Planning and preparation are just as important—and just as frequently neglected—at this level as they are at the meeting level.

Client planning is tough. A "client relationship" may consist of many crisscrossing lines going between multiple people on your team and multiple people at a client organization. Whatever it looks like, that connection between client and provider is either working or it's not, either shrinking or growing. How do you ensure that each client relationship achieves its fullest potential?

The obstacles are significant. Remember how powerful anchoring is? The client is anchored on what they have bought from you in the past, not what they should hire you for in the future. Meanwhile you and your team tend to assume that the client will call you when you're needed, probably using telepathy to know why they should be calling you. "Do great work, and the phone will ring" might work sometimes, but it won't grow the relationship as quickly as you'd like.

Many professionals let each client relationship wander in the woods— no compass, slow progress. Client planning is the map. It pinpoints your current position, the destination you seek, and the path from here to there.

Preparing for Dynamic Meetings

I spent years coaching my two daughters' softball team, the Red Hot Chili Peppers. We had fun, and even though we didn't always win the league title, we always improved.

Early on, I'd let little things slide. Take fielding a grounder. For young kids just learning the game, the ball isn't going very fast, and a fielder with poor form can still make a play 80 percent of the time. They can get away with having their feet together, standing straight up, slowly bending over at the waist, and still intercepting the ball rolling at a snail's pace toward their legs. During practice I'd consider correcting this. Then I'd think, *Hey, they're just learning,* and I'd let it go. (The problem was the other 20 percent of the time when the ball takes an odd bounce or comes in a hair lower than expected. If the girls weren't in a sound athletic position then, they'd miss the ball.)

In one of my first real games as a coach, things went south. We were on defense, ahead by one in the final frame, bases loaded. We just needed one out to win. The other team hit a slow roller to second. *Easy out,* I thought. Then, demonstrating the same poor form she'd diligently cemented in our practices, my second baseman casually leaned over at the waist. The ball took a small hop, using all its little energy left to *boink!* right a few inches and barely roll a few feet further. Two runs scored. We lost. Wins and losses didn't matter to me, but they did to the girls. They felt dejected, especially the poor player on second base. It wasn't her fault—it was mine.

We played how we practiced.

Things changed after that. I focused on teaching proper fundamentals. I would model what I wanted for every skill—fielding, throwing, batting. I made up little rhyming phrases to help the kids remember, like *lock, load, explode!* for the proper approach to hitting. We even had the girls critique each other's fielding stances and keep score of correct versus incorrect form. We made a game out of every skill, rotating stations in practice. My favorite was our annual field day, where we measured and scored the girls on every fundamental skill and gave prizes to the girls who amassed the most points. They couldn't control how big or strong they were, but they could control their practice of the fundamentals.

This sweat-the-details approach worked. Not only did we consistently improve the most, but the girls also had a blast. Some of the girls are in college now, and when I see them they'll still recite our cheer:

We are the Chili Peppers!

We are the Chili Peppers!

We are the Chili Peppers!

And we're HOT! HOT! HOT!

When it comes to client meetings, you'll play how you practice. Many trainees tell me they don't prep at all—they just figure something out with their colleagues in the cab. When our clients say they do take the time to plan—before they go through our training—they unknowingly plan to talk the entire time. This means they'll spend hours building a PowerPoint anchored on the last similar meeting they had. Then they'll spend the remaining time practicing what they'll say, whisper-narrating one boring graph after another. "Here are Q4 results after implementing this new methodology . . ."

We're going for a birthday experience for the client. When was the last time you asked for someone to narrate a thirty-slide PowerPoint for your birthday?

Instead, let's prepare to create a vibrant, interactive meeting, one that drives to a meaningful goal everyone is excited about. Because we'll play like we practice, let's practice the way we want the meeting to go: clearly defined goal, interactivity, and ready for anything.

Here are six steps for planning a client meeting with clear direction and memorable impact.

Goal. Write down your one goal for the meeting. Delivery meetings might have a dozen goals, but BD meetings should have only one. What's the reasonable next step for this client relationship? Having a goal in mind will give you the flexibility to run a dynamic meeting. Your conversation can ebb and flow naturally as you always—gently—steer to the goal. An example of a goal might be getting the prospect excited about pitching our mutually crafted give-to-get idea to their boss.

Frame. The frame is how you'll explain the meeting goal to the client right at the beginning in a way that makes the benefit clear to them. Have you ever been in a meeting without understanding why you're there or what the purpose is? Maddening, isn't it? You can't even focus on what's being said because you're so focused on solving the mystery. *Why am I here? What are we trying to accomplish?* Professionals rarely make this mistake in delivery meetings, but it happens frequently in business development. Instead, get the prospect's buy-in from the start. If they know what everyone is trying to accomplish, they will help you get there. You're a *team* trying to accomplish something, even in business development. No one wants to waste time in an unproductive meeting. When the prospect buys into your frame at the beginning, *great!* If they want to tweak it, *great!* Either way, you need clear direction. If your goal is to get sign-off on a give-to-get, your frame might be: "Today I thought we'd cover ways we could invest in our relationship. The team has developed three two-hour workshops we could lead for you on our dime. We're really excited about them. I consider the ideas 60 percent right at best, and we need your input. For the first twenty minutes we'd love to run all three concepts past you for your input. For the last ten minutes we could get your high-level thoughts on next steps, then finish by scheduling the next call to plan out where, when, and who should be involved. How does that sound?"

Changes. BD meetings vary in duration more than delivery meetings do. Sometimes they're cut short: "Sorry I'm fifteen minutes late. I also have to jump off five minutes early for my next call. What can we cover in ten?" Sometimes they go long: "This is really interesting. Mind if I pull in Jeff and Craig?" Think through what you'll do if you only get half the time you expect, as well as if the time doubles. This is a simple but effective way to be ready for any time changes. Also, what if you get changes in attendees? Think through how you will handle that. When a client throws you a curve ball—the ol' Uncle Charlie—you'll be ready.

Questions. You'll play how you practice. If you practice delivering a monologue, you'll deliver a monologue, and your client will fall asleep before intermission. Instead, practice asking great questions. Review the gravitas model, and think through the perfect questions to ask, ones that will tell you something you don't already know about your client's needs as well as demonstrating your experience and expertise. Get that client's pleasure center lighting up! Also, think through questions they might ask you; using your work on objections will help you here. Be ready for any question they might ask, and think about what questions you can ask in response, unearthing the true objection for anything they might bring up. Practicing your questions and the questions they might ask you will prepare you for a dynamic, interactive discussion.

Personalization. Run through each of the four thinking preferences and ask: How can I incorporate the language of this quadrant? Think of this as an audit of your prepared approach. Have you pulled in new ideas and strategies? How about analytics? Stories? Processes and next steps? Is there anything you can bring up to show or build more commonality? Think through the audience and the preferences you think they have. Lean toward those while making sure you cover all four.

Next, add any other personalization you can. Do you have mutual friends you can mention? Any funny stories to bring up? Do anything you can to make your business meeting enjoyable and fun. Science shows that not only do we enjoy meetings in which we laugh, but we actually *accomplish more* in them too.

Agenda and materials. Sadly, most people *start* here, polishing up that gorgeous PowerPoint. In many cases you don't even need one. We avoid them at all costs. What materials are truly needed to reach your goal? Once you've thought through the prior steps, this one will become clear.

Our clients probably use the **Dynamic Meeting Prep** worksheet more than any other we provide. Go get it. Meetings happen often, and effective meetings create efficient movement. Plan for them wisely, and you'll always make progress.

Strategically Strengthening Existing Relationships

The principles that drive meeting-level success apply to longer-term client growth, but with a twist. Sure, having a goal matters, but the execution needed to get there is more complex. The time frame for a BD meeting might be thirty minutes, maybe an hour. The time frame for client planning is a year or longer. This calls for more up-front planning work and a more detailed execution plan. The scope isn't a single meeting but an entire relationship.

You might be operating two levels below the person you really want to know at the client's company. The client might be purchasing certain things from your organization but not using your services in an optimal way. You might be providing a service in one business unit but not in others that could be helped by what you do. How do you strengthen relationships with the people you know and expand into new areas while you're at it?

This is where client planning comes in. For big opportunities it's critical to map out a long-term plan for a new client the moment you kick off the first paid engagement. This gives a clear sense of the potential lifetime value of that client, clarifying all subsequent decisions about prioritizing efforts and intelligently investing time.

Or, for existing clients who perfectly fit your targeting criteria, perform a high-level strategic analysis once a year. This client plan lets you see what you need to do—and, critically, not do—to accelerate growth in that client relationship. From there you can drill down to the details in your day-to-day work so that your to-dos are aligned with your BD strategy.

This is important if you're a solo practitioner because it helps you get unstuck. It's even more important if you're on a large team. Going through this process will get your entire team aligned, helping each person understand the overarching growth strategy *and* their role within it.

From the client side we face the anchoring effect we've already discussed. Once a client hires you for a specific service, they tend to think of you primarily for that service.

From our side we face two biases. A study by researchers Richard Robins and Jennifer Beer of UC Davis and UC Berkeley found that we humans generally assess our current position in life as better than it really is. In my work, when I'm working with clients on client planning, I see them fall prey to this perspective as well. *We already do _____ for this client, and that's great. Why rock the boat and try to get more?* But I think the second bias is even more powerful. As we've talked about several times, seller-experts have the bias toward doing the work, not growing.

So from the client side, they keep marching along, busy as can be, largely thinking of us for what we've been hired for in the past. And from our side, we keep thinking things are great and doing that same old work. This is why proper client planning is so important. Without it, things are heavily biased to stay the same.

Current State

This entire process is on the **Client Planning** worksheet, so grab that, or use a piece of paper divided into four quadrants. Now jot down an honest assessment of the client relationship from each of the four thinking styles. Use the chart on the following page for some sample questions to answer in each quadrant.

Despite the positive illusion research we just walked through, if you're in a group, it's natural to downplay what you've been doing well. Meanwhile I've seen countless groups avoid talking about problems because it might mean being hard on someone in the room. Be straight with yourself as you answer these questions.

On the one hand, celebrate and learn from your successes. If you've handled communication with a client particularly well, give yourself a

Current State

A. Analytical		D. Experimental	
How much did we bill this client in the last year? What was our margin?		What big thematic issues are happening at this client that they are trying to solve - and need our help? What is our brand at the client? What are we known for?	
B. Practical		**C. Relational**	
External: How efficient is our BD process at the client (ex: how well do we create demand and make it easy for our clients to hire us?) Internal: How efficiently do we work together internally to share information, strategize, measure and execute our BD efforts as a team?		Who are the top people that make our buying decisions at this client? How would we currently rank each of these people on the seven steps on the path to raving fan?	

BASED ON THE WHOLE BRAIN® MODEL OF HERRMANN GLOBAL LLC. © 2018 HERRMANN GLOBAL LLC

pat on the back, and more important, look at the procedures you put in place to make that happen. Likewise, be honest about your shortcomings. Maybe you need to bolster your relationship with the right influencers. Maybe you aren't working with the functional area of the client company with the largest buying potential. Maybe your relationships have gotten bogged down below the real levels where big purchases are made. Whatever the issues impeding growth, you need to call them out.

Be thorough and spend some time on this exercise.

Are you doing this with a group? The fastest way we've found to get through this is to have someone fill this out ahead of time and send it to everyone. Get everyone to agree to read it, then meet as a group to discuss changes. The entire point of this exercise is to build a future plan, not just to contemplate the past. When you get together, set a timer to limit the debate of the current state. Twenty minutes is plenty. We've found that if you don't limit it, groups will find comfort in discussing the past far more than is necessary. Every minute you dwell on the past is a minute you're not focusing on your future.

Future Vision

Now go back to the worksheets, or divide a second piece of blank paper into quadrants. Where would you like to be in a year with this client? Think about this question from both an opportunity and a relationship perspective. Where, thematically, does this organization need help? Where is the money? Who are the most powerful decision makers? What do your internal and external processes need to look like?

The idea here is to create a destination to drive toward. Don't worry about which aspects are more important yet. Just get started. Here are some questions to get you going.

Future Vision

A. Analytical	D. Experimental
How much can our revenue grow at this client next year, based on already scheduled projects and anticipated growth areas? What do we want our margin to be next year? **Sample Metrics to Consider Tracking** • Percentage of give to gets that lead to small projects • Dollar value of small projects • Dollar value of give to gets • Number of give to gets given • Number of strategy meetings we conduct that lead to engagements • Percentage of dollars invested to revenue dollars realized • Average client ROI from our engagements	Where will they allocate large budgets for our kinds of services in the future? What do we want our brand to be known for at the client? **Sample Metrics to Consider Tracking** • Number of client purchasing areas that hire us and number of purchasing areas that could hire us • Projects completed for other clients or industries that would help this client • Projects with this client that we could leverage with another client • Joint presentations with us and the client on innovative solutions we've built together
B. Practical	**C. Relational**
External: How can we help our client by making our BD process more efficient, including creating demand, using give to gets/small projects, proactively resolving objections, etc. Internal: How can we better utilize and align all of our internal resources to grow our business and be helpful to the client in the next year? **Sample Metrics to Consider Tracking** • Percentage of engagements that lead to repeat business • Average time from initial meeting to revenue realized • Percentage of BD meetings that lead to projects	Where do we want our relationship to be for the key buyers listed in the Current State (ex: What's our *team* Protemoi list, with each client contact mapped on the seven steps to raving fan)? **Sample Metrics to Consider Tracking** • Number of people on Protemoi List • Number of Raving Fans • Number of people within a client's company that we have a direct relationship with • Number of strategic partners we have referring us to the client • Number of C-Level people we know at the client's company • Client satisfaction scores on our services • Number of references who will speak on our behalf

When looking to the future, be sure to target the areas of the client organization that will actually invest in your offering, not just those where you have existing relationships.

As you finish this section, prioritize the most important ideas and finalize your vision.

Strategic Themes

Now that you know where you are and where you want to be with this client, you can develop one to three strategic themes for the coming year. No more than three—this will force you to focus your efforts. Grab your worksheet, or simply write your three themes on a piece of paper.

These goals should stem directly from your current state and future vision. Looking at the gaps you're trying to close, which will be the most meaningful? If you've had communication snafus with the client company that threaten the relationship, getting them addressed in the coming year may be a deciding factor in whether you see any more big projects with them. Your first strategic goal might be: "Client Communication: Create systems to ensure all client questions are answered within twenty-four hours and that we proactively reach out with updates on a weekly basis." It will take a number of smaller steps to get there, but by establishing that goal now, you can plan out how to manageably tackle it over the coming months.

This is just one example. Each client's plan depends on your current state and future vision, how aggressive you can afford to be, where the money is spent, and so on. Be creative, and emphasize the significant and meaningful opportunities, not just the easy ones. How can you evolve this client relationship, this year, to the fullest?

As you work through your themes, use what we learned about positioning in Chapter 3 to tighten your language. This will make your strategic themes more memorable, creating a mantra for yourself or your entire team. Here are some examples I've seen from our clients.

Proactive, procurement, and process. First and foremost, this team decided to work on being more helpful to its clients proactively; second, to build relationships with people in procurement (the purchasing department) roles; and third, to establish better internal BD processes, which included deciding which people owned which client relationships, and which give-to-gets they wanted to offer as well as improving team-wide communication.

Weed, seed, and feed. This client team wanted to wind down some services, break into new areas with their client, and continue to nurture important current relationships. You can't get snappier than this.

Fix, foundation, and future. This outsourcing team had client delivery issues. They decided to focus on fixing the existing issues, restoring the foundation of their most important relationships, and bringing in new team members to focus on the future. While the current team members focused on fixing problems, the newer team members could branch off, blazing a trail of new relationships throughout the organization.

No theme is perfect, but having a rough vision for the future is better than charging forward with none at all. Don't overthink this process; just decide what needs to change with your client relationship, and focus on the three things likely to have the greatest impact. You will refine your strategy over time as you see it in action.

Ninety-Day Tactics

Once you've established strategic themes, it's time to lay out the ninety-day tactics that will drive you and your team's actions over the first three months. You may not achieve the goals in their entirety in that time, but at the very least you can build some serious momentum. With the right tactics in play from the start, next year's current state evaluation will look very different from this year's.

The easiest way to map out tactics is to create a simple table with the following columns, or use a downloaded worksheet.

Why? Describe the link between this action and a strategic theme.

What? Describe the next right step needed.

When? Set a deadline for the next right step in the process.

Who? Pick the one person responsible to see it through.

Go through each of your strategic goals, and create action steps for the next ninety days with this client. Be sure strategic theme is covered with at least one action.

Once you've created every action you can think of, winnow the list down to what would be feasible but challenging to accomplish in ninety days. You may find that you can do more than you thought possible in that time. At that point you can shift your effort to other actions from this initial list for the next ninety.

The client team above that came up with the proactive, procurement, and process themes might have a few initial actions like this:

WHY	WHAT	WHEN	WHO
Proactive	Develop map of client relationships and who from our side leads each relationship.	Aug. 15	John
Procurement	Reach out to Bett in procurement to ask for meeting discussing our relationship.	Aug. 14	Helen
Process	Send calendar invites for ongoing ninety-day client planning execution meetings.	Aug. 18	Tena

Execute the Plan

Almost all our clients have been through the following client planning sequence:

Someone on the team says, "We need to meet about this client!" Everyone agrees. They agree that this client relationship should be growing faster than it has been.

All nine people on the client team sit around a table. Everyone takes a turn talking about what they know about the client, subtly talking about how well they know them. Sentences like "They'll call us when they need us" and "I haven't reached out to Chris yet because it's a tough time for him" are uttered. Time runs out before team can decide on any actions. The next meeting is scheduled.

Meeting number two comes. Only five people can make it this time because of "work emergencies" that popped up. They discuss the same things as they did during last meeting. One new introduction does happen. There's hope. The next meeting is scheduled.

Meeting number three comes. Only two people make it. They talk about football. Future meetings are canceled.

Wait two years, then return to step one.

This isn't much of an exaggeration. Without a process, this is what usually happens.

So how *should* you execute your plan? Every BD process requires coordination. If you're a sole practitioner, review each client plan on an ongoing basis, preferably during your set BD time. Track which actions have been taken as planned and which are falling behind. For each accomplished action identify the next right action to push toward that specific strategic theme. If you've achieved a strategic theme and have spare bandwidth, go back to your future vision and identify the next most important one to focus on with the client, along with the appropriate tactics.

If you run a team, create a periodic meeting to review client plans together. When creating ninety-day tactics, one person is always responsible for each action, so that stakeholder should update the team on the progress from the last period, celebrating wins and politely but publicly calling out negative or unexpected outcomes. (More on this in the next chapter, where we'll go *deep* on how high-performing teams function.)

Whoever leads the client team should collect everyone's progress, update the scorecard, and send it to everyone *before the next meeting*. When you push the retrospective review to email, it allows the in-person to be prospective. If needed, pick someone to nudge everyone to get their data in on time, give updates, and share information. This might or might not be a person on the team. It's usually someone with a high practical thinking style who enjoys reviewing the task list and moving things along. They can do this from behind the scenes so the core group can spend their time looking forward.

Once you're in the meeting use a countdown timer again. The team leader can pick a time everyone agrees on to limit the retrospective conversation, especially because the scorecard data has already been shared via email. If you meet for an hour, ten minutes should be plenty to celebrate past successes, thank people for great work, and ask if anyone who didn't get their piece done needs additional help.

Once the timer goes off, the leader can transition the meeting to brainstorming the most valuable actions for the coming time period. Finish the meeting by recapping next actions and agreeing on the overall plan. The key to progress is spending the bulk of the time looking ahead.

The quick celebration of incremental success creates a winning team mentality. The focus on the future keeps the energy and excitement high. When you do these things, people stay engaged. The team keeps showing up. Oh, and feel free to assign a few extra tasks to those who say they can't make it. That helps.

Essential Client Tactics

Business development tactics are separate from the tactics you use in your day-to-day work as an expert. At first you may not have a very clear sense of the specific things you might try to move your current state toward your future vision. As you put various tactics into motion and watch them advance your strategic themes, you'll find that some are more powerful than others.

Here I want to introduce you to some of the most powerful client growth tactics in the BD arsenal. Regardless of the industry or the nature of the service, these have proven themselves to be incredibly effective ways of growing stronger and deeper relationships with clients for the professionals we train. If you aren't sure where to begin when growing a client relationship or if the tactics you're using aren't delivering the kind of progress you expected, consider incorporating some of these into your client plans.

Ask for Advice

One of the best ways to deepen a client relationship—any relationship, really—is to ask for help. As Adam Grant's research has found, *getting help* can strengthen a bond with someone in similar ways to actually helping them. That's why this ask-for-advice technique is so powerful.

Best of all, if we can open ourselves up to it, this advice can be incredibly valuable. It's always good to get a different perspective, and your clients have a particularly useful one to share on your service and your BD efforts with them. Nobody else sees you from quite this vantage point, so listen carefully.

As your clients advise you and offer advice, they will also be learning more about your business and your target customer profile. This educates them; they'll begin to have better, more appropriate ideas for you and suggestions of others in their network who might benefit from your services.

If you're going to use this tactic with a client, frame it with importance. Don't just ask for some quick advice in five minutes as a broader conference call bleeds long; instead, ask your client to spend some dedicated time helping you, with the focus of the meeting only on this subject. Doing so elevates the importance of the conversation. If you tack this subject onto others, it won't seem important, and the client won't go as deep. Schedule a meeting solely to ask for the client's advice on growing your business. You'll be surprised how many clients will be happy to help.

Give the client a brief but concrete summary of where you plan to take your business in the coming year, and explain why you are coming to them for advice and support. When you get advice in return, particularly in the form of potential new clients, lock in next steps to make sure that each lead is followed up and that the client is kept up-to-date on where things land. Acknowledging and acting on client feedback are critical to this tactic's effectiveness. Asking for advice and then dropping the ball will leave things worse than where they started. When you do this right, you're simultaneously establishing new relationships and deepening the old ones.

A simple slide deck or short written document can be very effective.

Current state. As with the client plan earlier, this is a four-quadrant overview of where your business is today. What is the marketplace saying about you? Why is your service important and distinct? What are you not happy with?

Playing field. What does the rest of the industry look like? How does your service compare? Boil it down: How is your service unique? If you can convey this difference in a simple graph, so much the better.

Your strategy. Use all four quadrants to succinctly define what you're trying to do. "We are trying to [analytical results] by [experimental action] to [relational target market] through [practical steps]."

What doesn't work. Lay out what you don't do and what doesn't work for you. This adds clarity and helps distinguish you from your competitors.

Our expertise. Describe what you're really good at doing. Again, a graphic works best, one that takes a very process-oriented approach to explain how you provide your service in a way no competitor does.

The goal. Cover the financial and analytical results you're trying to achieve in the coming year. This is the numbers version of the story you've told so far, translated for the analytical thinkers in your audience. Your goal might be the target prospect, how many introductions you're trying to get, or how many give-to-gets you'd like to offer.

What we need. Finish on this slide for best results. Offer a table with two columns: Where We Need Help, and Benefit to the New Relationship. If the help you need is "five opportunities to beta test our new offering," the benefit might be giving that offering to the client without charge. If it's "three client success stories to showcase in a case study," the benefit to the client might be increased visibility wherever that case study appears.

These slides create clarity about where you're taking your business, solicit useful feedback on your plans from the people most directly affected by them, get clients interested in services they don't currently use, and give your loyal clients and raving fans more opportunities to help you. Remember: you only have to ask—these clients want to help!

Once you create the document, set up a lunch or a meeting specifically to go over it, allotting at least an hour to discuss your strategy and ask for advice around it. This is important and valuable for both sides. One of my clients develops an annual strategy for BD growth and then transforms it—minus some proprietary details—into an elegant, client-viewable document. Then he goes to his top six or seven loyal clients and raving fan clients, buys them a nice lunch, and shares the plan while asking for their advice.

Each time he does this, he tells me, he leaves the meeting with great ideas to grow his business as well as several good leads. According to him, he's never left a meeting like this without at least one valuable introduction.

The beauty of the ask-for-advice tactic is that you don't have to ask for a lead. By simply laying out what you're trying to accomplish in the coming year and putting out an honest request for advice, your clients will proactively offer their support.

Value Groups

One of my favorite ways to elevate relationships is by implementing a *value group*. A value group is a bit like a onetime forum (described in Chapter 6), but it meets regularly. While a forum generates most of its value from the great content provided, with a sprinkling of value from meeting peers, a value group emphasizes the meeting of peers, with content as a secondary value.

One of our clients is a large healthcare provider. They sell through third-party consultants and brokers. They created a value group of regional healthcare practice leaders at all the major consultants and brokers in their town. Although the speakers are always interesting, the main value for attendees is the ability to talk to their competitors. In this industry people often switch roles between the large employers, healthcare companies, consulting firms, and brokerage businesses, so it's always useful to meet each other. And before our client created this group there was no easy way to meet peers.

The group meets quarterly, always at a nice restaurant. One of the reasons it works well is that they only invite the top regional leaders to attend. Every meeting someone would ask if they could send a surrogate, but our clients would say no. In value groups, once you allow people to send "a person one level below," everyone does that, and your group will die a quick death. It's okay if not everyone can attend every meeting—just make sure that only the *right* people attend.

Other examples: One management consulting client of ours gets the CEOs of airlines together once a year. A commercial brokerage client brings together the CFOs of $100-million-and-up companies in his city on a quarterly basis. A confectionary producer invites retail front-end checkout lane buyers who love innovative products to get together semi-annually.

The benefits of value groups are immense, both for the clients and especially for the company putting it on. The clients get to meet each other and talk about relevant issues on an ongoing basis. You'll notice narratives and story lines that stretch from one meeting to the next. Meetings frequently begin with warm handshakes, hugs, and "Hey Sam! Whatever happened with that situation we talked about last time . . ."

Of course, the content in each meeting is important. It's an opportunity to showcase your own partners. Make it about the value, not promoting yourself, and people will keep coming back. As they do, you'll be elevating your relationships. You can target folks a level or two above your day-to-day contacts. As you increase the value, higher-level clients will start to come. Although it's true you need to put in hours of up-front work to organize a successful group, all that effort pays off in spades because, as the organizer, you become the star of the show. You gain instant credibility when you put together a value group that is truly valuable to everyone involved.

In getting a value group off the ground, you have the opportunity to design the perfect membership—raving fan clients, high-value prospects, highly connected influencers—scaled to just the right size for your goals. Some start with three or four members getting together for a simple dinner, others with a hundred or more attendees in an event space. You can efficiently add a tremendous amount of value for each attendee and customize the cadence to suit everyone's availability. Best of all, being able to offer a onetime invitation to one of your regular meetings gives you a hole-in-one tactic that can give a lasting boost to any key relationship, whether client or prospect.

Another twist on this approach is to build a board of advisors. This combines elements of both ask for advice and value groups. A board of advisors is a group of clients, prospects, and influencers assembled to give you ongoing feedback on how you're doing and ideas for what to focus on next. You don't need to be a Fortune 500 company to put a board together, either. Even sole proprietors can assemble these groups—as long as they deliver lots of value to the clients who sign on.

The main goal of a board of advisors is to get feedback and deepen critical relationships, but it can also be a great source of leads. A board can be set up for your company, for a single practice area, or even a single product or service.

How do you make a seat on your board of advisors so valuable that clients are willing to take regular time out of their busy schedules to participate? One company I know created a board for its outsourcing practice. They invited clients and a few key prospects to a meeting once a quarter. Everyone would fly in the afternoon before, with a grand dinner that night. Usually a high-value speaker would address the board members on a topic of interest in the industry. In the morning the group would discuss how things are going, current trends, and plans for the future. The company would always include a specific ask at different points in the presentation, similar to what you would do when asking for advice: "We need five new prospects in the tech sector to beta-test a new service, and only these five will get our best team and a special price." The meeting would end with everyone getting a top-notch boxed lunch for the ride back to the airport.

Each member of the board gets a regular opportunity to catch up on trends and other valuable industry info, network with others in the group, and hear a high-value speaker. It's no surprise that membership in this board is highly coveted and always a powerful gesture when the company wants to move a client relationship forward. Also, think back to Dr. Robert Cialdini's advice on the lure of scarcity. Use that here by *limiting* the number of seats on your board of advisors. Pick a number slightly lower than the number of people you think will have interest—everyone involved will benefit from an exclusive group.

Once you've assembled your board, leave one seat per meeting open for a prospect. This becomes an easy and effective way to deepen the relationship and introduce them to your raving fan clients. If you have a critical mass of clients, a good spot to hold regular meetings, and the resources to plan and run them, this might be the tactic for you.

Designing and implementing successful value groups and a board of advisors are similar. Here are the primary steps:

Focus. Start by picking a focus area for the group. For value groups think of a role a level or two above where you usually interact. If there are enough of those people in a geographic area (say, CFOs of Russell 2000 companies in Atlanta), add a geographic limitation. If not (say, CEOs of major airlines), don't worry about geography. For boards of advisors you might initially think this would be for your entire company. In fact, it's often best to single out a specific industry, practice area, product, or service. In either group determine the kinds of value you will offer the members. Thematically, what would be most interesting for this group?

Size. Pick the size that would be perfect, based on your focus area. Sometimes three or four people works best. Others, it might be hundreds. It depends on your expertise, how many people you want to meet, and how senior they need to be. If you're not sure, start small. It's easier to grow when you have a small group of A players to start with. Once you know how many people you'd like to attend the average meeting, bump that up by a percentage to account for the inevitable conflicts and no-shows.

Cadence. High-value clients are inevitably busy. (If your members have all the time in the world to attend the meetings, you're probably not aiming high enough with your targets.) Something from quarterly to bi-annually usually works best. You want members looking forward to the next one.

Cornerstone clients. This step is critical. When initially recruiting the group the first question everyone will ask is: "Who else is going?" Whose early involvement would help when recruiting everyone else? Select a few key clients to secure right off the bat. Get them involved in the planning. You know: build everything together. Once you get their involvement, getting others involved rolls downhill. Pro tip: We've had some clients partner with others to get these groups off the ground. Partnering with a local business school or a strategic partner that runs in the same circles but has a different expertise can be a great way to share networks and grow the group quickly.

Execution. Lay out the concrete action steps you need to take to get your group established, from branding the group to finding partners, from securing a location to setting a budget. As always, approach the planning process from all four thinking styles.

A value group or board of advisors is a powerful way to elevate your relationships and create an ongoing, easy way to establish powerful touchpoints. Once you've set one up, you can use it for all kinds of things, from lead generation to relationship building to industry networking. And because you built it, you'll be the star of the show.

•

There's power in planning. Planning will help you aim higher and execute through the unexpected. It will help you deepen relationships and generate the highest ROI on your time. With these tools, you're now ready to plan efficient client BD meetings and employ effective client growth strategies.

Now it's time for a small celebration of your own. Pat yourself on the back—you've come a long way. You've now devoured nearly all the topics needed to be individually successful at business development. Whether you're a professional service provider at a big firm or a graphic designer launching a business, an account manager leading the company's biggest relationship or an attorney raising money to start a public advocacy not-for-profit—if you serve clients with hard-earned expertise, the Snowball System will help you grow your business.

If you're a solo practitioner or solely responsible for all client relations at your company (*and* you're happy to remain that way), you now have everything you need to succeed. Stick to the system, and before you know it, you're going to be fielding a steady stream of ideal prospects and promising opportunities.

Not everyone can be an island unto themselves, though. Bigger deals require teams of people to work together, crafting the perfect solution while interfacing with prospects through a web of relationships. Larger client relationships need teams of experts working in harmony to service and grow their work. Many complex solutions even require teams of experts *across* organizations to work together.

Working on and leading teams requires a new set of skills. In sports, the best players rarely go on to become the best managers. Successful leaders of sports teams possess their own expertise, a mastery of everything from team strategy to one-on-one motivation. And the best contributors on teams *help each other* in powerful ways, creating a winning team mentality across the team's culture. The best BD teams are similar, with great leaders designing and executing a growth plan and great team members doing their part to help everyone be better, together.

That's what's left: taking what you've learned as an individual and applying it across a group of people to create a high-performing team. There's no feeling better than being a part of a winning, growing team. Next, I'll show you how to do it.

CHAPTER 10

Creating Momentum in Teams

• • ●

BIG THINGS HAPPEN in teams. Bigger deals require teams to pitch them. Bigger clients require teams to service them. Bigger products and solutions require teams to implement them. And teams require leadership and collaboration. What's right for the individual might not be right for their team.

You know I love the St. Louis Cardinals. Imagine if their leadership went bonkers and decided to do everything they could to get the most talented players to win next year *and next year alone,* selling every single asset they had in the process. Everything is on the table: trading their current players, trading their young talent in their farm system, spending all their available cash—*everything.* Doing so would result in acquiring great talent, much of which might only have one year remaining on their contract. They'd have a lot of great players locked in for next year, but little after that.

The good news? They'll probably have the most talented team in baseball next year. The bad news? They've got one year to win the World Series. After that, there's no bench strength, no money, and the players with contracts expiring will leave.

Now imagine this twist: they fire their managers and coaching staff and don't allow any of their newfound talented players to talk to each other. They tell everyone: "We've got the most talented individuals, so we don't need a manager leading the team. We don't need coaches to help you improve and hold you accountable. We don't need any collaboration.

You're the best individuals, so just go out and play your own game, and we'll win."

This is my worst nightmare. They wouldn't win. Without an overarching strategy, every person would fight for who starts, who pitches next, and who gets the desirable spots in the batting order. Without accountability, people would start slacking off on their workouts, putting in less effort, and not improving. Without an ongoing process for preparing for games, people would start "doing their own thing," not practicing for anything requiring more than one player. And the worst part? Without collaboration, the team would fall into chaos, arguing, blaming each other, and fighting over why they lost the night before and what to do differently for the next game.

That scenario was my imagination, right? It felt so awful that it was hard for a Cardinals fan to write. But without some effort, your internal teams can fall into the same situation: great individual talent with a losing formula on a team that's no fun to be on.

Great teams require leaders to lead as well as team members to do their best to contribute. Each person acting in their own best interests doesn't work. Sure, everyone needs to excel, but they need to excel *in a way that helps the team.*

Working to deploy the Snowball System across teams is my favorite thing to do, largely because the people I'm working with see so much success. Whether you work in a small business with a few employees, a practice area within a professional service firm, or a large account servicing a Fortune 100 corporation with many other experts, this chapter will teach you how to get everyone on board with the system, working effectively together for best results.

These skills also work for client teams. These are sometimes the hardest groups to manage because the experts, structurally organized by products, practices, service areas, and/or geography, can report through many different managers. In most cases there's no "official" reporting structure governing a client team. Remember the story in the last chapter about how these teams can quickly fall apart after only a few meetings, until only two people show up and spend the time talking about football? There's a better way. Next, we'll build on the client planning strategies in the last chapter to show you how to make teams work and to make them fun in the process (hint: the two go hand in hand).

This chapter will also help someone who *wants* to be in these roles. The best way we've found to get promoted is to start exhibiting the behaviors needed for the job you want. We've had our clients use the methods in this chapter to start a client team and drive success where there was no leadership or coordination before. There's nothing like driving positive change to drive a positive change in people's opinion of you.

To get breakthrough results on a team, you need *every* team member using this system. The Snowball System is an all-in, cooperative approach to handling clients. The focal point is a team leader. The leader is the coxswain of the rowing team and needs everyone to pull together to glide down the river. The last thing you want is one team member's careful planning and preparation with a client stymied by the misdirected efforts of another. The question is: How do you get everyone pulling in unison, and how do you keep a Snowball System team going once you've done so?

The great thing about using a comprehensive system like Snowball is that you're not operating on intuition anymore—it's all here in the book. My clients call it their "common language" across teams and organizations. By having the team read this book, they'll know exactly what to do. Instead of ten people arguing for forty minutes about whether a strategic investment is worth pursuing, everyone will already know what a give-to-get is, and you'll pick the perfect one in ten minutes. Having a common language drives effectiveness. Maybe your first step as a team member is a bulk book order. That will make your team and my editor, Colleen, very happy. But there's much more to cover to ensure your success.

Team members need clarity about what success looks like—and each team will have unique goals. In this chapter I will cover setting a growth strategy for your team, identifying the behaviors needed to implement that strategy, choosing leading and lagging indicators to measure, and designing a process to keep the focus on growth, celebrating success every step of the way. These elements hit everyone's thinking styles, align the culture around accountability and continuous progress, and establish a fun, winning-team mentality. If you're on a team, this might be this book's most important chapter. The stakes are higher.

Developing a Strategic Plan for Growth

Effective teams deftly use all four thinking preferences. They keep a close eye on the numbers and incorporate them into decision making. They use systems, processes, and cadences to streamline operations. They incorporate every team member's point of view and communicate with each in the way that best suits them. And, *as a team*, they craft and communicate a vision for the future. Productive teams begin with a strategic growth plan, and the best teams build their plan together.

A good strategic plan helps align everyone's activities with the larger goals of the organization. Having an explicit plan also helps avoid one of the common missteps of teams: expecting everyone else to "just know what to do." That's the fast track to disappointment. When we don't have a plan, people are rowing in different directions at different cadences. When we *do* have a plan, things just flow.

One of my all-time favorite teams was back at Hewitt. I was fresh in my role as a managing consultant, just making the transition from expert to seller-expert, when I caught a lucky break. A seasoned managing consultant, Andy, took me under his wing. We agreed to colead four client teams for a year, and after that, we'd sort out which two we'd lead independently. That year with Andy was one of the most important of my career. I won because I could learn from someone I admired who was ten years my senior. Andy won because he was having a lot of success and wanted to give back.

One of the four clients stood out to me. They were a global financial services company—one of the biggest in the world. I really clicked with their chief people officer. She was new in the role and ready to set the world on fire. We had lots of upside too. Although we did some great work in one main practice area, the rest of our work was episodic, with frequent team changes spanning across several of our practice areas. Great talent, but little coordination.

Andy and I decided to focus on three things: we permanently staffed the team in *all* our major practice areas (even the ones where we didn't have active work), focused on offering give-to-gets to introduce these new team members, and continuously shared what we were learning across the team. I knew so much less then: we didn't have fancy rhyming strategies, didn't know what a give-to-get was, and didn't have a model in the firm for doing this. Our plans were intuitive and a big risk for us. At the time Hewitt didn't do these things for clients who weren't *already* big. We made a big bet that we could help this client immensely and grow the business. If we didn't, we were going to hear about it.

It worked. The client loved our investment mindset and saw the value our people brought. We grew the account nearly ten times in just a few years, providing some of the most complex global consulting Hewitt had done to date. The work was so cutting-edge and impactful that the chief people officer landed on the cover of *Hewitt Magazine*. We even built a sophisticated partnership model that quantified the value we were adding and allowed the client input on which investments we'd make next. It was a frequent-flyer program of sorts, where the client would build credits and spend them as they wished in new areas. They loved it, and I loved building it with them.

But the best part for me was seeing our internal team flourish. It wasn't always easy, but we were always moving forward, always helping this important client with a "we can do anything" mentality. It was our team's *strategy* that propelled us. And we had a blast fulfilling our potential. The strategy worked so well that it became a model for other client teams across the globe. I still keep in touch with nearly everyone who was on that team.

This was my first experience leading a big client team, and I loved it. My biggest lesson? A little coordination goes a long way. The coxswain might not have an oar in the water, but their role has a huge impact.

The best way to start developing this kind of focused alignment on a team is with a strategic plan. Again, build it as a group, either starting from scratch or having a person or small subteam create a "60 percent right" version, sharing it, and working with everyone over a few iterations to complete it. Doing so creates buy-in and educates the team on the *why* behind each strategic element.

It can seem like a time-saver to have one person craft the entire strategy to completion, but that doesn't work well. We've tried it. Most times it actually takes *longer* to get everyone on board. That's because everyone wants to add value. If you give someone something complex that's 100 percent completed, there's only one way to add value—to poke holes in it. For larger or more complex teams, starting with the 60-percent-right draft can save time, but don't go farther than that before getting the team's input. We've talked about how building everything together with clients creates buy-in—it turns out that using the IKEA effect is the best way to create buy-in internally too, and you don't need Allen wrenches to do it.

Letting the team take it home is where the magic happens.

Creating a strategic plan for your team follows the same general process as the one for a client-based strategic plan, as we saw in Chapter 9. Here's a quick recap, with a few changes to match the broader team perspective:

Current state. Have the team create an honest assessment from each quadrant: strategic, financial, process, and relationships. What is our reputation, our brand? What are our current financials and other metrics? How effective is our BD process, externally and internally? What is the state of our most important relationships, both internally and externally?

Future vision. Where would you like your team to be a year from now in terms of business development? Be realistic based on your own experience with how ambitious you think you can be in a one-year time frame. How should your team's brand shift? Where do you want your numbers to be in a year? What can you improve about the team's BD processes, internally and externally? What should change with your relationships over the next twelve months?

Strategic themes. Now that you know where you are and where you want to be in a year, decide on three strategic themes to organize and direct the team's efforts. No more than three. This will force you and your team to focus on the highest priorities. When *everything* is "of the utmost importance," nothing is important. Your strategic themes can apply to any aspect of your BD efforts.

Let's say your team has been doing things the normal way: starting with pitching their stuff, not investing in prospects, and following up by nagging: "Did you get my email following up on my voicemail following up on the proposal?"

This team might reorient with three key themes:

- ✦ Start all BD meetings with listen and learn, creating meaningful conversations instead of delivering boring pitches.
- ✦ Create demand using give-to-gets.
- ✦ Perform better follow-up communication that adds value and fosters the relationships instead of nagging.

Once you get agreement across your broad themes, get creative to shorten them to make them more memorable, maybe using rhyming or alliteration. The team above might choose:

- ✦ *Learning mindsets* drive perfect
- ✦ *give-to-gets* and then we always
- ✦ follow up with *assets*

Their strategy: Learning mindsets, give-to-gets, assets.

Each team's strategic plan will be different. Be creative, and focus on what's most significant and meaningful to the team.

Once you've identified your team's strategic themes for the coming year, don't just type them up, paste them on the wall, and expect them to be achieved. Instead, ask yourself what new *behaviors* will be required from every member of the team to achieve them.

In our example above, the team needs to learn to ask great gravitas questions. This sounds easy, but it can be hard to break years of "show up and throw up" habits. Over the course of the coming year the team might spend time together regularly to develop insightful questions, build a shared database of them, and share results as they put them to use. Every small improvement can be shared across the team. Sharing success is fun and builds momentum.

This team would work together on their plans for the other two strategies as well—designing new give-to-gets and amassing assets. They could collaborate on implementation: figuring out when and how to offer them for best results. Team members can take on elements of the project based on their thinking preferences. Practical thinkers could work on the process, relational thinkers could report on client experiences, and so on.

I've seen hundreds of teams become energized about making their strategies work. I've seen people volunteering for extra night and weekend work just to move things forward. I've seen people's passion power big breakthroughs.

Coaching for Success

Winning teams have something else in common: everyone gives everyone coaching. Every person sees things. Every person has the potential to help out another. When every person is helping every person get better at every opportunity, positive change happens faster.

I think peer coaching is even more powerful than manager-to-subordinate coaching. As a peer, each person provides the fresh perspective of someone who understands the role and its objectives. A peer isn't influenced by performance goals or prior managerial biases—they see each moment for what it is. And the math is powerful. There are ten times the opportunities for peers to coach each other over manager-only coaching. Peer coaching is both very effective and there's more of it. It's simple: high-performing teams coach each other. They get better together.

Remember the "Losada ratio" from Chapter 4? It applies here too. High-performing teams have a positive comment-to-constructive comment ratio of 5.6 to 1. You might also remember that medium-performing teams had a 2-to-1 ratio, and the lowest-performing teams actually had more constructive comments than positive. I love the Losada ratio of 5.6 to 1 because it gives a team a tangible benchmark. The key is to promote the positive, look for any small movement in the right direction, then provide authentic, positive praise for that behavior.

Now let's widen our view to the whole team. For each behavior the team identifies, you'll get one of three responses from each team member: (1) adopt the new behavior well, (2) not adopt it at all, or (3) adopt it incorrectly. Each represents a coaching opportunity. If the team member adopts the new behavior seamlessly, don't just take it for granted—offer positive reinforcement. *People run toward praise.* If the effort isn't noticed and rewarded right away, the tendency is to assume the team didn't really care about the new behavior and to backslide to the old, more comfortable approach. Habits are hard to break.

If the team member does not adopt the new behavior or adopts it incorrectly, it's up to anyone who witnessed it to have a follow-up conversation right away. Learning a new skill or habit takes time. Perhaps they forgot. Perhaps there are obstacles to completing the new behavior that you weren't aware of. In an open and nonjudgmental way ask the team member how the new behavior is going and then—as always—really listen to what they have to say.

For the bigger coaching conversations there is an amazingly effective way to walk through the thinking preferences. See the following model.

It works like this:

Whole Brain® Coaching Model

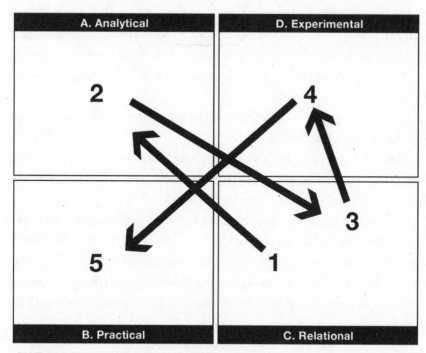

BASED ON THE WHOLE BRAIN® MODEL OF HERRMANN GLOBAL LLC. © 2018 HERRMANN GLOBAL LLC

Relational. Start with them. If you're offering positive reinforcement, let them know how much it meant they did X. If it's constructive, let them know you're offering some feedback because you care and see how they can improve.

Analytical. Be completely objective—and *specific*. If positive, give a metric or the dollar value of an impact they made. If constructive, be specific about what could change and by how much. Numbers are specific. Words like "a lot" aren't.

Relational. Pull back to them and ask open-ended questions about how they feel about the news, whether it was positive or constructive. You might have a back-and-forth here in this step, either celebrating the success or discussing the constructive feedback. Either way, stay here until it's time to look forward.

Experimental. What should we do about it? If positive, can we promote this story with others? Can the person share what they did with the team? If constructive, what does your team member think needs to happen to fix things or to improve the next time? Keep this at a high level until you start to home in on a specific action.

Practical. Now build a plan to implement: Who's going to do what by when?

Let's run through two scenarios using the model, one for positive and one for constructive feedback.

Here is an example of positive feedback. Tiffani offered a promising new prospect a give-to-get, executed it well, and got a verbal commitment for a $30,000 opportunity. Time to celebrate!

You might high-five in the car on the way back to the airport. Then you get specific. According to your quick calculations, a client with a breakthrough project like this might have a five-year added revenue of over $10 million. There's a lot more to do, but it will never happen without closing out this first project, and this first project wouldn't be happening without Tiffani's give-to-get.

Ask Tiffani how she feels about this, like what it might mean for her career or, if it's appropriate to talk about money, what the bonuses generated on growth might mean for her family. Then, an experimental idea: ask her how she'd like her success to be promoted internally. Maybe you can mention it to her boss. Or maybe to this team's leader. Can we show-case this on a team call? Would the division president like to know? Can others in the organization learn from this? Decide on a strategy. Then finish with next steps and to-dos. When everyone's helping each other like this, it creates a winning team mentality and personal bonds that last forever.

Now a constructive example. Jim is talking too much in BD meetings, struggling with the behavior of listen and learn. You've been in three pros-pect meetings with him, and things aren't changing. You might bring this up right after that third meeting, in the car on the way back to the office. You could start with the fact that you're disappointed: you prepped to-gether with questions, and for the third time Jim didn't use them.

Now, the specifics. You monitored the one-hour meeting and esti-mated the amount of time Jim talked: forty-eight out of sixty minutes. Be clear and specific. It's easy to fall back on vague feedback using words like "a lot" or "many." That only starts an argument—each person has a dif-ferent view of what "a lot" means. Forty-eight out of sixty. Next, get back to empathy with an open-ended conversation about how Jim feels about this. Listen. See what the issues are. Once you discover what's underlying this behavior, move to experimental thinking to collaboratively build a strategy with Jim. Finish with practical next steps.

Whether positive or constructive, this model works well, and you don't need to be someone's boss to use it. It's one friend helping another. Use it, and you'll crush coaching.

Celebrating Success

One of the most frequently overlooked aspects of business development is the celebration of success. Most organizations recognize big wins, but few celebrate the small, incremental successes that truly drive growth over time.

The brain loves rewards. The brain isn't selective about what counts as a reward either—food, money, symbolic tokens, or simple social rewards like a compliment or the opportunity to talk about yourself. (We love talking about ourselves, remember?)

A celebration is a reward. By praising the accomplishments of a member of your team, you are contributing to forming healthy behavioral patterns. You're actually making it easier for them to adopt and implement the right BD behaviors by offering a kind word. Kind words work. Some of our clients have initially been turned off by the word "celebration," comparing it to hollow cheerleading with pom-poms, as though it's unprofessional to call out a win. That's not what we're talking about here. We're talking about *authentic praise* from someone they respect. It's free. It reinforces the behavior. It deepens the relationship.

Don't hold back. If you want to see more of a behavior, reward it. Great opportunities for celebration include:

+ completing the week's Most Important Things
+ forming a significant new business relationship
+ leveraging a raving fan relationship for a referral
+ targeting and meeting a new prospect
+ successfully executing a give-to-get

These small things are a big deal. Imagine if my Cardinals only celebrated victories and nothing else—no high-fives, no cups full of water to the face after a home run. That would make for some lousy baseball. Thankfully they celebrate all the little things that lead to the big win— the perfectly executed bunt, the double play that was turned, the catcher smoothly framing a pitch that resulted in a strikeout. I watch a lot of games, and I see the guys high-five in the dugout after all the little things. They are celebrating throughout the game, and they even have a name for it: the Cardinal Way. They've created a brand for consistently doing the little things right.

Celebrate small wins in small ways across the team. You might order donuts for the conference room when everyone on the team has completed their MITs for the month or when total BD hours hit a certain milestone. Whatever you choose to track as a team, measure it and celebrate any improvement. Being human, we find it easier to notice the missed opportunities and failed experiments. Instead, always be on the lookout for the small wins each day, and take every opportunity to celebrate them.

Doing this creates a winning team mentality. It creates momentum. *You seriously can't do this too much.* It racks up more 5.6's in the bank, giving you license to get more constructive in the future.

Putting the Snowball System into Practice

Every team member has various levels of responsibility for measuring, monitoring, and mentoring the team to achieve greater results and create a better buying experience for your clients. It's up to the team to define its measures of success, determine how your team will report progress, attend regular team meetings, and coach each other to success. This is another area where people buy into what they help create. Let's cover some best practices to get the team started, but as always, get the team to adjust these to fit. Consider this your 60-percent-right version, ready for you to evolve and perfect with your teammates. After you add your own flair and finish, everyone will feel a part of the plan.

We've talked about how most companies track lagging indicators like revenue generated, units or projects sold, number of new clients, and so on. Although these are important and certainly can't be ignored, they aren't under the complete control of your team members. What's more, it can take time to see how your efforts are translating—you might not really know whether you're off track until it's too late to recover for the current quarter or year. These are important things to track, but more is needed.

Popular activity-only indicators track employee activity level without actually revealing impact. Only measuring the number of outbound phone calls or emails, for example, doesn't really tell the team about the *quality* of an account manager's relationship with a prospect, the status of an opportunity, or the next step in a buying process. These are just easy things to track and reward. Kelly made ten calls and Todd made nine— does that mean Kelly grew the business more effectively?

Instead, focus on the leading indicators that truly correlate with successful business development. Here is a set of indicators with a proven track record. In my experience, when these numbers rise, the lagging indicators will rise over time too. As you evolve you can modify this list to fit the needs of your team, but it's a good place to start.

+ MITs chosen and completed
+ hours of BD time
+ give-to-gets offered and accepted
+ leads generated that fit your targeting criteria
+ current number of raving fans and, more broadly, the team's collective
  Protemoi List, including the step each person is at

Not all of these are worded in a way that is 100 percent in a single person's control, so you'll need to slice them into smaller pieces that fit with the next steps for your unique team. These indicators reveal not only the team member's general activity level but also the progress being made toward advancing key relationships and opportunities. I also like it when teams choose a nice balance of quality (like MITs decided on as a team) and quantity (like aggregate BD hours). Pay attention to your portfolio of leading indicators—the best overall group might not be an aggregation of the best individual ones. You want a nice balance.

This process of measurement and reporting doesn't need to be exact or ideal to start. You can always change things as you evolve. The key in the beginning is *getting started*. Given that, there is one important thing left: it's best to measure the *right metrics subjectively* rather than the *wrong metrics perfectly*.

I love subjective measures when they are the right ones. Choosing them drives *great* conversation. One of our clients tracked how many *meaningful client BD conversations* they had. They wanted to deepen the relationships they already had, moving clients from solid working relationship (where most of their relationships had stalled out) to loyal client and raving fan. The internal dialogue they had over what counted as a meaningful conversation was incredibly useful. The team was winning with every word. The team debated and defined the metric, then they were bought in, dead set on having those kinds of conversations. Somewhat subjective? Yes. More effective than tracking client outreaches, which, for them, would have nagged clients without adding value? Definitely.

You can always refine things over time. At first you can celebrate with the team when everyone has checked in, when everyone has submitted their data. Reporting can be a thankless task—make it a game, make it fun, and your team will start looking forward to each week's or month's review. You'll want to show everyone's data publicly. Going over the results in the spirit of friendly competition can be very motivating.

Above all, it's important to be patient with the team. All of them are learning how to implement the Snowball System while also learning how to communicate and coordinate with each other.

What if you're leading the team? This is an entirely new level of business development for any rainmaker. You have new behaviors to establish too. What behaviors do you want to focus on yourself? What leading indicator metrics would show *your* progress? How can you celebrate your own incremental improvement? Turn the process on yourself, and you'll accomplish many things at once, including increasing your empathy for your team.

Back to the team. Here are some key questions to ask everyone as you establish better team communication around business development.

+ What tools will your team use to report progress (email, IM, CRM, an app, shared documents, etc.)?
+ What team data will you report and on what cadence?
+ Who will be responsible for collecting data and creating team reports?
+ When will you require team members to submit their data?

Think through these choices as a group. You can always fine-tune as you go, and always remember the magic words: think big, start small, scale up.

Bringing It All Together

Let's get practical. At this point your team has read *The Snowball System*, settled on a strategic plan, and picked some leading indicator measurements to track. Your team's next step is to get everyone on the same page.

The best way to do this is through a Snowball launch session. This is a team activity designed to get everyone in alignment.

For this meeting you will want to bring:

+ the strategic plan
+ the new behaviors the team has agreed to
+ the approach to tracking and reporting indicators
+ any expectations of team members for using the system's rituals
+ how the team has agreed to celebrate success

Most teams have covered many of these things at this point, especially if you built the strategy together with them, but maybe not everything. The perfect time for the official launch meeting varies. Sometimes you can do all these things in one meeting, and with others it's a series of meetings.

If you've nailed down most of these things already, a two-hour launch meeting can tie everything in a bow and propel you forward. You might not need two hours—feel free to modify this agenda for a perfect fit. The key element is that people are going to have questions and this meeting is set to review everything and provide answers. Clarity is key. Once the team is clear on how the Snowball System will be implemented, decide on any necessary next steps and explain the schedule for monthly meetings moving forward.

Here's how a typical launch meeting might look, but again, feel free to modify to fit your needs:

Twenty minutes: Review the strategic goals of your team, with emphasis on your current state, future vision, and strategic themes. Be sure to elaborate on *why* the team will be doing things differently.

Twenty minutes: Discuss the behaviors you'll want to see across the team. Cover the definitions for each, and give examples of what each looks like.

Twenty minutes: Discuss the measures you'll use to track the behaviors. Cover the concept that no measure is perfect but that the team has agreed to these as a start, and recap that important, somewhat subjective measures are better than less important accurate ones. Be ready for people to complain about capturing and submitting data—*it will happen every time,* even if they've already agreed. Expect "I'm too busy!" Share how they can track things quickly and submit painlessly. And hit the true issue under many people's comments here: They're scared. They're scared of showing their activity levels, they're scared of being judged, and they're scared of change. Remind them of high-performing sports teams and how measurement is a big part of their success. You'll all be improving together, and the data you'll be collecting will be key.

Thirty minutes: Have each team member discuss where they're going to focus next and where they would like help. These should be a bit more conceptual than the MITs, which are closer to the granular-task level. No matter what, make sure each person is talking about the future, looking forward. Teams that spend their time looking backward, summarizing the things they've *been doing,* die a quick death, usually not making it to the third or fourth meeting cycle.

Twenty minutes: Cover the upcoming schedule: next meeting, data reporting deadlines and methods, and how everyone can help by celebrating incremental success. Everyone can look for and share the bright spots, the incremental progress. Have the group decide on the best ways to do this. Celebrate celebrating.

Ten minutes: Finish with each person telling the group their number-one most important thing for the upcoming time period and number-one area where they'd like help. This should go quickly—a fast-paced, positive closing of commitments. Have the leader capture these.

Ongoing meetings are similar, but with a shorter time frame. One important aspect of this is sending the combined team data out to everyone well before the meeting. Set the expectation that everyone should review it ahead of time and come with questions. That critical step lets you spend the majority of the meeting time looking forward, not back.

A typical team meeting agenda might look as follows:

Five minutes: Review strategic goals.

Ten minutes: Review past time period's metrics and lessons learned. Highlight successes and where the team needs to improve. Remember to balance highlighting leading indicators (Jim asked six gravitas questions in our recent meeting, and we learned X) with lagging indicators (Tiffani landed a $30,000 small project that could result in a $10 million stream of work!). Both are important.

Fifteen minutes: Review one Snowball System tool or technique. Do a deeper dive on one concept, usually letting a team member showcase their success. This has elements of learning, evolving skills, and celebration.

Twenty-five minutes: Team members share planned *future* MITs and help needed.

Five minutes: Quickly recap next steps, next meeting, and due dates for next month. End on a positive.

This monthly team meeting will be invaluable, both for keeping the team in alignment with your strategic goals and for helping each member learn from the successes and failures of the others and gradually hone their rainmaking skills. Also notice how future focused it is—almost every minute is looking forward. Even the metric review is largely looking forward: quickly review what happened, and then focus on what we learned and what we should do next.

If you lead the team, you might augment the team meeting with monthly thirty-minute one-on-one coaching sessions with every team member. This is an opportunity to focus on each team member's particular challenges and opportunities. You can use this time to:

+ discuss and celebrate successes;
+ identify what's working well, what isn't, and what can be done differently in the coming month;
+ figure out where you or other team members can help; and
+ review MITs in depth.

The one-on-one meetings are where you can really dive deep with each person, inspiring them to accomplish more than they ever thought possible.

We helped one team, and I'll never forget the experience.

It was a business process outsourcer whose growth had stalled out. The firm took on repetitive processes at scale—for example, running all the real estate contracts for a retailer with thousands of locations. Their deals were big and ongoing. What struck me was their client list. It was a huge percentage of the Fortune 50, the biggest companies in America. As we dug into their situation, listening and learning all the way, we found that, although they had marquee clients, their "wallet share"—as they called it—was small at nearly all of them. What was going on? It appeared to be the BD paradox spread across an entire team. All their initial fast-paced growth had created a situation in which the *servicing* of the client work was getting in the way of getting more. They had huge clients, tremendous room for growth, but little momentum.

We started with training. We covered all the Snowball System principles. Our team could see the lightbulbs going off with each one. These new skills were the beginning—but more was needed. Working with the entire team, we focused on three leading indicators and skills.

The first measure clarified quantity: hours spent per month on business development. The team members had to both service clients and grow them, and they had said the servicing was taking a lot of time for months, pulling them away from growth activities. Hours spent on BD time might seem like an odd measure at first because it's not an "action" someone can take, like offering a give-to-get or asking for an advance. But measuring BD hours can shed light on the *quantity of effort* a person is making toward growth activities. In general, the more BD hours, the better. BD hours are especially important to measure for people who own both client servicing and growth because it's *so easy* to fall back on the servicing at the expense of growth.

The second measure focused on momentum: the team started asking for the next BD step *in the one they were in* instead of asking for the next step and trying to schedule it on email like they had been doing. They started securing the date, time, and location of the next client meeting in person whenever possible. (Remember the thirty-four-times factor for in-person asks versus email?) This was a great *quality* measure.

The third measure was tailored to create demand: the team started focusing on offering give-to-gets. We prioritized expansion areas by client. Then we picked specific give-to-gets to offer. We even practiced offering the give-to-gets by role-playing the benefits in all thinking styles. This was another great *quality* measure.

We developed all these measures with team involvement, creating buy-in. The conversations over what counted as a BD hour were amazing—dissecting things like a client lunch where servicing and BD topics were both covered. (In that case, if they talked with a client at lunch for an hour about existing work and fifteen minutes about new potential work, they'd count fifteen minutes.) Even what counted as a give-to-get was specific to them. Their team had expertise too, but we decided as a group to *not* count give-to-gets they completed themselves. Their logic was that they needed to create demand for *other* experts, not themselves. So although they decided they should attend all give-to-gets, the focus should be promoting other experts. The group had great debates over each measure, and we made progress with every word. Debating and defining the measures was a critical part of success.

The debate over data collection was classic too. "We're too busy. We don't have enough time for business development as it is. How will we find time?" We worked through these things together and focused on *just getting started*. Scribbling daily data on a Post-it Note each night before leaving work works fine. Once we got over that hurdle, we created a simple way to submit weekly data.

So, what happened? The numbers tell the tale.

Total BD hours spent across the team improved drastically and, amazingly, continued to improve every month: 109, 281, 484, 505, 683, 835, and 883! The actuary in me gets excited about patterns like this. That's a *710 percent improvement* over eight months. Here's what happened: once senior leadership saw how *little* time their team was spending on business development in the first month, they fixed some nagging service delivery issues. You can see that started to take hold in month two, as the team went from 109 to 281 BD hours—more than double. Those little nagging issues were completely fixed by month three, with 484 BD hours, and then we were off to the races. After that, the team was focusing *much* more on BD activities, becoming more efficient and trying to beat their prior personal bests.

Total meetings requested bounced around a little bit, going from 114 and 159 in the first two months to 258 and 203 in the last two. The big improvement wasn't the number of meetings asked for but the percentage *accepted*, which rose from 54 to 96 percent. Wow! Asking more helped, but asking *effectively* helped more. The impact of both, along with focusing on more BD hours in aggregate, had a compounding effect: the number of BD meetings held in month one was 68. In the last month, 188.

The give-to-get measure was my favorite, but it didn't turn out like I expected. Before we started tracking the measures, I expected all of them to steadily improve, but the number of give-to-gets offered didn't. The number offered each month actually went *down*: 38, 24, 13, 18, 20, 15, 10, and 18. I would have thought this was very weird had I not been around to see why. Were people not trying? Were the clients not receptive to my favorite approach? The answer was none of the above. With about a three-month lag, the initial give-to-gets were so effective that they sold so much new business that *it swallowed up all their capacity.* The average number of new contracts in the first four months was thirty-three—in the second four months, sixty-seven. In only eight months they brought in more than double the business.

The team had so much success so quickly that they had to take a break from our program. All their capacity for new projects was taken, so we paused our yearlong program after the eighth month. That's a good problem to have.

My favorite part wasn't the results, however. It was how we got there: Everyone a little scared to try something new and expanding outside their comfort zone. Everyone pitching in, building an inventory of what was working. Everyone sharing as they learned. We had a magical feeling—we were all making a difference on a winning team.

Believe me, there were plenty of struggles along the way, especially in the beginning. It's unquestionably hard for people to add more to their plate (tracking metrics), try new things (offer give-to-gets), and be more transparent (sharing their data across the team). But you know what's really hard? Being on a miserable team that's stuck in neutral. High-performing sports teams work hard and have a blast doing it. If you want breakthrough results, it's what your team should do too.

·

Great sports teams have a lot in common: A common vision. An established mode of operation. A shared commitment to the vision. The team members believe in each other, in the goal, and in the strategic plan to get there. Great teams measure everything, from leading indicators like workouts and dietary data to specific activities on the field. And of course they measure lagging indicators, like wins and losses. They have a process for evaluating progress and setting goals. Everyone on the team is looking to give immediate feedback when things happen, high-fiving the little positives and pointing out what can be improved.

It can take a long time to build a legacy, but every iconic team starts somewhere. The best started with less than what they had in the end—because they improved. It might have been hard to build momentum and alignment in the beginning, but the very best do all these things, day in and day out. They're excited about their future. They're excited about their progress.

Follow these guidelines, and your team will do more than they ever thought they could. You'll build momentum. You'll inspire each other. You'll challenge each other. It will be hard at times, but each person will feel part of something bigger. They'll grow and accomplish new goals. Everyone wants to be a part of a winning team. This system creates just that.

Getting the Snowball Rolling

• • ●

WHAT DOES SUCCESS look like to you?

Personally, I see my success in terms of *relationships*. I love serving clients who need and appreciate my expertise. I love teaching this system to brilliant but stymied experts and watching it unlock all the potential within their businesses. I love working with the leaders of large organizations on deploying this system across hundreds of experts, people they care about and want to invest in. And I love collaborating with my amazing team and all the terrific friends and strategic partners we've made over the years. Our friends become clients and our clients become friends. Interacting with them, introducing them to each other, helping them all succeed—that's what drives me.

Most of all, I love spending time with my wife and daughters, secure in the knowledge that business is good. I can do this because of the momentum I've built using these methods. I still worry too much—I'm a recovering people-pleaser—but I can now get off the treadmill at the end of the day. I don't bring too much work home with me because when I'm home, work is still working. Our raving fans are out there doing our best marketing for us. Things don't grind to a halt the moment I take off my sport coat and put on my Ultimate Frisbee workout gear.

I love getting new leads through our Lead Generation efforts, and it's a thrill to listen and learn to a new prospect's problem and figure out some way to help, even if Bunnell Idea Group isn't the solution. Meanwhile our existing clients keep coming back because we're in touch regularly, always looking to give them more value, always communicating in the way that best suits their thinking preferences. At BIG our formula is simple: we *listen* to our clients, seek to *understand* what they need, and then do whatever it takes to *deliver* it. (If there's a better path to long-term success, I have yet to find it.)

More than a decade ago I left the HR consulting world behind to build BIG. A few years into building the company I got to the point where I was keeping myself busy. In fact, if I was being honest with myself, I knew the business *was* me. Plus, I was running a second company with a friend. Unsurprisingly, neither it nor BIG was thriving as they should. I had plateaued. So I sold my share in the other business back to my friend and went all in on BIG. I created a clear vision for the company I wanted to build and the life I wanted to lead while building it. In the process I designed my own system for creating such a vision: I called it a Life Blueprint. I still look at the now-tattered Moleskine notebook where I created mine.

The first page has a few quotes and a picture.

"All achievement, no matter what its nature or purpose, must begin with an intense, burning desire for something definite."

—NAPOLEON HILL

"Bad luck doesn't like persistence. When it runs across persistence, it goes away and finds someone else."

—UNKNOWN

"I even have a superstition that has grown on me as a result of invisible hands coming all the time—namely, that if you do follow your bliss you put yourself on a kind of track that has been there all the while, waiting for you, and the life that you ought to be living is the one you are living. When you can see that, you begin to meet people who are in your field of bliss, and they open doors to you. I say, follow your bliss and don't be afraid, and doors will open where you didn't know they were going to be."

—JOSEPH CAMPBELL

I would read these quotes often. The picture was even more meaningful. It was a 1968 picture of Bob Gibson, a St. Louis Cardinals pitcher I
had worshipped while growing up. Gibson owned that year. In 2016 the
average number of complete game shutouts for a team's *entire* pitching
staff was a little more than one. In 1968 Gibson himself threw *thirteen* and
finished *twenty-eight* games himself, a feat unheard of today. His earned
run average was 1.12. Unhittable. He won the Cy Young Award for best
pitcher. He won the regular season MVP Award. The picture is of Gibson
in action, just releasing the ball, throwing so damn hard he nearly goes
horizontal.

That picture meant one thing to me: *the desire to be the best.*

Below all this inspiration I scribbled down a vision of what I wanted
my life to look like in ten years, including a high-level description of BIG
and of what I wanted our family to look like. I wrote about what I wanted
my relationships to be like with Becky and my daughters. I even wrote
down specific goals for cash flow and net worth, a description of where
we would live, and the family rituals I wanted to keep doing or build on,
like our annual Daddy Robot Day trip with each daughter and the annual
Bunnell Movie I made of each year's family adventures, premiering on
New Year's Day.

After completing my Life Blueprint I was a little embarrassed to walk
through it with Becky. I felt like a geeky goal weirdo returning from a
hyped-up self-help conference held in a football stadium. But I fostered
the courage and walked her through what I had written. She loved it. She
was behind me, she believed in me, and I found that was exactly what I
needed.

Remember, from back in Chapter 1, how important having a *why* is?
My why, what was driving me, was a desire to create the best future for
my family. Short term, that meant designing the perfect environment for
everyone to thrive. Long term, it meant showing my daughters Gabby and
Josie that you can run at your fears, take the harder path, and build something great. They were young, but they were paying attention—watching,
learning, absorbing. I *had* to succeed for them. *The desire to be the best.* Not
for me really, but for those two young women I love so much.

That Life Blueprint changed everything. The progress that happened afterward didn't come because of some phenomenal stroke of luck—although I've been very lucky. Or through Herculean effort—although I've put in plenty of midwestern-y good, hard work. The progress occurred because I was always moving in an incremental fashion toward my vision. The vision painted a picture of where I was headed, those extremely ambitious goals. I had no idea if it was even possible to hit the ten-year numbers I had written down. But each week I knew I was moving in that direction, slowly, one step at a time. Edwin Locke taught us goals matter. Teresa Amabile showed us that the happiest and most successful people celebrate incremental progress. This was pure behavioral psychology in action.

Celebrating incremental progress used to be the hardest part for me. My brain is wired for coming up with far more ideas than I could ever check off my list. This brought me down sometimes. I'd end a day or a week thinking only about what I *didn't* get done. I had to hack my own habits to counter this. I started forcing myself to write down all the things I'd gotten done, all the progress I made, in my notebook every Friday afternoon.

Over time this ritual evolved. Now I do it all electronically, using a journaling app. I tally metrics, summarize progress, even include photos of the fun things that happened during the week. This process is a lifesaver, anchoring me on the successes of the week instead of on the things I wish I'd done. Spending a few minutes writing down the week's progress is all the celebration I need, and it ends my workweek on a high note. The habit I once resisted is now so strong that I haven't missed a week in years. When I first started, it felt like a chore, something that got in the way of "real work." Now it's a cemented habit, something I look forward to. I love this time.

Then there's the growth. Walt Disney once said something that deeply resonates with me: "We don't make movies to make money, we make money to make more movies." I feel that way about BIG. For lots of cultural reasons we don't talk openly about money in America, and I wish we did. There's so much misinformation. What appears to be true with people and money rarely is. The person living in a nice house and driving a fancy new car might be leveraging it all, filing for bankruptcy the moment one small thing goes wrong. Meanwhile someone else down the street, in a similar home and with the same cars, might have far more cash in the bank than they need, a financial margin that gives them an inner calm and the potential to do whatever they want.

That's the person I admire: the one with a margin, a buffer. I remember thinking that my Blueprint's financial goals were incredibly aspirational. They felt impossible—I wrote them down anyway. I clearly remember flipping my pencil around to erase and lower those goals before finally deciding to stick with them. *No,* I decided. *That's what I want to achieve, and ten years is a long time. I'll figure out how to do it.*

I ended up being wrong—by quite a bit, actually. I didn't reach those financial goals in ten years. I reached them in eight. Not only that, we beat them that year by over 60 percent.

I remember reading back through the notebook at the time, astonished that things had grown that far, that fast. In a way accomplishing those goals created a new problem: I had plateaued again. I was doing all the things I'd hoped to be doing, but new ideas were still surfacing. For example, I'd always wanted to write a book. I wanted to impact more people in other ways too. We'd been successful taking our programs to larger and larger organizations, but there were still so many more people out there who would benefit from the system. In the beginning it had made sense to start with large organizations where one opportunity might affect hundreds of people, but what about entrepreneurs? Freelancers? People just starting out who don't have the money for our training courses?

I needed new goals and a new vision. I found an online course called The Focus Course, and I signed up. It was amazing. That work led to a new vision, a new ten-year plan. I discovered that I was doing a lot of work that others could do instead, so we implemented a plan to free up more of my time to do the deep work with the highest value: creating content like this book. What seemed impossible before came together with a plan.

Craft the vision. Pick the short-term leading indicators, the things you can control. Set a cadence to review tactics and execution. Celebrate incremental progress.

Let's get back to *you*. Let's review and make sure you're on track with your vision, your plan. Go back to the personal strategic plan you started in Chapter 1. Also, pull out the rituals list you created. Now that you've read the entire book, we can beef that plan up. I want you to finish this book with a plan to crush your goals and have fun doing it.

A well-crafted strategy is only half the battle. Knowing yourself well and setting up the right habits—while removing the wrong ones—brings a strategy to life. The war is won in the trenches. The tactical decisions you make every day will free up or squander the time you have for business development: "I'll send this email after lunch. I just want to catch up on this other, less important thing." But then the afternoon comes, and you're in a postlunch coma. "No way am I writing that email now. I'll get to it first thing in the morning, when I'm fresh. Man, that pizza was good, though." Rinse and repeat. Next thing you know, you've missed a vital opportunity. Build ironclad habits of execution, and watch your business grow.

Review your plan from the very beginning of learning this system. What's changed for you as you've worked your way through the book? Is your future vision the same? If it's changed in light of a deeper understanding of business development, mark it down. Goal setting really works—often better than we expect. Make sure you've put your ladder against the right building before you start to climb.

The most effective way to stay on track with goals is to track your progress. Decide on leading and lagging indicators to watch. Lagging indicators are the ones you probably already have to measure and report on if you're part of an organization—revenue, originations, deals closed, production. The patter is different across industries, but it usually comes down to revenue, profits, and deals won. These are your results; they lag behind the efforts you put in to achieve them. You don't have complete control over them, but they do reflect your efforts, so there's no ignoring them. Select a handful of key lagging indicators that you can review regularly on your BD "dashboard."

Leading indicators measure the things you *can* control: the actions you take to drive new business, develop client relationships, and bring opportunities to fruition. Your leading indicators might be anything from the number of MITs you get done each week to the percentage of Protemoi people you've reached out to this month. Think broadly about what you'd like to motivate yourself to do. Hours spent on business development, asks you've made to move deals forward, give-to-gets offered—there are many possibilities. Pick two or three to start. Ask yourself: If I do these things, week in and week out, do I think my business will flourish? If the answer is yes, give them a shot. I find I tweak mine each quarter; they're not set in stone. The important thing is just to get started.

Between your leading and lagging indicators, you'll be able to take the pulse of your BD progress. By watching the interplay between them, you'll have a better sense of which actions are effective at driving results. The best part? Leading indicators are motivational. By focusing on what you can control and not worrying about the things you can't, you keep progressing. It's the difference between focusing on *offering* give-to-gets (fun, can be done today, relatively easy) and worrying about making your annual target (stressful, long term, hard to figure out what to do next). I rarely think about making our annual numbers, but I think dozens of times a day about making "asks" to keep projects moving. That's because I track that leading indicator, I want to keep those numbers in an acceptable range, and it's a thrill to get close to or even beat my weekly record.

Remember what we discussed back in Chapter 10: better to track an important leading indicator subjectively than track a bad one accurately. Pick or evolve your metrics now. This is an important decision to get the snowball rolling.

Putting the Snowball System into Action

Now let's switch gears from analytical to practical thinking. There's no single BD routine that will work for everyone. These tools apply broadly to many different types of professionals, from people who always need a big funnel of new leads to those who simply need to elevate a handful of key relationships to deliver more value. That said, I can offer some guidelines on cadence that will help you integrate the Snowball System into your work life. Adapt this approach to suit your needs and your strategic goals.

Download the **Snowball System** worksheet for a visual of how all these pieces fit together. It's a poster that summarizes this process. Our training clients frequently attach this to their wall to remind them of what they should be doing. One of my favorite clients, Robb, proudly displays his faded, tattered poster every time I'm in his office. It makes us both happy. And guess what? Robb is a rainmaker.

BD activities can be pushed off a day here and a week there. Don't let that happen. Place some kind of reminder where you can see it—this poster is perfect for that.

Remember rewards. Every ritual on your list needs one. Even if it feels silly, treat yourself. Your brain will notice, and you'll find it easier and easier to stick to each habit over time. It's good to have a friendly relationship with your brain.

Annually and Quarterly

The purpose of annual and quarterly reviews is to set a direction. Life and business move quickly—if you want to build momentum toward your goals, you can't afford to wait 364 days between strategic reviews. You want enough time to pass so that you can see long-term change happening but not so much that you need to make big course corrections each time.

Every three months schedule a few hours when you can sit without distractions and review and revise your personal strategy from Chapter 1. What's your new current state? Has your future vision changed? Are there some practices and behaviors that no longer serve you and belong on your to-don't list? With business development it's easy to miss the forest for the trees. The few hours you spend at thirty thousand feet will be some of the most valuable investments of time you can ever make.

This is also the time to review growth strategy plans for your long-term, high-value clients.

It takes me about two hours to do this for BIG, and it's some of the best time I spend every year. I enter my review in my journaling app and tag the entry as Annual Summary or Quarterly Summary so I can find old ones quickly.

Your process will evolve to suit your needs. Here's the complete list of what I do.

Tally leading indicators and lagging indicators. I've chosen to take the time to do this myself and not delegate it. Entering the numbers myself gives me deeper insights than if I handed them off to someone else.

Analyze the data for trends. I always get important insights from this. Maybe the numbers are higher or lower than I thought. Maybe I realize I need a new metric to track or that I need to retire one that's not relevant anymore. Even if things are going great, there's always something new to improve.

Summarize my results. I ruthlessly compare what I'd set out to do in the prior quarter against what I actually accomplished. I grade myself from A to F in areas borrowed from Shawn Blanc's The Focus Course: spiritual, physical, relationships, rest and recreation, vocation (i.e., BIG), and economics.

Look forward. After the look back I set goals for the next quarter. This includes specific goals in each area, business and personal. Over the years I've learned that less is more. It's counterintuitive, but I've found that the fewer goals I have, the more likely I am to meet each one.

Pick leading indicators. I'm always looking to have the fewest, most predictive leading indicators. Right now, I measure four: hours spent on business development, MITs completed, a subjective 1-to-5 score of how much I'm enjoying my work, and the number of asks for the advance. These four measures are working great for me right now and are easy to tally. They measure quantity of effort (BD hours), quality of effort (MITs completed), enjoyment (the 1–5 score), and how proactive I am (asks).

Always remember the mantra: Think big, start small, scale up. It's better to start with one paragraph and one metric than to try something elaborate and quit halfway before you get rolling. Start small and get going. You can add more later.

Believe it or not, I really struggled with this process at first. You might come away from having read this book thinking I'm a big practical guy, but it's actually my lowest preference by far. I used to *loathe* having a self-set meeting on my calendar every quarter. I felt like it was getting in the way of real work—I was too busy!

In the beginning I started small and tried to see it through an experimental lens: an hour of brainstorming and strategizing. That attitude got me started, and over time I fell in love with the practical aspects. As you have success doing this, you'll look forward to it more and more.

Monthly

Most businesses operate on some sort of monthly cadence, so this is probably the best pace to focus on two things: your lagging indicators and your relationships.

Are you on track to meet the expectations of your organization? If not, is it because something prevented you from taking your planned actions during the previous month? Or is it because you took those actions and they didn't have the intended effects? What needs to change in the coming month?

Cross-reference your long-term strategic goals from your quarterly review against your to-do list. Are you acting on each goal at the tactical level? For example, if one of your goals was to create a strategic partnership this quarter, do you have concrete action steps broken out toward that objective? Often we'll complete a step and, in our rush, neglect to specify the follow-up task. Now's the time to check on your progress and make sure that every goal has an incremental step lined up for execution.

Check in on your Protemoi List. Have you added value for each and every person on your list this month? If not, what percentage did you get to? If you regularly whiff your Protemoi outreach, is it possible your list is too long to handle?

Remember: the people on your Protemoi List are *first among equals*. Although every client and prospect deserves attention, each of your Protemoi people is at a higher priority because they have a serious impact or potential impact on your business. These are not just the people you know and like. In fact, several of them should be people you still don't know or don't know well but whose goodwill could help dramatically grow your business. Now is the time to decide: Is there anyone who needs to be added or removed?

This monthly sequence typically takes me about an hour. I try to add value with Protemoi people I haven't yet connected with that month, but sometimes I don't get that far and just note their names and the way I'll proactively be helpful to them over the next week or so.

I don't document the monthly review in my journal: for me this one simply generates tasks that get added directly to my to-do list.

Weekly

The weekly review is where I find the magic happens. I never miss the weekly review, and I feel uncomfortable, almost lost, if I can't do it on Friday and need to pick it up over the weekend.

My focus here is to revisit my quarterly goals, to jot down all the progress that happened in the prior week, summarize anything I was unhappy with, and document my goals for the upcoming week.

I type this up in a journal entry, tag it Weekly Summary, and finish it off with a few pictures of the week. My work pictures might be a selfie in front of a new prospect's building or a fun keynote speech in front of a room full of clients. My home pictures might be my wife, Becky, beating me in a board game or a picture of our miniature donkey, Louie Hamilton, rolling on the ground, giving himself a dirt bath. I *need* this weekly ritual to combat my tendency to focus on what didn't get done. This is my celebration of the week, and the pictures are the piece that brings back the positive emotion. It connects me with my why and is probably the most important time I spend each week. Seeing the asks I made, entering the time I spent, attaching those pictures of work and family, all snapshots of incremental improvement—all of it focuses me on positive progress. Teresa Amabile would be proud.

Sometimes I'm disappointed in myself during my review too. Maybe I didn't do something I needed to do or got too involved in something another team member could have handled. Any of these could be a sign I've drifted off course. The beauty of this review is that I've only drifted for a week at most. Before I developed this habit I spent entire *quarters* drifting off course! The world is always pulling us into doing the wrong things—it doesn't share our priorities. Far better to realize you're off track within a week and course-correct. So when I do have a bad week, I am oddly happy. I vent in the journal and come away motivated to do much better next week.

No matter how the prior week went, the most important element of the weekly review is to be proactive. Be sure to go over your Opportunity List. Are you clear on what the next step is for each opportunity and how you're going to get there?

Set the MITs for the week to come—three is plenty. Getting those three done each week without fail will be vastly more effective than what most people do: write down ten, twenty, or more tasks that are "all important" and then do five or six of the less valuable but easier ones. Or worse, just let your email inbox be your to-do list and spend all day greasing the squeaky-wheel clients and letting your most important opportunities and relationships die on the vine because they aren't bugging you.

Some of the professionals we train say that a weekly review is too frequent. Maybe it is for some. If that's the case for you, feel free to try biweekly. For me BD activities change quickly. A short email from a client can change the priority of a most important thing immediately. Plus, the ability to manage your schedule depends on the rhythm of weekdays and weekends. It's easiest to ask yourself: How many hours do I have available to spend on BD next week? This leads to: What are the MITs I can get done with that amount of time? It's much harder to look out further than a week.

Rainmakers make the time to focus their efforts. They don't say, "I don't have time to work on BD next week." They say, "I only have an hour for BD next week, so what's the most important thing I can fit in?"

Daily

The goal at the daily level is to push the ball forward on your BD efforts at your earliest opportunity. Do the hardest thing first.

If you aren't able to make even a little progress here, you may not be slicing your incremental steps small enough at the weekly level. First and foremost in any workday do the Most Important Things. Push those forward. Focus on business development first—not "after lunch" or "in that opening at 3:30." There's nothing like checking one of those off your list—after that, your day-to-day work rolls downhill. Once any MITs are out of the way that day, use your BD time to send an asset to a Protemoi person or move an opportunity forward.

Fifteen or twenty minutes in the morning on business development may not sound like much, but multiply that by five days a week, fifty weeks a year, and you're going to be shocked by how much you can get done. Rainmakers don't spend enormous amounts of time on business development; more often they're just very consistent about doing it and very focused during the time they do spend.

One of my favorite clients developed a great daily ritual. She writes down the most important BD task she has each day on a Post-it Note and sticks it on her computer. She rewards herself with coffee right after that. Then she doesn't let herself leave her office that day until that task is done. The reward for her is the satisfaction of peeling the note off, crumpling it up, and tossing it in her trash can. Today she's a rainmaker bringing in millions of dollars a year. Those Post-it Notes might be among the most valuable on the planet. And she told me she's never had to sleep in her office.

·

We seller-experts are unique. No one else juggles as much—deepening our knowledge, managing client teams, developing relationships, delivering on client needs, running the business. It's no wonder BD skill building gets shelved and the tactics tabled. Days become weeks, weeks become months. Before you know it, growth stalls.

One common fear I hear from people in my training sessions is that if they actually put the Snowball System to work, they're going to have too many leads to handle, too many opportunities to manage, too many relationships to maintain. Rarely does a high-level professional come into my training without already feeling, to some degree, overwhelmed. Sure, we all want to close deals, make revenue, and get promotions, but in the heat of the workday, more of *anything* can feel like a bad idea.

Here's some good news: focusing on business development is the one habit that can positively impact all the others. In *The Power of Habit* Charles Duhigg calls these *keystone habits*. These are the habits that positively impact many other habits and improve results across the board. Do these well, and many good other things will happen naturally.

Business development habits are keystones to broader success. A growing business is easier to manage than a stalled one with no margin for error. A full pipeline of leads is much easier to manage than a scanty one. Hundreds of raving fans are easier to nurture than a handful. A little attention goes farther when you're in high demand. It means more because others know how busy you are.

Growth is the medicine that cures nearly every ill. It deepens your knowledge because you're talking to more clients. It helps you manage your internal teams because it provides new opportunities for all. It helps you develop relationships because you know more people and are the hub of a desirable network. And it helps you run the business because you have strong profits to invest in exciting new products, services, and people. Growth creates more growth, and it's a lot more fun than shrinking.

Here's more good news: the amount of time you need to invest in pure BD efforts is modest considering the return you can expect. Twenty or thirty minutes a day, one hour weekly, a couple of hours monthly, and half a day or so every quarter (and of course the time needed to efficiently close all those opportunities coming in). That's probably less time than you're spending taking old friends to lunch, checking social media, and obsessing over your fantasy football lineup. This system will make you so much more efficient at business development that you'll actually free up time. Less busy-ness, more business.

Best news of all? You'll live the life you want to live. More than anything I've seen, getting good at bringing business in correlates to success: Promotions. Expanding your team. Getting the meatier work you want. Raising your prices. Getting that big bonus. Being indispensable. Leading a winning team. Feeling great.

Think back to your *why* in Chapter 1, the underlying reason you want to become great at growth. It was something important to you, something deep. My why is showing my daughters you can design and build the life you want. It's not easy, and that's *exactly* why it can be so meaningful. You can start a company in your closet and can grow it to where you're teaching people all over the world. When you have setbacks, you can overcome them. When you make mistakes, you can find other paths to success. When you hit plateaus, you can break through them. You can work hard and love doing it. You can build an awesome team of people and integrate them into your life as trusted friends. You can celebrate progress and still find a way to improve next time. You can build expertise and assets and use them to help others. You can work with some of the smartest people in the world and improve their lives.

I love that my daughters see how they can create the life of their dreams. They can change the world in their own personal way. I can already tell that they will. And I can hardly wait to see them do it.

That's my why.

What's yours?

Acknowledgments

I am grateful for what I am and have. My thanksgiving is perpetual.

—HENRY DAVID THOREAU

I have a worry about this book, and it's an odd one.

I don't worry about whether it will sell. My goal was to write something I could take pride in. I achieved that goal, and that's enough for me.

I don't worry if it will receive favorable reviews. I know this system works, and that's enough for me.

I don't worry about giving our prized techniques away for the price of a book. I know they will help people, and that's enough for me.

What I worry about is that I won't have sufficiently thanked the people who made it possible.

As I painstakingly incorporated each element of the Snowball System into the manuscript, I found myself wanting to thank the individual responsible for inspiring that particular technique or for teaching it to me in the first place. Throughout the writing process I fought the urge to thank all the other wonderful people whose encouragement, support, and wisdom have gotten me to this point in my life. Unfortunately, the format of a book—well, the patience of its readers—made that inadvisable.

So I'm stuck thanking people here, way in the back of the book. All I can say is, were it up to me, I'd have put my acknowledgments smack at the top of Chapter 1 and then continued with call-outs throughout the text. (You're probably glad it *wasn't* up to me.)

I need to start with my parents. In many ways they taught me the seller-expert model. My dad is a completely authentic guy. You can always count on him to guide you to what's right for you, regardless of what's right for him. He makes friends with nearly everybody, finding commonality in no time at all, starting with that bright red Cardinals hat he wears every single day. My dad is the seller.

My mom taught child development for nearly thirty-five years at the same school, always deepening her own expertise—a quiet role model for the entire Fort Wayne Community School System. I have a 1970s picture of her energetically leading her class, and the bulletin board she made in the background says, "Improvement starts with I." The apple didn't fall far from the tree. When my mom falls in love with a subject, she goes deep, whether it's guiding students, gardening, or genealogy. My mom is the expert.

I learned many things from my mom and dad. Above all, I learned perseverance. It was never easy for us as a family, but we always made it, always found a way. I'm grateful they raised me in rural Indiana, teaching me how to treat people right, invest in myself, and live by a midwestern work ethic. My mom and dad provided the perfect start for me, struggles and all, and I still learn from them to this day.

Next is easy: my wife of over twenty-five years, Becky. I'm a peculiar person at times, frequently becoming so infatuated with a new topic or skill to master that, honestly, I can go off the deep end. It's Becky who keeps me grounded. She knows when to push back on my nutty curiosity and provides the perfect words to keep me on an even keel. She's the wise sage in my corner, my secret weapon.

Next, my two daughters. I didn't realize when I had kids that I'd learn so much from them. I always thought I'd be the slightly eccentric, modern version of TV dads like Wally Cleaver and Andy Griffith, imparting insightful words of wisdom five minutes before bedtime like clockwork. It hasn't happened that way at all. I'm the one who's always learning. Gabby and Josie have taught me about determination, hard work, empathy, inclusion, and even the art of training miniature donkeys. Most of all, having these two amazing daughters has taught me what love is. I can't thank them enough.

Then there's a whole team of people who have helped this book be the best it can be. My fantastic agent, Lisa DiMona, has added insights at every turn. Some people told me "agents don't matter." They were wrong. Lisa mattered—a lot. Dave Moldawer is a writing genius, helping craft and edit the book proposal and manuscript. Rob Whitfield, now CEO of Ferrazzi Greenlight and one of my favorite training participants ever, helped with the section on Protemoi. Colleen Lawrie has been a fantastic editor and publishing expert, not only giving the right advice but also knowing how to give it. And thank you to my team at Hachette Book Group who helped get the book polished and to the presses, especially my project editor, Sandra Beris; my copy editor, Josephine Moore; and my marketing director, Lindsay Fradkoff.

I certainly can't forget the great team at Bunnell Idea Group, with Darla Ward being the biggest contributor. She's amazing, the best thing that ever happened to BIG. Debra Partridge, Bradley Humbles, Matt Kress, Marshall Seese Jr., Graham Reeves, Austin Ward, Shane Ward, Macey Smith, and Ryan Grelecki have all had a big impact on BIG, among many, many others. Katrina Johnson, PhD, has provided invaluable research advice over the years. Many times, we learn from our clients too. John Hightower taught me the phrase "Think Big, Start Small, Scale Up," long ago, and I use it nearly every day. And although Herrmann International isn't part of BIG, the folks over there feel like members of the team because they've been such great partners. Ann Herrmann-Nehdi and her entire team are fantastic. Thanks to all of you.

That leaves me with the most stressful part: thanking everyone else who has helped me my entire life. Or at least as close to everyone as I can get. I've struggled with how to list the right people, keeping things both interesting and reasonably short. While on a run one day, thinking about all the people I'm grateful for, I started trying to select three words that would encapsulate my debt to them. This gratitude game was so much fun, I decided to use it here, with a few inside jokes added just for enjoyment.

To keep this section from ballooning into a stand-alone memoir, I limited myself to the fifty most important people contributing to my career.

That made it really hard. (Sorry, awesome person who would have made the fifty-first spot. You know who you are.)

Here goes, in roughly chronological order:

1. Grandpa Goodrich—Kept my promise.
2. Becky Genth—Always helped me.
3. Aunt Tena—Longtime role model.
4. Uncle Ben—Opened the outdoors.
5. Bob Gibson—Desire for greatness.
6. Dave Mendez—Eighties metal forever!
7. Chris Weidler—Sorry: tone-deaf.
8. Cindy Desjean—Influenced my math.
9. Doug Crandell—My writing inspiration.
10. Ball State University—Great learning experience.
11. Guy Driggers and Mike Engledow—Saw my future.
12. Kerry Harding—I'd ask WWKD?
13. Delta Tau Delta Fraternity—Taught me sooooo . . .
14. Bill Taylor—Always moving, growing.
15. John Rhoades—Gave once-in-a-lifetime opportunity.
16. Bill Borchelt—Brother, another mother.
17. Anne Harris—Path to Hewitt.
18. Craig Dolezal—Believed in me.
19. David Batten—DMD! Studying! Life-friend.
20. Andy Hiles—Amazing BD mentor.
21. Michael Murphy—First BD inspiration.
22. Brian Cafferelli—Perfect tag team!
23. Jason Jeffay—Cubs *stink*, forever.
24. Bob Brubaker—Board game tonight?
25. Jim Buckley—So much awesomeness.
26. Dawnette and Paul Hewitt—Great friends, always.
27. Mike R. Lee—Taught people management.
28. Robb Stanley—Amazing counsel, friend.
29. Jay Schmitt—First BIG client!
30. Russ Osmond—Learned *so* much.
31. Larnie Higgins—Designer. Developer. Doer.

32. Coffee—My best friend.
33. Ned Morse—The best ideas.
34. Scott Harris—Wise outside counsel.
35. Warren Shiver—Let's keep sharing.
36. Bonneau Ansley—You inspire me!!
37. Chris Graham—Love your mind.
38. Shawn Blanc—Are we related?
39. Chris Dawson—Keep pushing me.
40. Merrick Olives—Admire your priorities.
41. Minsoo Pak—Big ideas, forever!
42. Sandy Lutton—Always helpful, happy.
43. David Nygren—So, so good.
44. Spencer Borchelt—Where to start?
45. Mike Duffy—Mutually beneficial, defined.
46. Adam Grant—Your research rocks.
47. Denie Sandison Weil and Frank Weil—What a connection!
48. Dian and Mike Deimler—Inspirational life designers.
49. Amy Hiett—Perfected our path.
50. Louie Hamilton—Lifeless, without donkeys.

Resources

Introduction

I'm a big fan of Dan Pink's work. To go deeper in his work on business development, see Dan Pink, *To Sell Is Human: The Surprising Truth About Moving Others* (New York: Penguin, 2013).

Business development is a teachable skill. For the research on why expertise is something people learn I recommend Anders Ericsson and Robert Pool, *Peak: Secrets from the New Science of Expertise* (Boston: Houghton Mifflin Harcourt, 2017). Or, if you'd like to listen to a podcast summarizing their work, I highly recommend *Freakonomics Radio*, "Peak Project," http://freakonomics.com/peak.

Chapter 1

For the research on psychological momentum, see S. E. Iso-Ahola and C. O. Dotson, "Psychological Momentum: Why Success Breeds Success," *Review of General Psychology* 18, no. 1 (2014): 19–33.

For an easily digestible and comprehensive overview of how we spend much more time on autopilot than we realize, see Charles Duhigg, *The Power of Habit: Why We Do What We Do in Life and Business* (London: Random House, 2014).

For much, much more information on everything whole-brained, check out Ned Herrmann and Ann Herrmann-Nehdi, *The Whole Brain*

Business Book: Unlocking the Power of Whole Brain Thinking in Organizations, Teams, and Individuals, 2nd ed. (New York: McGraw Hill Education, 2015).

For an overview of Dan and Chip Heath's work on change, including the elephant metaphor for how we think, see Chip Heath and Dan Heath, *Switch: How to Change Things When Change Is Hard* (London: Random House, 2013).

Chapter 2

For a summary of Teresa Amabile's work on incremental progress see Teresa Amabile and Steven Kramer, *The Progress Principle: Using Small Wins to Ignite Joy, Engagement, and Creativity at Work* (Boston: Harvard Business Review Press, 2011).

For Locke's original study on the power of goal setting, see Edwin A. Locke, Karyll N. Shaw, Lise M. Saari, and Gary P. Latham, "Goal Setting and Task Performance: 1969–1980," *Psychological Bulletin* 90, no. 1 (1981): 125–152.

My favorite David Maister book is David Maister, Charles Green, and Robert Galford, *The Trusted Advisor* (New York: Free Press, 2004).

For a short and inspirational read on the power of Ken Blanchard's raving fan concept, see Ken Blanchard and Sheldon Bowles, *Raving Fans: A Revolutionary Approach to Customer Service* (London: HarperCollinsEntertainment, 2011).

For more on the primacy effect, see "Serial-Position Effect," Wikipedia, https://en.wikipedia.org/wiki/Serial-position_effect.

For a comprehensive deep dive into how much stronger the negative is than the positive, see R. F. Baumeister, E. Bratslavsky, C. Finkenauer, and K. D. Vohs, "Bad Is Stronger Than Good," *Review of General Psychology* 5, no. 4 (2001): 323–370.

I highly recommend Keith Ferrazzi and Tahl Raz, *Never Eat Alone: And Other Secrets to Success, One Relationship at a Time* (New York: Crown Business, 2014).

Chapter 3

Here is the preeminent and original book on positioning: Al Ries and Jack Trout, *Positioning: The Battle for Your Mind* (New York: McGraw Hill Education, 2014).

Here is the original study on the power of three in messaging and marketing. I found it highly readable and insightful: Suzanne B. Shu and Kurt A. Carolson, "When Three Charms but Four Alarms: Identifying the Optimal Number of Claims in Persuasion Settings," *Journal of Marketing* 78, no. 1 (January 2014): 127–139.

For the core research on how much we can typically remember, see J. N. Rouder, R. D. Morey, N. Cowan, C. E. Zwilling, C. C. Morey, and M. S. Pratte, "An Assessment of Fixed-Capacity Models of Visual Working Memory," *Proceedings of the National Academy of Sciences* 105, no. 16 (April 2008): 5975–5979.

Chapter 4

Here is Burger's work on commonality: Jerry M. Burger, Nicole Messian, Shebani Patel, Alicia del Prado, and Carmen Anderson, "What a Coincidence! The Effects of Incidental Similarity on Compliance," *Personality and Social Psychology Bulletin* 30, no. 1 (January 2004): 35–43.

For more on the mere-exposure effect, see "Mere-Exposure Effect," Wikipedia, https://en.wikipedia.org/wiki/Mere-exposure_effect.

If you'd like to dig into more recent research in the mere-exposure effect that aligns with this chapter, see R. F. Bornstein, D. R. Leone, and D. J. Galley, "The Generalizability of Subliminal Mere Exposure Effects: Influence of Stimuli Perceived Without Awareness on Social Behavior," *Journal of Personality and Social Psychology* 53, no. 6 (1987): 1070–1079.

Or this: Xiang Fang, Surendra Singh, and Rohini Ahluwalia, "An Examination of Different Explanations for the Mere Exposure Effect," *Journal of Consumer Research* 34, no. 1 (June 2007): 97–103.

I cannot speak highly enough about Adam Grant's research. Although there are several studies I could recommend, the most easily digestible way to dig into his work is to read Adam Grant, *Give and Take: Why Helping Others Drives Our Success* (New York: Penguin, 2014).

Here's the specific research on the power of a sincere thank-you: A. M. Grant and F. Gino, "A Little Thanks Goes a Long Way: Explaining Why Gratitude Expressions Motivate Prosocial Behavior," *Journal of Personality and Social Psychology* 98, no. 6 (2010): 946–955.

I love Losada's research on high-performing teams. Here's my favorite study: Marcial Losada and Emily Heaphy, "The Role of Positivity and Connectivity in the Performance of Business Teams: A Nonlinear Dynamics Model," *American Behavioral Scientist* 47, no. 6 (2004): 740–765.

For more on the concept that unexpected surprises are more powerful, see David B. Strohmetz, Bruce Rind, Reed Risher, and Michael Lynn, "Sweetening the Till: The Use of Candy to Increase Restaurant Tipping," *Journal of Applied Social Psychology* 32, no. 2 (2002): 300–309.

Chapter 5

Cialdini's work on what influences us as humans is a must-read. I recommend his seminal work as a first step. This is fantastic: Robert Cialdini, *Influence: The Psychology of Persuasion* (New York: Collins, 2007).

Chapter 6

For the research on the power of a face-to-face ask, see M. Mahdi Roghanizad and Vanessa K. Bohns, "Ask in Person: You're Less Persuasive Than You Think over Email," *Journal of Experimental Social Psychology* 69 (March 2017): 223–226.

Chapter 7

For further exploration of Tamir's research on how it feels to talk about yourself, see Diana I. Tamir and Jason P. Mitchell, "Disclosing Information About the Self Is Intrinsically Rewarding," *Proceedings of the National Academy of Sciences* 109, no. 21 (May 2012): 8038–8043.

For more on how experts can become closed-minded over time, see V. Ottati, E. Price, C. Wilson, and N. Sumaktoyo, "When Self-Perceptions of Expertise Increase Closed-Minded Cognition: The Earned Dogmatism Effect," *Journal of Experimental Social Psychology* 61 (November 2015): 131–138.

To go further into the power of curiosity and how it's an intrinsic motivator, see P.-Y. Oudeyer, J. Gottlieb, and M. Lopes, "Intrinsic Motivation, Curiosity, and Learning: Theory and Applications in Educational Technologies," *Progress in Brain Research* 229 (2016): 257–284. Also see Mathias J. Gruber, Bernard D. Gelman, and Charan Ranganath, "States of Curiosity Modulate Hippocampus-Dependent Learning via the Dopaminergic Circuit," *Neuron* 84, no. 2 (2014): 486–496.

If you want to be seen as a trusted advisor, read Patrick Lencioni, *Getting Naked: A Business Fable About Shedding the Three Fears That Sabotage Client Loyalty* (San Francisco: Jossey-Bass, 2013).

Chapter 8

Here's the research on how we tend to highly value things we create. I found this core-level research highly readable and interesting: Michael I. Norton, Daniel Mochon, and Dan Ariely, "The IKEA Effect: When Labor Leads to Love," *Journal of Consumer Psychology* 22, no. 3 (July 2012): 453–460.

Here's Goldsmith's book that includes some great information on the FeedForward concept: Marshall Goldsmith with Mark Reiter, *What Got You Here Won't Get You There: How Successful People Become Even More Successful* (Boston: Hachette, 2014).

If you'd like to skip the book and simply read a short article on FeedForward, see Marshall Goldsmith, "Try FeedForward Instead of Feedback," Marshall Goldsmith | FeedForward, www.marshallgoldsmithfeedforward.com/html/Articles.htm.

Here's the most interesting study I've found on commitment: J. L. Freedman and S. C. Fraser, "Compliance Without Pressure: The Foot-in-the-Door Technique," *Journal of Personality and Social Psychology* 4, no. 2 (1966): 195–202.

Also, Anthony Greenwald and his research team found that when people tell others what they plan to do, it enhances the chance of them doing it: Anthony G. Greenwald, Catherine G. Carnot, Rebecca Beach, and Barbara Young, "Increasing Voting Behavior by Asking People If They Expect to Vote," *Journal of Applied Psychology* 72, no. 2 (1987): 315–318.

Here is some great research on how people focus on price as a predictor of quality: Maria L. Cronley, Steven S. Posavac, Tracy Meyer, Frank R. Kardes, and James J. Kellaris, "A Selective Hypothesis Testing Perspective on Price-Quality Inference and Inference-Based Choice," *Journal of Consumer Psychology* 15, no. 2 (2005): 159–169.

For more on how creating levity in financial conversations reduces the chance of negotiation, see Terri R. Kurtzberg, Charles E. Naquin, and Liuba Y. Belkin, "Humor as a Relationship-Building Tool in Online Negotiation," *International Journal of Conflict Management* 20, no. 4 (October 2009): 377–397.

Much research shows that buyers look to price as a key indicator of quality. (Expensive = good. Cheap = bad.) Here's an easy-to-read study with simple and memorable examples: Maria L. Cronley, Steven S. Posavac, Tracy Meyer, Frank R. Kardes, and James J. Kellaris, "A Selective Hypothesis Testing Perspective on Price-Quality Inference and Inference-Based Choice," *Journal of Consumer Psychology* 15, no. 2 (2005): 159–169.

For more on how specific prices get less pushback than rounded ones, see M. F. Mason, A. J. Lee, E. A. Wiey, and D. R. Ames, "Precise Offers Are Potent Anchors: Conciliatory Counteroffers and Attributions of Knowledge in Negotiations," *Journal of Experimental Social Psychology* 49, no. 4 (July 2013): 759–763.

For a broader discussion on behavioral economics, I highly recommend Dan Ariely, *Predictably Irrational: The Hidden Forces That Shape Our Decisions* (London: HarperCollins, 2009).

Chapter 9

Here's the study on how we generally assess our current situation from an overly positive state: Richard W. Robins and Jennifer S. Beer, "Positive

Illusions About the Self: Short-Term Benefits and Long-Term Costs," *Journal of Personality and Social Psychology* 80, no. 2 (2001): 340–352.

It wouldn't be funny to make up the idea that humor improves meeting productivity. See Nale Lehmann-Willenbrock and Joseph A. Allen, "How Fun Are Your Meetings? Investigating the Relationship Between Humor Patterns in Team Interactions and Team Performance," *Journal of Applied Psychology* 99, no. 6 (2014): 1278–1287.

Chapter 10

Dr. Losada and Heaphy's work, "The Role of Positivity and Connectivity in the Performance of Business Teams: A Nonlinear Dynamics Model," comes up again here in Chapter 10.

If you want to dig deeper into how tracking leading indicators can "gamify" individual or team performance, I highly recommend Jane McGonigal, *SuperBetter: The Power of Living Gamefully* (New York: Penguin Books, 2015).

Conclusion

I found The Focus Course to be one of the best things I've ever done for myself. Check it out at The Focus Course, https://thefocuscourse.com.

I've already referenced Duhigg's *The Power of Habit*, above. It comes up here again in our discussion of keystone habits.

Want a Jump-Start?

Bunnell Idea Group training classes propel people further, faster.

Going deeper than any book can, our expert facilitators will guide you: deepening your knowledge, giving you feedback along the way, and perfecting your approach.

Our classroom training is called GrowBIG®, and the experience is insightful, interactive, and fun—you'll leave with a complete plan to take your skills to the next level, covering every last aspect of business development.

- ✦ On your own? You can attend a public workshop.
- ✦ In an organization? We can tailor the course to your needs and come to you.
- ✦ In a *really* large organization? We can train *your* people to train *your* seller-experts, allowing you to quickly scale and institutionalize the growth mindset.

All these approaches drive results.

We also consult. Our consulting helps design specific programs so you'll achieve your unique goals.

Or you might want to start small by getting your HBDI® Assessment. It's the simplest step with the quickest payoff.

Check out Bunnell Idea Group's services at www.bunnellideagroup .com, or give us a call today at 404.260.0780.

You can probably guess what our approach will be when you reach out: *we'll focus on being helpful.*

Index

Mo Bunnell is a speaker, consultant, and the founder and CEO of Bunnell Idea Group (BIG). He helps organizations grow by teaching their highest performers how to bring in more clients and more revenue. Over the course of his career he's worked in every area of business development and used this knowledge and experience to build the GrowBIG® business development system, resulting from years of testing and peer-reviewed research into why people buy and what makes the buying process happen faster, in greater volume, and with more enjoyment. BIG has trained over ten thousand seller-experts in various roles all over the world—working solo, in high-end professional service firms, and in large, global Fortune 500 companies, including Aetna, Boston Consulting Group, and Sotheby's. He lives in Atlanta with his wife, two daughters, and a miniature donkey.

You can learn more about Mo at www.mobunnell.com.

31901064532965